AMY BALFOUR, RAY BARTLETT, GREGOR CLARK & ASHLEY HARRELL

Contents

FIRES

Summer wildfires have become a regular occurrence in California, and some trails may have been affected since this guidebook went to print. Always check fire warnings (www.fire.ca.gov) when hiking in the summer, and confirm that trails are still open.

COVID-19

We have re-checked every business in this book before publication to ensure that it is still open after the COVID-19 outbreak. However, the economic and social impacts of COVID-19 will continue to be felt long after the outbreak has been contained, and many businesses, services and events referenced in this guide may experience ongoing restrictions. Some businesses may be temporarily closed, have changed their opening hours and services, or require bookings; some unfortunately could have closed permanently. We suggest you check with venues before visiting for the latest information.

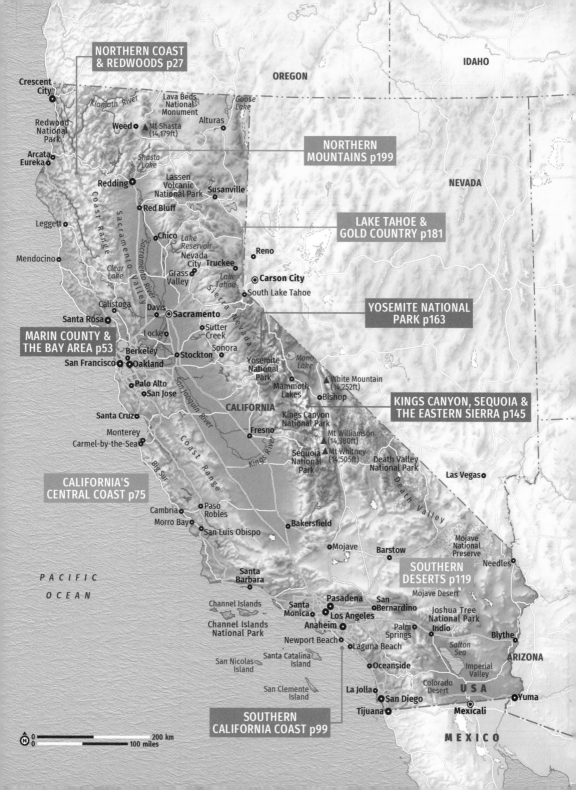

NORTHERN COAST & REDWOODS p27

NORTHERN MOUNTAINS p199

LAKE TAHOE & GOLD COUNTRY p181

YOSEMITE NATIONAL PARK p163

MARIN COUNTY & THE BAY AREA p53

KINGS CANYON, SEQUOIA & THE EASTERN SIERRA p145

CALIFORNIA'S CENTRAL COAST p75

SOUTHERN DESERTS p119

SOUTHERN CALIFORNIA COAST p99

IDAHO

OREGON

NEVADA

CALIFORNIA

ARIZONA

USA

MEXICO

PACIFIC OCEAN

Crescent City

Redwood National Park

Arcata
Eureka

Leggett

Mendocino

Calistoga

Santa Rosa

San Francisco
Berkeley
Oakland

Palo Alto
San Jose

Santa Cruz

Monterey
Carmel-by-the-Sea

Cambria
Morro Bay
San Luis Obispo
Paso Robles

Santa Barbara

Channel Islands
Channel Islands National Park

San Nicolas Island
Santa Catalina Island
San Clemente Island

Santa Monica
Newport Beach
Laguna Beach
La Jolla

Oceanside

San Diego
Tijuana

Pasadena
Los Angeles
Anaheim

San Bernardino

Palm Springs

Indio

Joshua Tree National Park

Blythe

Salton Sea

Imperial Valley

Colorado Desert

Yuma

Mexicali

Mojave Desert

Mojave National Preserve

Needles

Barstow

Mojave

Bakersfield

Death Valley National Park

Las Vegas

Death Valley

Mt Williamson (14,380ft)
Mt Whitney (14,505ft)

Sequoia National Park

Kings Canyon National Park

Fresno

Bishop
White Mountain (14,252ft)

Mammoth Lakes

Mono Lake

Yosemite National Park

Sonora

Sutter Creek

Locke

Sacramento
Davis

Stockton

San Joaquin River

Coast Range

Sierra Nevada

Kings River

Big Sur

Clear Lake

Santa Rosa

Grass Valley
Nevada City
Truckee
Reno
Carson City
South Lake Tahoe
Lake Tahoe

Chico
Lake Reservoir

Red Bluff
Redding

Lassen Volcanic National Park
Susanville

Shasta Lake

Weed
Mt Shasta (14,179ft)
Alturas

Lava Beds National Monument
Goose Lake

Klamath River

Coast Range

Sacramento Valley
Sacramento River

N
0   200 km
0   100 miles

A hike is more than just a walk in the woods in California. It's a full-blown body-and-mind immersion. Yeah, yeah, what does that mean? It means laughing when the mist from Vernal Fall drenches your last clean shirt on the Giant Staircase. Or yelling with surprise as a gray whale breaches calm waters along the rugged Northern Coast. Or wiping your brow as you estimate the distance of a palm tree oasis across a desert canyon. Even a simple forest stroll has a pull-you-in charm in California. Rest assured, you *will* place your palm against a centuries-old sequoia while exploring the Giant Forest in the Sierra Nevada. Yes, we felt it 'breathing' too. The 60 day hikes in this book will swing you up to alpine lakes and granite summits then down to striking cityscapes and sunset-ready coasts. Just grab your hiking boots and your sunscreen.

Highlights

GEM LAKES, KINGS CANYON, SEQUOIA & THE EASTERN SIERRA

Gorgeous alpine lakes reflect jagged Sierra Nevada peaks on this high-altitude ramble through the Little Lakes Valley. **p156**

BIG SUR BLUFFS & BEACHES, CALIFORNIA'S CENTRAL COAST

Big Sur's quintessential coastal trail serves up phenomenal Pacific Ocean views en route to a pair of wild and secluded beaches. **p92**

BOY SCOUT TREE TRAIL, NORTHERN COAST & REDWOODS

Tucked in a far-flung corner of the remote Northern Coast, this idyllic trail through soaring old-growth redwoods is a blessing of solitude and wonder. **p44**

VERNAL & NEVADA FALLS, YOSEMITE NATIONAL PARK

Thunderous waterfalls and soaring granite peaks mark this classic loop as it climbs the Giant Staircase on the Mist Trail and descends on the John Muir Trail. **p174**

LOST COAST TRAIL: NEEDLE ROCK TO WHALE GULCH, NORTHERN COAST & REDWOODS

This cinematic coastal trail has sights for nearly every mood: invigorating grassy bluffs, bright summer wildflowers, dramatic frothy seas, moody elk, and a mettle-testing mountain climb. **p48**

LANDS END TO THE GOLDEN GATE, MARIN COUNTY & THE BAY AREA

Enjoy unparalleled perspectives of California's favorite bridge and immerse in local life as you pass joggers, fishers and kayakers on this iconic urban trail. **p66**

CINDER CONE TRAIL, NORTHERN MOUNTAINS

Live your own Tolkienesque adventure as you navigate the Fantastic Lava Beds and the Painted Dunes on your journey into the crater of an ancient volcano. **p206**

RUBICON TRAIL, LAKE TAHOE & GOLD COUNTRY

An exhilarating roller coaster, the Rubicon Trail swoops and swerves though the forest on the shores of Lake Tahoe then brakes at a Scandinavian castle. **p190**

HELLHOLE CANYON & MAIDENHAIR FALLS, SOUTHERN DESERTS

A chance to see bighorn sheep, a lush palm oasis, a gazillion thirsty bees and a stunning desertscape make this hike more heavenly than hellish. p128

POTATO CHIP ROCK TRAIL & MT WOODSON, SOUTHERN CALIFORNIA COAST

Popular for a reason, Potato Chip Rock's lovely, varied terrain features gorgeous views, a pretty reservoir, and of course the Potato Chip selfie op. p106

Best For...

RICHARD BIZICK/SHUTTERSTOCK ©

MEXCELL90/SHUTTERSTOCK ©

👀 BIG VIEWS

From rugged cliffside beaches to blackened lava beds to sprawling lake-and-mountain tableaus, gobsmacking landscapes are a reliable backdrop.

BASS LAKE, WILDCAT & ALAMERE FALLS
Sandstone cliffs stretch for miles along wilderness beaches in Point Reyes National Seashore. **p68**

SENTINEL DOME & TAFT POINT
Enjoy expansive views of Half Dome (pictured above) and terrifying sheer cliffs on this Glacier Point Rd loop hike. **p170**

LASSEN PEAK
From the summit of an active volcano, see volcanic peaks, lakes and a lush former wasteland. **p208**

PACIFIC COAST TRAIL & MT JUDAH LOOP
See alpine lakes, a ski resort, Sierra peaks and reminders of a pioneer tragedy from atop Mt Judah. **p188**

WILDROSE PEAK TRAIL
Your reward after this strenuous Death Valley climb? Panoramic views of the Mojave Desert. **p138**

🥾 ESCAPING THE CROWDS

It's hard to find solitude on top-notch hikes near the city. Which means you'll likely have to drive an hour or two for quiet contemplation.

GARRAPATA GETAWAY
This Big Sur park (pictured above)sweeps in dramatic coastal cliffs and a hidden remnant of redwood forest. **p86**

LOST COAST TRAIL: MATTOLE TO PUNTA GORDA LIGHTHOUSE
An abandoned lighthouse sets the tone for a lonely sojourn across a windswept beach. **p42**

SOUTH GROVE TRAIL
This quiet trail unfurls beneath 2000-year-old sequoias in a lovely park deep in the Sierra Nevada. **p184**

HELLHOLE CANYON & MAIDENHAIR FALLS
Eighty miles from San Diego, this trail rolls deep into a desert canyon to a seasonal waterfall. **p128**

HUNTING HOLLOW TO WILLSON PEAK
Get lost in hilly, oak-dotted grasslands in one of California's largest and least-visited state parks. **p90**

 ## POST-HIKE CHEER

Kick back and share stories about your trail adventures.

GREEN GULCH, PIRATES COVE & MUIR BEACH
Enjoy a post-hike libation at the Pelican Inn (pictured above), a British-style pub. **p64**

EAGLE FALLS & EAGLE LAKE
Sip beers with locals at South Lake Brewing Company. **p186**

MENDOCINO HEADLANDS TRAIL
Walk into Mendocino for a beer at Patterson's Pub. **p40**

TEMESCAL CANYON
Drive north along the coast to Neptune's Net, a beer-and-seafood joint. **p108**

MONTAÑA DE ORO
Go brewery-hopping in the lively college town of San Luis Obispo. **p80**

 ## WILDLIFE

Look for wild animals from the coast to the Sierra.

LOST COAST TRAIL: MATTOLE TO PUNTA GORDA LIGHTHOUSE
Sea lions, elephant seals and hundreds of bird species. **p42**

PINNACLES HIGH PEAKS LOOP
Scan skies above volcanic spires for California condors. **p88**

TOKOPAH FALLS
High-altitude boulders are hot spots for pika and marmots (pictured above). **p152**

CORTE MADERA TRAIL
Watch for warblers, woodpeckers and jays. Foxes, coyotes and bobcats are more elusive. **p110**

TOMALES POINT TRAIL
Tule elk wander the hills between Tomales Bay and the Pacific Ocean. **p60**

 ## COASTAL VIEWS

California features 840 miles of ocean coastline, and snowy peaks hug alpine lakes.

POTATO HARBOR
Take in stunning views of cliffs and coves, and watch for whales and dolphins off Santa Barbara. **p97**

PATRICK'S POINT LOOP TRAIL
Pretty sights abound: sea-polished agate, seaside bluffs, tidepools and a pine forest. **p32**

BIG SUR BLUFFS & BEACHES
Experience seaside cliffs, towering redwoods and remote beaches. **p92**

RUBICON TRAIL
This Lake Tahoe path (pictured above) dips from forested slopes to a lively beach. **p190**

With Kids

CALIFORNIA FOR KIDS

California is a fantastic destination for family-friendly hiking. Along the coast, younger kids can explore critter-filled tide pools, while kids of all ages gape at enormous redwoods. Wildlife spotting is fun for all ages in the Sierra Nevada, with cute pikas and marmots popping up here and there among the boulders. In the desert, jackrabbits and lizards scamper about. An appealing lineup of adventures should keep older kids engaged as they tackle granite domes and challenging trails in Yosemite (pictured above), Kings Canyon and Sequoia National Parks. The hardest part of any family trip may be choosing where to go.

ACCOMMODATIONS

Camping is superb across the Golden State. Campsites at national and state parks are inexpensive, and they are typically located in scenic locations, many times near a trailhead. Loads of family-friendly amenities and activities are often available, especially in national parks. Campgrounds in national forests may be lacking in amenities beyond pit toilets and fresh water, but the scenery is often top-notch. Private campgrounds, while more expensive than their public counterparts, may have more family-friendly amenities on offer, like swimming pools, movie nights or bike rentals. Hot showers and a coin-operated laundry are often available too. Private campgrounds tend to cater to RVs (recreational vehicles),

with full electricity, water hookups and dump stations.

Motels and hotels in outdoorsy towns typically have rooms with two beds or an extra sofa bed. They may have rollaway beds or cots, usually available for a surcharge (request these when making reservations). Some offer 'kids stay free' promotions, which may apply only if no extra bedding is required. When booking, be sure to request the specific room type you want, although requests aren't often guaranteed.

WHAT TO PACK

Bring broken-in hiking shoes and your own camping equipment. Outdoor gear can be purchased or sometimes rented from local outdoors outfitters. But the best time to test gear

Taking Kids on the Trail

- Keep kids within earshot (if not sight) of adults. They may want to rush ahead, but it's very easy to miss a necessary junction or take a wrong turn.
- Dress them in bright-coloured clothes and have each one carry a flashlight and a safety whistle. Make sure they know what to do if they get lost (for instance, stay put and periodically blow the whistle).
- Dress kids (and yourself) in layers so they can peel off or pull on clothing when needed.
- Bring lots of high-energy snacks and drinks, even on short outings.
- Children are just as vulnerable as adults to altitude sickness at higher elevations. They may not know what it is they're feeling, and they may not let you know. Familiarize yourself with symptoms (headaches and nausea are common) and watch for them. If your child shows symptoms, descend to lower elevations.

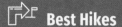 ## Best Hikes

- Tennessee Valley (p56), Marin County & the Bay Area
- Tokopah Falls (p152), Kings Canyon, Sequoia & the Eastern Sierra
- Big Tree Loop Trail (p30), Northern Coast & Redwoods
- Hellhole Canyon & Maidenhair Falls (p128), Southern Deserts
- Sunset Cliffs (p102), Southern California Coast

is before you take your trip. Murphy's Law dictates that wearing brand-new hiking shoes always results in blisters, and setting up a tent for the first time in the dark isn't easy. And don't forget the sunscreen.

KEEPING IT FUN

Active, adventurous and environmentally aware parents are often eager to share those interests with kids. Take care though not to turn a diversion into a chore. For example, don't make your kids memorize 80 different rocks; that's no fun. At national parks, consider participating in organized activities, such as junior ranger programs and nature walks, or visit kid-friendly spots, like nature centers. Kids usually like when other kids are around. Hiking is great exercise, though parents should gauge their children's abilities and choose hikes carefully.

REGIONAL HIKING TIPS

Northern Coast & Redwoods, Marin County & the Bay Area Don't let your kids approach wild elk, which can be aggressive.

Northern Coast & Redwoods Keep a close eye on the seas while hiking on the sand on the Lost Coast. Large waves can come in unexpectedly.

Northern Mountains Keep kids close on the Bumpass Hell Trail. If they fall off the boardwalk or take a wrong step, they can scald themselves.

Yosemite, Kings Canyon & Sequoia National Parks Ask rangers about current conditions before letting your kids jump into rivers in the Sierra Nevada, particularly in the spring. Currents can be much stronger than they appear and drownings are common. Obey all signage.

Yosemite National Park Be extra cautious around viewpoints, such as Taft Point, which has a railing at the cliff's edge but none around the periphery, and the adjacent Fissures – giant cracks in the granite that plunge thousands of feet. The same goes for the summits of peaks and domes.

National & State Parks; National Forests Don't let your children feed wild animals, no matter how cute. If chipmunks, squirrels and bears are regularly fed, they can lose their fear of humans, causing them to become a nuisance and potentially a risk to the public.

Forest Trails & Channel Islands Watch out for poison oak.

Accessible Trails

For the most part, hiking trails across the Golden State are designed for use by fully able walkers. Federal, state and local parks are taking greater care every year, however, to meet the access needs of disabled travelers and older hikers. And though it's not possible for wheelchair travelers or those with mobility issues to cross rugged terrain to reach remote sites, many of California's most striking vistas and geological features can be accessed via short paved trails from nearby parking lots.

ACCESSIBLE PATHS

Paths in forests and mountains are often rocky and steep, and many can be slippery after a rain shower. Expect creek crossings in the mountains and soft soil near rivers and streams. Trails improve in urban areas, where you'll often find well-maintained multiuse greenways crisscrossing the city. Paved trails along beaches and lakefronts are also common.

NATIONAL PARKS

National parks have done much in recent years to improve accessibility. The websites for all nine national parks in California include a page dedicated to accessibility issues. Yosemite, Kings Canyon, Sequoia and Lassen Volcanic have also prepared comprehensive accessibility guides that can be downloaded as a pdf from their websites.

Many national parks offer services that are helpful to blind/low vision and deaf/hard of hearing visitors. Some parks will need a heads-up before providing these services, however, so check the park website to see if you need to call first.

With the exception of rough-and-tumble Channel Islands National Park, which is reached by boat, all national parks have accessible trails and most have accessible campground and lodging options. In Yosemite National Park, Yosemite Valley has an extensive network of easy and paved trails with gorgeous views of granite domes and towering waterfalls. The eastern section of the Lower Yosemite Fall Trail is accessible to wheelchairs and has a fall viewing area.

Shuttles in Yosemite and Sequoia National Parks are wheelchair accessible. You can rent wheelchairs at both parks.

CALIFORNIA STATE PARKS

Each park in the California state park system has a dedicated webpage describing its accessible features. You can also search by specific accessible amenities – campgrounds, trails, picnic

Resources

Accessible Nature (www.accessiblenature.info) Shares links to federal, state and local parks across the US, with separate tags for accessible trails and easy-walking trails.

Access Northern California (www.accessnca.org) Extensive coverage of accessibility features for various trails from the Northern Coast to San Francisco and the Bay Area.

A Wheelchair Rider's Guide to the California Coast (www.wheelingcalscoast. org) Spotlights accessible trails and their features at parks along the California coastline.

Wheelchair Traveling (www.wheelchairtraveling.com) Search accessible outdoor activities in California at a global travel site.

Lake Tahoe Basin Management Unit (www.fs.usda.gov/ltbmu) Forest Service webpage with helpful overview of accessible recreation sites around Lake Tahoe.

Best Trails

Big Tree Loop Trail A crushed gravel trail leads to the Big Tree, a 350ft-high redwood. p30

General Sherman Tree & Congress Trail Paved path to the world's largest tree and into the Giant Forest. p148

Montaña de Oro Wheelchair-accessible Bluff Trail crosses low cliffs along the central coast shoreline. p80

Muir Woods Boardwalks and hard paths loop through a coastal redwood grove. p58

---

areas, exhibits, etc – to see which parks provide them (www.access. parks.ca.gov).

LAKE TAHOE

Although there isn't a paved trail looping around the entire 72-mile perimeter of Lake Tahoe, plans for constructing one are afoot. In the meantime, you'll find paved paths beside sections of the lake and along the Truckee River, which feeds into it. Be aware that these trails can get crowded in warmer months.

Just over the state line in Nevada, the Tahoe East Shore Trail (pictured) is a 3-mile paved path linking Incline Village with Sand Harbor State Park. Dotted with interpretive signage and scenic viewpoints overlooking the lake, the trail meets standards set by the Americans with Disabilities Act for wheelchairs. On the north shore near Tahoe City, the scenic Truckee River Bike Trail is another good option. It is part of the 23-mile Tahoe Trailways Bike Path (www.tcpud.org/trails), a popular multi-use trail network along the north and west shores. There are several wheelchair-friendly trails beside the lake at the Taylor Creek Visitor Center in South Lake Tahoe.

OLDER HIKERS

Hiking is a popular activity for all ages in California, and for many people it develops into a lifelong love affair. Most of the hikes in this book should be suitable for moderately fit hikers of all ages, although some of the harder trails involve more unstable terrain and cover considerable distances, so it's important to be realistic about your own ability.

• Hiking poles are a very handy accessory for older hikers, as they give you a firm platform when covering unstable terrain.

• Hilly or rocky trails can be very hard on the hips and knees, so choose level routes if you have hip and knee problems.

• When you're doing your research and planning, remember to think about issues such as building in regular rest stops, access to toilets, location of car parks and so on.

• If you plan to hike in several national parks or recreation areas on your visit, consider buying a Senior Pass (www.nps. gov). The Annual Senior Pass ($20) covers admission to four parks for a year while the Lifetime Senior Pass ($80) allows unlimited visits. The Senior Pass is available to US citizens and permanent residents 62 years of age and older.

Essentials

CLOTHING & EQUIPMENT

Layering A secret of comfortable hiking is to wear several layers of light clothing, which you can take off or put on as you warm up or cool down. Most hikers use three main layers: a base layer next to the skin, an insulating layer, and an outer shell-layer for protection from wind, rain and snow.

Sun Protection In the desert and at high altitude you can sunburn in less than an hour, even through cloud cover. Use sunscreen (with an SPF of 30 or higher), especially on skin not typically exposed to the sun, reapply it regularly and wear long sleeves. Apply sunscreen to young children and wear wide-brimmed hats.

Footwear Running shoes are OK for hikes that are graded easy or moderate. However, you'll probably appreciate, if not need, the support and protection offered by hiking boots for more demanding walks. Buy boots in warm conditions or go for a walk before trying them on so that your feet can expand slightly, as they would on a hike. Bring a pair of sandals for camp if you're backpacking, and for fording waterways.

Daypack (30L–40L) Consider bringing a small backpack for carrying water, snacks, matches, a first-aid kit, insect repellent and a flashlight or headlamp.

Map & Compass Smartphones can be unreliable, so always carry a good paper map of the area in which you are hiking, and know how to read it. Before setting off, ensure that you are aware of the contour interval, the map symbols, the magnetic delineation (difference between true and grid north), plus the main ridge and river systems in the area and the general direction you are headed. Buy a compass and learn how to use it. The attraction of magnetic north varies in different parts of the world, so compasses need to be balanced accordingly, and for your destination zone.

HIKING SAFETY

• Allow plenty of time to accomplish a hike before dark, particularly when daylight hours are shorter.

• Study the route carefully before setting out, noting possible escape routes and the point of no return (when it's quicker to continue than turn back). Monitor your progress against the time estimated for the hike, and keep an eye on the weather.

• Leave details of your intended route, the number of people in

Trail Etiquette

Mind your manners Keep noise levels low and cell-phone usage to a minimum.

On the trail Stay on the trail. Greet others you meet. Horses and pack trains have right of way.

Be courteous Provide assistance if someone needs help.

Proper preparation Prepare yourself for challenging and emergency situations.

Respect nature Don't break branches from bushes or trees. Don't remove any fossils or plant (such as pine cones) or animal products from where you find them.

Be mindful of animals Don't feed wild animals and never leave food unattended.

Clean up Dispose of waste, human and otherwise, properly.

In the campground Respect private property and never leave fires unattended.

Resources

National Park Service (NPS; www.nps.gov) Gateway to America's national parks.

California State Parks (www.parks.ca.gov) Information about 280 state-run parks.

National Park Service Mobile Apps (Yosemite, Kings Canyon and Sequoia) Maps and current park details for your smartphone.

AllTrails Mobile App Follow previously recorded hikes or create your own.

Oh, Ranger! ParkFinder Mobile App Covers activities across federal and state parks and federal recreational areas.

Modern Hiker (www.modern hiker.com) In-depth coverage of California hiking trails.

your group, and expected return time with someone responsible, and let that person know when you return.

• Hiking alone adds additional risk, especially if you get injured or get lost. If hiking solo, be extra vigilant about leaving your hiking itinerary with someone. Consider bringing a GPS device with emergency satellite notification capabilities.

• Make sure you have a relevant map, compass and whistle, and that you know the weather forecast for the area for the next 24 hours. In the mountains, always carry extra warm, dry layers of clothing and plenty of emergency high-energy food.

• Desert hiking comes down to three things: hydration, hydration, hydration. Which means bring extra water, know exactly where you are on the trail,

and turn around when you've finished half your supply. And remember that the desert can get cold after dark.

• Be mindful of your surroundings when taking photos and selfies. There have been fatal accidents on trails in California as hikers try to capture the perfect photograph of themselves in dangerous spots.

WHEN TO GO

• For most of the state, the best time for hiking is April through October, although at lower elevations you can easily hike year-round.

• One major exception is the desert, where summer (June–September) is the low season. Desert wildflowers usually bloom from late March through April. October has comfortable

temperatures and skies are typically clear. In summer temperatures exceed 100°F (38°C).

• You'll encounter the biggest crowds across most of the state from the end of May through August, when children are out of school and families take vacation. Most national and state parks are at their busiest.

• Waterfalls hit their peak in the Sierra Nevada in June, as the snow melts and rivers rise.

• In the spring and early summer wildflowers bloom down coastal hillsides, across mountain meadows and along desert sands.

Hiking in
California

With its epic scenery, California is an awe-inspiring place to hike. And though the state has scenic drives galore, exploring by foot allows you to experience the state's iconic highlights: strolling coastal bluffs, trekking past Joshua trees, scrambling up craggy peaks, navigating lava beds and hugging the world's tallest, largest and oldest trees.

NATIVE CALIFORNIANS

Human settlement began in Native California as early as 19,000 years ago, and communities flourished side by side. Native Californians passed knowledge of hunting grounds and turf boundaries from generation to generation in song, in at least 100 distinct languages. Today, re-created native villages and original petroglyphs, or rock carvings, are fascinating links to the past.

Over centuries, each nation became uniquely adapted to local ecosystems. Northern coastal fishing communities such as the Ohlone, Miwok and Pomo built snug, subterranean roundhouses and sweat lodges, where they held ceremonies, told stories and gambled for fun. Northern hunting and fishing communities like the Hupa, Karok and Wiyot constructed big houses and redwood dugout canoes, while the Modoc traveled between summer tipis and winter dugouts. Kumeyaay and Chumash villages dotted the central coast, where they fished and paddled seaworthy canoes all the way to the Channel Islands. Southern Mojave, Yuma and Cahuilla nations developed irrigation systems for farming in the desert, and made sophisticated pottery to conserve precious water.

By the time Europeans arrived, 300,000 Native Californians were flourishing here. Their first encounter did not bode well. When English sea captain Sir Francis Drake harbored briefly on Miwok land north of San Francisco in 1579, shamans saw their arrival as a warning of apocalypse. The omens weren't wrong, just off by a couple of centuries. By 1869, a century after Spanish colonists arrived, California's indigenous population would be decimated by 90%, due to introduced European diseases, conscripted labor, violence, marginalization and hunger in their own fertile lands.

Today you can explore a reconstructed Yurok village on the Patrick's Point Loop Trail (p32) on the Northern Coast and check out petroglyphs on the Barker Dam Nature Trail (p142). In Yosemite Valley, the Indian Village of the Ahwahnee is a reconstructed Southern Sierra Miwok community.

JOHN MUIR & YOSEMITE

On a weekend visit from San Francisco to Yosemite Valley in the spring of 1868, Scottish immigrant John Muir found his calling as a naturalist. The following year he returned to begin a monumental experiment in the observation of nature. He wandered, most often alone, into the highest realms of the Yosemite backcountry,

Though not a scientist by training, Muir looked at the natural world with a keen curiosity. From his prolific and florid writings on nature one might see him as a poet among naturalists, but over time his pen turned increasingly toward the political aims of the growing conservationist movement. Muir's articles and lobbying efforts were the foundation of the campaign that established Yosemite as a national park in 1890. Muir founded the Sierra Club in 1892 and devoted his life to defending California wilderness against the encroachments of dams and urbanization.

After backpacking with Muir in Yosemite in 1903, President Theodore Roosevelt was convinced to preserve additional sections of Yosemite as a national park. Yet despite Muir's passionate objections, Woodrow Wilson commissioned Hetch Hetchy Reservoir in 1913 to funnel water from Yosemite to the Bay Area. In drought-prone California, tensions between land developers and conservationists still run high.

The 211-mile John Muir Trail overlaps with a section of the Vernal & Nevada Falls Loop (p174) in Yosemite National Park. Tuolumne Meadows was a favorite spot of Muir's and he called it a 'spacious and delightful high-pleasure ground.'

PACIFIC CREST TRAIL

The Pacific Crest National Trail (PCT; www.pcta.org) stretches 2650 miles from Campo, CA, on the US–Mexico border to Manning Provincial Park in British Columbia, Canada. It hugs the crest of the glacially carved Sierra Nevada in California and the volcanic Cascade Range in Northern California, Oregon and Washington, crossing six national parks.

In California the trail skirts the Mojave Desert along the Tehachapi Mountains and then enters the southern Sierra, where it joins the John Muir Trail in Sequoia National Park, just west of Mt Whitney. Leaving the park via Forester Pass (13,120ft), the trail's highest point, it continues through Kings Canyon National Park. After passing Devils Postpile National Monument, the path enters Yosemite National Park at Donohue Pass and diverges from the John Muir Trail at Tuolumne Meadows. It crosses

PREVIOUS PAGE: SEQUOIA NATIONAL PARK
ON THIS PAGE: TOP: BLACK BEAR
BOTTOM: ANZA-BORREGO DESERT STATE PARK

Dorothy Lake Pass as it exits Yosemite, then travels over Sonora Pass, Ebbetts Pass, Carson Pass and Echo Summit. Entering the popular Desolation Wilderness west of Lake Tahoe, the trail passes Alpine Meadows and Squaw Valley ski resorts en route to Donner Summit. It undulates though deep river valleys in the northern Sierra and continues to Lassen Volcanic National Park, marking the southern extent of the Cascade Range.

As a thru-hike, the entire trail takes five months to complete. You can hike on the PCT on the Pacific Coast Trail & Mt Judah Loop (p188) near Lake Tahoe.

CALIFORNIA'S FAUNA & FLORA

Although the staggering numbers of animals that greeted the first foreign settlers are now distant memories, you can still easily spot wildlife thriving in California. Some are only shadow populations, and some are actually endangered – all the more reason to take the opportunity to stop by California's designated wildlife areas to appreciate their presence and support their conservation.

BEARS

Though a grizzly adorns the state flag, the species was hunted to extinction in California in the 1920s. Only black bears live in the state today, and California's mountain forests are home to an estimated 30,000 to 40,000 black bears, the grizzlies' smaller cousins. Despite their name, their fur ranges in color from black to dark brown, auburn or even blond. These burly omnivores feed on berries, nuts, roots, grasses, insects, eggs, small mammals and fish, but can become a nuisance around campgrounds and cabins where food and trash are not secured.

Bears are active throughout the Sierra Nevada, and are especially prevalent in Yosemite. Yosemite's bears are notorious for breaking into cars and raiding campgrounds and backcountry campsites in search of food. To keep bears at bay at night, the park service in Yosemite requires you to remove all scented items from your car, including any food, trash, and products such as gum, toothpaste, soap and sunscreen, and place it in a bear locker – a large metal storage locker found in most major parking lots and at every Yosemite campsite. During the day, the best practice is to store these items in the food lockers while you hike. Otherwise, cover anything in your car that even looks like a cooler or food. In Yosemite failure to use food lockers can result in a fine – not to mention the possibility of your car windows being shattered and upholstery ravaged by a hungry beast. Elsewhere in the Sierra you'll find lockers at national park trailheads and campsites and the most troublesome USFS (United States Forest Service) trailheads. Check current storage requirements online for each park or national forest, as they may differ.

In undeveloped areas stay at least 50yd from a bear. In developed areas, try to scare it off with aggressive yelling and loud noises. If confronted, don't drop your backpack – that's probably what the bear wants and it will likely lead to more problems for other people (and, ultimately, the bear). Never run from a bear either. You'll only trigger its instinct to chase, and you cannot outrun a bear. You can and should fight back if attacked. Use any means available – throw rocks or sticks or hit it with your gear. Fortunately, it's extremely rare for a bear to make an unprovoked attack on a human.

WHALES

Once threatened by extinction, gray whales now migrate in growing numbers along California's coast between December and April. Adult whales live up to 60 years, grow longer than a city bus and can weigh up to 40 tons, making quite a splash when they leap out of the water. Every year they travel from summertime feeding grounds

Almost an Island

Cut off from the rest of North America by the soaring peaks of the Sierra Nevada, California is as biologically distinct as an island. Under these biologically isolated conditions, evolution and local adaptation have yielded unique plants and animals ranging from bristlecone pines in the north to Joshua trees in the south. California ranks first in the nation for its number of endemic plants, amphibians, reptiles, freshwater fish and mammals. In fact, 30% of all plant species, 50% of all bird species and 50% of all mammal species in the USA can be found here.

in the arctic Bering Sea down to southern breeding grounds off Baja California then all the way back up again, making a 6000-mile round trip.

Look for whales while hiking the Patrick's Point Loop Trail (p32), Mendocino Headlands Trail (p40) and Trinidad Head Loop Trail (p38) along the North Coast.

REDWOODS & SEQUOIAS

California is home to two of the most enormous species of trees on earth: the giant redwood, also known as the coastal redwood, and the giant sequoia. Though similarly impressive in scale, there are distinct differences between the trees. Redwoods are the tallest trees in the world and they have slender trunks. They can grow more than 350ft high and typically live 500 to 700 years. Sequoias are the largest trees in the world by volume and they have hefty trunks, which can reach 26ft in diameter. Sequoias can live 3000 years. Their habitats differ too. Redwoods stretch along the Northern California coast for an almost continuous 450 miles. Giant sequoias grow in groves on the western slopes of the Sierra Nevada at elevations between 4000ft and 7000ft.

Peer up at redwoods on the following trails: Big Tree Loop Trail (p30), Boy Scout Tree Trail (p44), Tall Trees Grove Loop Trail (p46), Muir Woods (p58), Dipsea, Steep Ravine & Matt Davis Loop (p62), and the Garrapata Getaway (p86). You'll find sequoias beside the South Grove Trail (p184) in the Gold Country and the General Sherman Tree & Congress Trail (p148) in Sequoia National Park.

WILDFLOWERS

The famous 'golden hills' of California are actually native plants and grasses that have adapted to local conditions over millennia, and learned to dry up in preparation for the long hot summer. Many local plants have adjusted their growing cycles to long periods of almost no rain, growing prolifically during California's mild wet winters, blooming as early as February, drying out in early summer and springing to life again with the first rains of fall.

In Southern California's desert areas, wildflower blooms usually peak in March, with carpets of wildflowers covering lowland areas of the state into April. Visit Anza-Borrego Desert State Park, Death Valley National Park, the Antelope Valley California Poppy Preserve and Carrizo Plain National Monument for some of the most spectacular annual wildflower displays.

As snows melt later at higher elevations in the Sierra Nevada, Yosemite National Park's Tuolumne Meadows is another prime spot for wildflower walks and photography, with blooms usually peaking in late June or early July.

LAY OF THE LAND

California is the third-biggest US state after Alaska and Texas, covering more than 155,000 sq miles – if it were a country it would rank as the 59th largest in the world. It shares borders with Oregon to the north, Mexico to the south, Nevada and Arizona to the east, and has 840 miles of glorious Pacific shoreline to the west.

GEOLOGY & EARTHQUAKES

California is a complex geological landscape formed from fragments of rock and earth crust squeezed together as the North American continent drifted westward over hundreds of millions of years. Crumpled coastal ranges, fault lines rippling through the Central Valley and jagged, still-rising Sierra Nevada mountains all reveal gigantic forces at work, as the continental and ocean plates crush together.

Everything changed about 25 million years ago, when the ocean plates stopped colliding and instead started sliding against each other, creating the massive San Andreas Fault. This contact zone catches and slips, rattling California with an ongoing succession of tremors and earthquakes.

MOUNTAIN RANGES

On the eastern side of the Central Valley looms California's most prominent topographic feature: the Sierra Nevada, nicknamed the 'Range of Light' by conservationist John Muir. At 400 miles long and 70 miles wide, this is one of the world's largest mountain ranges, punctuated with 13 peaks over 14,000ft high. The vast wilderness of the High Sierra (mostly above 9000ft) is an astounding landscape of shrinking glaciers, sculpted granite peaks and remote canyons. This landscape is beautiful to look at but difficult to access, and it was one of the greatest challenges for 19th-century settlers attempting to reach California.

The soaring Sierra Nevada captures storm systems and drains them of their water, with most of the precipitation above 3000ft turning to snow, creating a premier winter-sports destination. Melting snow flows down into a half-dozen major river systems on the range's western and eastern slopes, providing the vast majority of water needed for agriculture in the Central Valley and for the metro areas of San Francisco and Los Angeles.

At its northern end, the Sierra Nevada merges imperceptibly into the volcanic Cascade Range, which continues north into Oregon and Washington. At its southern end, the Sierra Nevada makes a funny westward hook and connects via the Transverse Ranges (one of the USA's few east–west mountain ranges) to the southern Coast Ranges.

THE DESERTS & BEYOND

With the west slope of the Sierra Nevada capturing most of the precipitation, lands east of the Sierra crest are dry and desertlike, receiving less than 10in of rain a year. Some valleys at the eastern foot of the Sierra Nevada, however, are well watered by creeks, so that they're able to support livestock and agriculture.

At the western edge of the Great Basin, the elevated Modoc Plateau in far northeastern California is a cold desert blanketed by hardy sagebrush shrubs and juniper trees. Temperatures increase as you head south, with a prominent transition on the descent from Mono Lake into the Owens Valley east of the Sierra Nevada. This southern

High & Low

California claims both the highest point in the contiguous US (Mt Whitney, 14,505ft) and the lowest elevation in North America (Badwater, Death Valley, 282ft below sea level; pictured below). And they're only 90 miles apart, as the condor flies.

hot desert (part of the Mojave Desert) includes Death Valley, one of the hottest places on the planet. Further south, the Mojave Desert morphs into the Colorado Desert (part of Mexico's greater Sonoran Desert) around the Salton Sea.

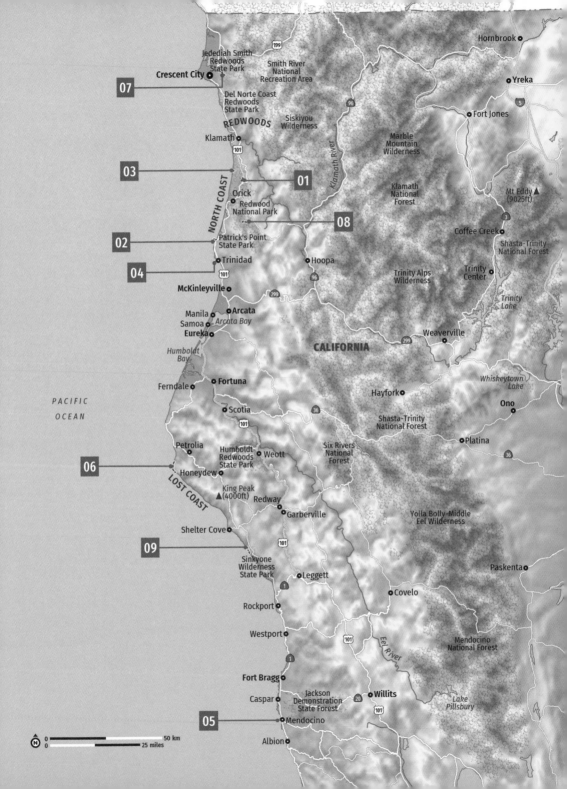

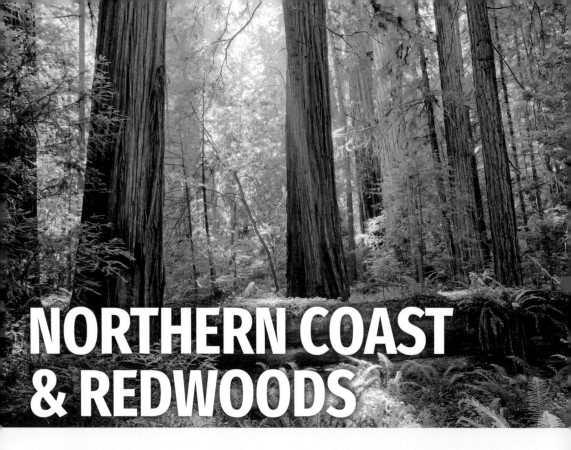

NORTHERN COAST & REDWOODS

Explore
NORTHERN COAST & REDWOODS

On California's Northern Coast, the trees are so large that the tiny towns along the road seem even smaller, and the rest of the scenery is pure drama: cliffs and rocks, tranquil lagoons and frothing seas, legendary salmon runs and wild elk. It's telling that a stretch of this shoreline became 'lost' when the state's highway system deemed the region impassable in the mid-20th century. Whether you're hiking in the majestic forest or by the crashing sea, you'll want ample time to saunter and bask in the haunting natural grandeur of it all.

TRINIDAD

Cheery, wind-whipped Trinidad perches prettily on the side of the ocean, combining upscale mid-century homes with a mellow surfer vibe. Somehow it feels a bit off-the-beaten-path even though it's the loveliest base for exploring the southern end of Redwood National and State Parks, with top-tier lodging. Most inns and motels line Patrick's Point Dr, north of town, and are family owned and welcoming, with fabulous ocean views.

ARCATA & EUREKA

The Northern Coast's most progressive town, Arcata surrounds a tidy central square that fills with college students, campers, wanderers and tourists. And just to the south, on the edge of the largest bay north of San Francisco, the city of Eureka's got strip-mall sprawl surrounding a lovely historic downtown, along with an interesting community of artists, writers, pagans and other free-thinkers. Every brand of chain hotel is located along this corridor of Hwy 101, and there are also some affordable options just north of Arcata and south of downtown Eureka on a suburban strip.

SHELTER COVE

The only sizable community on the Lost Coast, Shelter Cove is surrounded by the King Range National Conservation Area and abuts a large south-facing cove. The tiny seaside subdivision offers an airstrip in the middle, and flying in certainly beats the other way of arriving, via a steep, winding dirt road. Regardless, Shelter Cove has a solid selection of campgrounds, inns and hotels, but you'll need to book in advance, particularly over holiday weekends.

MENDOCINO

Leading out to a gorgeous headland, Mendocino is the Northern Coast's perfect, salt-washed village, with B&Bs surrounded by rose gardens, white-picket fences and New England–style redwood water towers. Standards are high in stylish Mendocino and so are prices; two-day hotel minimums often crop up on weekends.

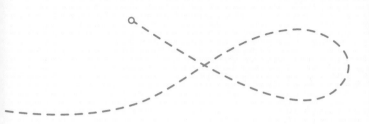

 ## WHEN TO GO

The summer months are the driest time of year, and therefore ideal for spectacular day hikes in the redwoods or along wild-flower-dotted valleys and bluffs. Moving into fall the weather remains warm and the sky is at its clearest, making this the perfect time for a hike on the Lost Coast. It rains quite a bit in wintertime, but from December to April keep a look out for gray whales migrating off the coast, and in early spring you may spot mothers with their calves.

 ## WHERE TO STAY

Finding accommodations in this region is rarely a problem, although those cute B&Bs in the coastal resorts get booked up fast on weekends by San Franciscan weekenders. Camping or cabin stays can be a truly memorable experience in these parts with a plethora of state and national parks offering forested campgrounds among some of the world's oldest and tallest trees. Motels are another option, and considerably more plentiful on Hwy 101 than elsewhere.

 ## WHAT'S ON

Mendocino Whale Festival (www.mendocinocoast.com/mendocino-whale-festival; ⊙Mar) Spot these magnificent mammals as they head north for Alaska.

Kinetic Grand Championship (www.kineticgrandchampionship.com; ⊙May) Essentially a human-powered sculpture race.

Reggae on the River (www.reggaeontheriver.com; ⊙Jul) Humboldt County's annual reggae music extravaganza.

 ## TRANSPORT

Although Hwy 1 is popular with cyclists and there are bus connections, you will almost certainly need a car to explore this region. Those headed to the far north and on a schedule should take Hwy 101, the faster, inland route, and then cut over to the coast. Windy Hwy 1 hugs the coast, then cuts inland and ends at Leggett, where it joins Hwy 101. Neither Amtrak nor Greyhound serve cities on coastal Hwy 1.

01

BIG TREE LOOP TRAIL

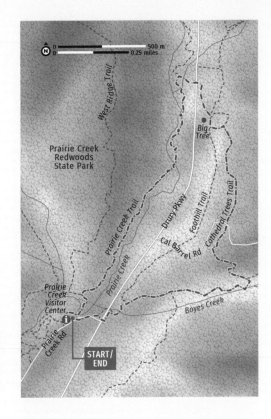

DURATION	DIFFICULTY	DISTANCE	START/END
3-4hr return	Easy	3.2 miles	Prairie Creek Visitor Center

TERRAIN	Crushed gravel (wheelchair accessible)

This three-trail combo is a highly accessible and popular sampler of the region's natural beauty, complete with superlative upland and lowland redwoods, a fast-moving creek and seasonal wildflowers. It features the Big Tree (one of the region's tallest) and offers a pleasing variety of environments. The only downsides are the trail's popularity, particularly in the summertime, and the noise from Drury Pkwy, which tends to increase on weekends.

The loop begins at the **Prairie Creek** Visitor Center. Head for the large wooden footbridge and cross Prairie Creek, then hang a right on Prairie Creek Trail. The path winds through a couple of redwood groves on its way to the main attraction: the

Big Tree, also known as the Big Tree Wayside. One of Prairie Creek's largest redwoods, the Big Tree stands more than 350ft high and is 21ft in diameter. It's thought to have existed for upwards of 1500 years, and you'll find it circled by a wooden platform in a small, isolated clearing, which most people visit before returning to the nearby parking lot.

It's far lovelier to continue hiking along the **Cathedral Trees Trail**, which climbs deeper into a dense, upland redwood forest. The trail eventually descends, crossing Cal Barrel Rd and continuing through some remarkable lowland redwoods. Soon you'll arrive in a meadow surrounded by large redwoods, after which you'll tunnel beneath Drury Pkwy (alternatively, you can scale an embankment and cross the street). The visitor center is just beyond the crossing.

02

PATRICK'S POINT LOOP TRAIL

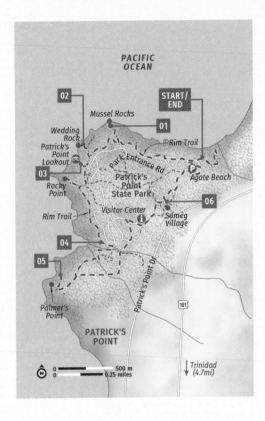

DURATION	DIFFICULTY	DISTANCE	START/END
3-4hr return	Easy	4 miles	Agate Beach Overlook

TERRAIN	Sidewalks, dirt, gravel, rocky outcrops

Patrick's Point State Park packs big-time beauty into a mere 640 acres of sandy beaches and coastal bluffs, and this dreamy loop links all of the headland's most scenic features. We're talking dramatic seaside cliffs, curious tide pools, a reconstructed Yurok Indian village and an agate-studded shore. In addition to the inanimate attractions, visitors regularly spy pelagic creatures and migratory birds from atop the inimitable Wedding Rock.

GETTING HERE

You'll definitely need wheels to visit this park. From the town of Trinidad, drive 6 miles north on Hwy 101 to exit 734 (Patrick's Point Dr), then it's a quick right onto the road that leads into the park. There's a day-use fee of $8 per vehicle. Camping is possible but in the summer it's in high demand. You'll pass a

visitor center by the entrance, after which you'll stay to the right, continuing until you reach Agate Beach parking area.

STARTING POINT

From the Agate Beach parking lot, where there are public restrooms, you can begin with an immediate detour down the stairs to Agate Beach, where stray bits of jade and sea-polished agates peek out of the sand. Climb back up the stairs to begin the trail.

01 Walk west along the road and eventually you'll reach a turnoff on the right for the Rim Trail. Follow the path through the **fern-filled meadow**, taking in the stunning views of the coast. The **Mussel Rocks** spur trail leads to a postcard-pretty view of some rocky islets.

02 Continue southwest through the meadow along the Rim Trail and soon you'll reach

Sumêg Village

Sumêg is an authentic reproduction of a Yurok village on what used to be tribal land, with redwood plank family houses, a sweathouse and a dance pit where Native Americans gather for ceremonies. In the native plant garden you'll find species for making traditional baskets and medicines. Follow the directions on the signs and respect this site, as local tribes consider it sacred.

The name Sumêg means 'forever,' and was selected to emphasize the hope that the village would educate future generations and preserve the Yurok tribe's heritage and culture for years to come. None of the original structures from the 1800s survive, but an all-Yurok crew built the replica in 1990.

Best for

COASTAL VIEWS

ASHLEY HARRELL/LONELY PLANET ©

a turnoff for **Wedding Rock**, the most popular lookout in the park. It's an epicenter of coastal romance (people frequently get married here) and a prime viewing spot for passing birds and for marine mammals. There are some good side trails, but the main path follows a steep staircase cut into the rock.

03 Return to the Rim Trail and continue across a ridge, through a gully and up some stairs. Optionally, veer off the main path again to **Patrick's Point Lookout** or **Rocky Point** (two more rocky outcroppings with mind-blowing views)

then rejoin the Rim Trail and continue south.

04 Wander south and mind your footing: one part of the trail has collapsed down the bluff. The trail veers west, crossing a couple of footbridges with **stunning views** of waterfalls, valleys and beaches below.

05 Continue on through a bishop pine forest and on to **Palmer's Point**, which offers scenic overlooks and a path down to a sand cove that also features some magnificent tide pools.

06 Walk along Palmer's Point Rd past the visitor

center and on to **Sumêg Village**. From here, it's just a short walk north back to the Agate Beach parking lot.

TAKE A BREAK

There are so many wonderful places to enjoy a picnic in these parts that it would be a crime not to stop by a grocery store along the way and pick up provisions; most have a deli counter where you can buy sandwiches and homemade soup. If you want to treat yourself, the eclectically adorned **Larrupin Cafe** (☎707-677-0230; www.thelarrupin.com; 1658 Patrick's Point Dr; mains $32-47; ◷5-9pm) serves up sought-after mesquite-grilled seafood and meat.

03

FERN CANYON LOOP TRAIL

DURATION	DIFFICULTY	DISTANCE	START/END
1-2hr return	Easy-moderate	1.1 miles	Fern Canyon parking lot

TERRAIN	Creek bed, logs, forest floor

Oversized ferns and fuzzy mosses drip down the walls of this narrow, dramatic canyon that Steven Spielberg appropriately selected as a filming location for *The Lost World: Jurassic Park*. The enchanting feature of Prairie Creek Redwoods State Park has also been designated a World Heritage Site and International Biosphere Reserve, so don't be surprised if you end up sharing it with a sizable crowd, particularly in the summertime.

GETTING HERE

From Hwy 101, you'll take the turnoff about 2 miles north of Orick for Davison Rd. You'll follow the paved road through Elk Meadow, after which it will become a dirt road, and then you'll continue for about 6 miles to Golf Bluffs Kiosk. Here you'll pay the $8 fee to enter, then continue for 3 more miles

that are somewhat bumpy and include a couple of stream crossings before reaching the parking lot. Note that in the rainy months, the creek crossings may be impassable for cars without 4WD. Meanwhile, in the summertime the parking lot can fill up fast, so you'll want to arrive early to guarantee yourself a spot.

STARTING POINT

Welcome to one of the busiest spots in all of Redwood National and State Parks, and for good reason. From the parking lot (which offers public restrooms) you'll head north on the Coastal Trail toward Fern Canyon. Before starting out, be sure you've got appropriate footwear: the trail intersects on many occasions with a winding, pebble-filled creek and it's likely that your lower extremities will get wet. You may also want to consider adding another longer trail to this relatively short hike, as there are some very good options nearby.

01 Winding through **beach meadows** and along the base of a bluff, you'll come to a **lush, forested area** and nearby springs may create soggy conditions underfoot. Eventually you'll cross a portable footbridge over Home Creek, unless of course you're visiting between October and April, when the bridges are removed. There are several trails that can be accessed from this area, but when you see the yawning entryway into **Fern Canyon** on your right, you'll definitely want to head toward it.

02 Entering the canyon, you'll notice that its 30ft walls are festooned in **living wallpaper**, including five different kinds of **ferns**. Keep a look out for the emerald-green sword ferns, velvety five-fingered ferns and delicate lady ferns, which tend to be the crowd favorites. The sandy footpath is oftentimes submerged beneath the cobbled creek (pictured), and you'll either have to get your feet wet, use big logs installed as balance beams or ask a friend for a piggyback ride. Above the canyon walls you'll notice Sitka spruce and other conifers soaring high, and if you look closely at the walls, you may spy a **salamander** or a **frog**.

03 The canyon narrows as the walls become ever more vertical, and depending on what the rainy season brought in, you may have to hop over some fallen trees. If the winter has been particularly wet, the tree limbs, trunks and other debris inside the canyon can really pile up. This is a great area to wander around, getting a closer look at the fern foliage and admiring the stretches of **canyon wall fronted by trickling water**. (There are a couple of particularly Instagram-worthy examples of this.) Eventually you'll reach an area where, at the time of research, a huge downed tree made it look like the trail ended.

Roosevelt Elk

Roosevelt elk roam the coast and forestland up against Fern Canyon, and encountering these majestic creatures is as enchanting as it is worrisome, particularly during their six-week mating season from August to October. Bulls can weigh up to 1000lb and can do damage with their antlers and powerful legs, while cows with calves can also become aggressive. Human-elk conflict has been on the rise in Northern California recently, and scientists are now making a large-scale effort to study and understand the elk in hopes of identifying solutions. Do your part in protecting yourself and the elk by staying at least 75ft away while admiring and photographing them.

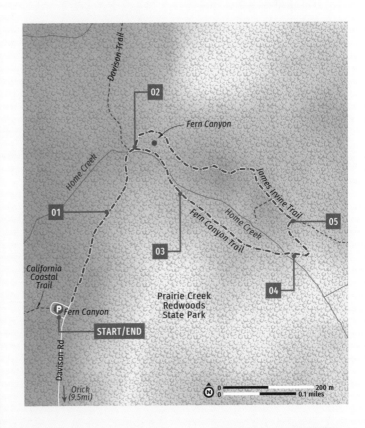

You'll actually need to climb up and over this tree to continue the journey deeper into the canyon.

04 The trail starts to climb a bit, and you'll want to stay to your left and veer off to a **flight of natural stairs**. (Note that you may need to slosh through the stream to get to the base of the stairs.) As you ascend the twisting trail out of the canyon and onto its rim, you'll get some lovely **views of the canyon from above** and be surrounded by spruce and alder. Eventually you'll reach a boardwalk over a spring-fed bog, and that gives way to a downgrade and some flights of stairs that will return you to the canyon entrance. Alternatively, when you reach the stairs you can ignore them and double back through the canyon, which also takes you back to the loop's start point.

05 Because the Fern Canyon Loop Trail is just over a mile long, you may want to add on a nearby trail to enhance and prolong the experience. The easy stretch of the **California Coastal Trail** to the north is ideal for spotting **Roosevelt elk** and a few waterfalls over the bluff, including **Gold Dust Falls**. You can also combine that with some redwood action on the **West Ridge and Friendship Ridge Trails**, from which you can hear the crashing sea (and occasionally see it on clear days). Alternatively, you could add the **James Irvine–Miner's Ridge loop** (pictured) to your itinerary. The 19th-century gold-mining trail offers 9 miles of old-growth redwoods, a spruce forest and a gushing river.

ASHLEY HARRELL/LONELY PLANET ©

 ## Eureka!

The yellow-gold-colored bluffs near Fern Canyon gave this stretch of coastline its name, Gold Bluffs Beach, but as it happens, there's also real gold to be found here. After early settlers discovered gold dust in the hillsides in the 1850s, mining operations moved in and Yurok tribes who had been living in the area for centuries were brutally forced out. By the early 1900s, removing the gold proved too laborious, without the profits to justify the work. Prospectors moved on, and the land was donated to the Save the Redwoods League to preserve the adjacent coastal forests. In remembrance of that history and just a couple of miles from Fern Canyon, a waterfall dubbed Gold Dust Falls plummets 80ft over the side of the bluff.

 ## TAKE A BREAK

There aren't many sit-down restaurants near Redwood National and State Parks, but one delightful exception is **Snack Shack** (✆707-458-4937; 12079 Redwood Hwy, Orick; burgers $7-21; ⏰11am-6pm Tue & Sun, to 8pm Wed-Sat), where you can grab an elk burger, some tater tots and a milkshake and chow down at an outdoor picnic table. Note that the burgers are made of farmed elk (not the famous, wild Roosevelt elk).

04

TRINIDAD HEAD LOOP TRAIL

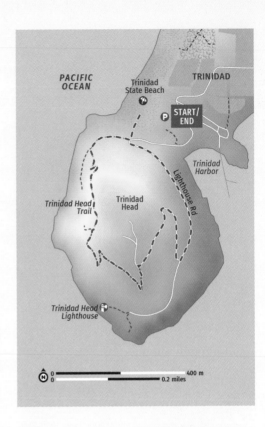

DURATION	DIFFICULTY	DISTANCE	START/END
1-2hr return	Easy-moderate	1.7 miles	Trinidad Beach parking lot

TERRAIN	Pavement & gravel

Trinidad Head boasts some of the loveliest coastal views in California, and yet the trail is easily accessed and fairly unchallenging to complete. Standout features of this rocky headland include windblown evergreens, a crashing sea in all directions and the occasional gray migrating whale, dolphin or harbor seal. Although the trail can be crowded, there are a great many viewpoints that each offer large wooden benches, and lots of spur trails as well.

Park at **Trinidad State Beach** and definitely consider strolling the boulder-strewn shoreline before climbing the staircase at the southern end of the parking lot to access the trail. You'll begin by crossing a narrow strip of land with **views of the rugged Humboldt**

coastline to the north and **tranquil Trinidad Harbor** to the east.

The trail goes counterclockwise round the head, starting off on a paved service road with a fairly steep incline. You'll amble beneath **tunnels of foliage** and eventually the path levels out somewhat and arrives at a **series of lookouts** over the sea. The vistas include some incredibly scenic rocky islets, such as **Flatiron Rock**, where large colonies of seabirds live and poop (hence the white rocks).

You'll notice quite a few spur trails, and these lead to still more lookouts where the bramble has parted. Don't wander into the brush, as there's quite a bit of poison oak in there, but do split off the main path for some rewarding explorations. As you come around the loop, the historic town of **Trinidad** becomes visible to the east, and soon you'll be back at the start.

05

MENDOCINO HEADLANDS TRAIL

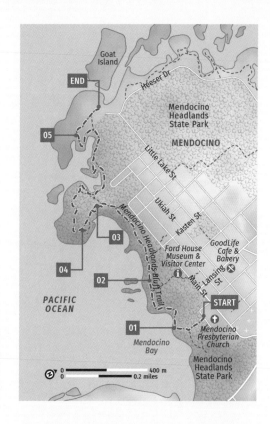

DURATION	DIFFICULTY	DISTANCE	START/END
2-3hr one way	Easy-moderate	4 miles	Presbyterian Church/ Heeser Dr

TERRAIN	Coastal bluff

Just steps from the romantic seaside enclave of Mendocino, this convenient but spectacular trail follows the dramatic edge of the headland and is flanked with berry bramble, wildflowers and cypress trees perched over dizzying cliffs. Ocean views include rock formations and dramatic arches, and there's also an option to descend to picturesque coves and relax in the sand.

GETTING HERE

Once you're in Mendocino, getting to this trail couldn't be easier: just walk toward the sea. The trail runs the length of Mendocino Headlands State Park, and we recommend hiking it from east to west (starting at Mendocino Presbyterian Church on Church St), but it can also be hiked west to east. There are several parking areas near different

stretches of the trail, meaning you can also drop in on those sections without hiking the whole thing.

STARTING POINT

Before setting out, drop by the **Ford House Museum & Visitor Center** (☎707-937-5397; www.mendoparks. org; 45035 Main St; ◷11am-4pm) for maps, books, information and exhibits, including a scale model of 1890 Mendocino, in a historical setting with Victorian-period furniture and decor. Then head a block east to the intersection of Main and Church Sts, where there's parking if you need it. Walk south on Church St, past Mendocino Presbyterian Church, which eventually turns into a gravel trail through a meadow toward the sea.

01 Stroll among the high grasses and beneath the occasional conifer to the first **lookout over the sea**, where a wide swatch of coastline can be spied through the parted bramble.

Mendocino History

Built by transplanted New Englanders in the 1850s, Mendocino thrived late into the 19th century, with ships transporting redwood timber from here to San Francisco. The mills shut down in the 1930s, and the town was rediscovered in the 1950s by artists and bohemians. Today the culturally savvy, politically aware, well-traveled citizens welcome visitors, but eschew corporate interlopers – don't look for a Big Mac or Starbucks. Instead the town is full of cute shops and has earned the nickname 'Spendocino,' for its upscale goods. To avoid crowds, come midweek or in the low season, when the vibe is mellower – and prices more reasonable.

Best for

POST-HIKE CHEER

PICCHU PRODUCTIONS/SHUTTERSTOCK ©

02 Winding along the edge of the rocky headland, you'll encounter **sandy coves**, **rocky islands** and perhaps even a **passing whale**. There are several short spur trails to **cypress-studded viewpoints** that are lovely around sunset, and often deserted. If you look back to the north, you'll notice the town's distinctive architecture peeking above the tall grasses.

03 Here's the first opportunity to descend some stairs to a **wide, sandy beach**. From the shoreline you'll have a view of a yawning tunnel through the rocky outcropping and out to sea, along with some elaborate driftwood structures that are particularly fun for kids.

04 After climbing back onto the bluff, you'll pass a **protected coastal dune** and also a number of **impressive arches** (pictured) that have been slowly eroded by the sea. In this spot you can listen to the foamy green sea lapping against hollowed-out caverns.

05 As the vegetation begins to disappear in this rockier home stretch, some **spectacular tide pools** may be visible on the edge of the headland, depending on the tide. Continue to the parking lot on Heeser Dr and cut back through town to return to your car or accommodations.

TAKE A BREAK

Before setting out on your hike, stop by **GoodLife Cafe & Bakery** (707-937-0836; www.goodlifecafemendo.com; 10485 Lansing St; light meals $6-10; 8am-2pm) and pick up a locally roasted fair-trade coffee and maybe some avo toast or a breakfast sandwich to go. Then you can nosh when you reach that perfect bench on the headland offering a panoramic ocean view.

06

LOST COAST TRAIL: MATTOLE TO PUNTA GORDA LIGHTHOUSE

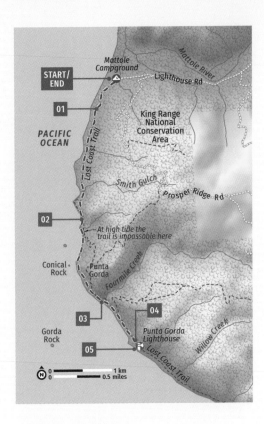

DURATION	DIFFICULTY	DISTANCE	START/END
4-5hr return	Moderate	7 miles	Mattole Campground

TERRAIN	Coastal bluff, rocks, sand

An abandoned lighthouse, remnants of shipwrecks, curious tide pools and an abundance of wildlife including sea lions, elephant seals and some 300 bird species are highlights on this spectacular stretch of the Lost Coast Trail. The footpath is mostly level, traversing beaches and crossing over rocky outcrops and coastal bluffs.

GETTING HERE

From Hwy 101 exit at Garberville, South Fork/Honeydew, or Ferndale. You'll then follow the signs toward Petrolia, eventually turning on Lighthouse Rd toward the sea. The drive takes at least two hours from the highway regardless of where you exit, and is very twisty and challenging (but quite scenic!). Some stretches are dirt and there are many potholes. Mattole Campground's parking lot offers restooms and drinking water.

STARTING POINT

The trail begins from Mattole Campground, just south of the mouth of the Mattole River. As you set out on the gray sand beach, the wind is likely to be at your back, and depending on the time of year, it may be strong. Keep in mind that on the return, you will be walking into this wind. Save some energy.

01 You'll spend the first couple of miles walking through **coastal dunes**, where jackrabbits and rattlesnakes are known to hide behind chunks of driftwood and among the dune grass and wildflowers. Hiking by the sea can be a challenge for some; be sure you've got good hiking boots and consider gaiters to prevent sand from getting in your shoes.

02 As you round Punta Gorda, the trail draws closer to the crashing sea and the sand is more tightly packed. For this portion of the hike,

The Longer Hike

Hiking the full 24.6 miles of the Lost Coast Trail within the King Range is a classic California experience. Within this 68,000-acre natural playground, the terrain is so extreme that engineers building Hwy 1 bypassed it entirely. This is a true wilderness, and it comes with unique challenges. Overnight camping requires a permit, available through www.recreation.gov, and these sell out weeks or months ahead. You'll also need a bear canister and a tide chart, as some stretches of the trail become impassable at high tide. Hiking with the wind means going north to south, from Mattole Campground to Black Sands Beach. Optimal times are weekdays in early June, late August, September and October.

Best for

ESCAPING THE CROWDS

you'll need to be hiking at low tide, when **tide pools filled with sea creatures** will become visible. Watch closely and you may spot a **playful sea lion** lounging on the rocks.

03 Nearing **Fourmile Creek**, which is fairly shallow in the summer and considerably deeper in the wintertime, you'll notice a **private cabin** on the shore. This is one of a few that were grandfathered in when King Range became a National Conservation Area in 1970.

04 Up on a bluff, the abandoned **Punta Gorda Lighthouse** (pictured) comes into view. High winds and rocky shoals led to untold numbers of shipwrecks here, prompting the lighthouse's construction in 1910. Its isolation earned it the nickname 'the Alcatraz of lighthouses;' don't hesitate to climb into its tower and pretend you're a lonely keeper.

05 Down toward the shore you'll find a resident colony of **northern elephant seals**. They weigh up to 4500lb and can easily crush a person, so you'll want to stay at least 165ft away. For endless entertainment, watch from a safe distance as they snort and fight with each other, then turn back north for the return, and get your windbreaker ready.

TAKE A BREAK

If you are heading for the Lost Coast Trail you'll definitely need to pack sufficient provisions, and there's a general store in Shelter Cove (the only sizable community in the region) to grab last-minute items. There are several places to eat and drink in the town, but **Gyppo Ale Mill** (📞 707-986-7700; www.gyppo. com; 1661 Upper Pacific Dr; mains $10-20; ⊙ 4-8pm Mon-Fri, noon-8pm Sat & Sun), a craft brewery and from-scratch kitchen, is the most delightful.

07

BOY SCOUT TREE TRAIL

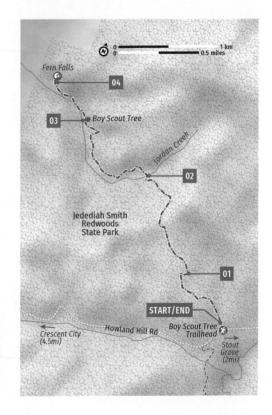

DURATION	DIFFICULTY	DISTANCE	START/END
3-4hr return	Moderate	5.6 miles	Boy Scout Tree Trailhead parking lot

TERRAIN	Uneven forest floor, many tree roots

If it was possible to curate the perfect redwood day hike, including a range of environments, old-growth trees and very few people, the result would look a lot like the Boy Scout Tree Trail. The quiet, little-explored trail is tucked into Jedediah Smith Redwoods State Park, the northernmost expanse of Redwood National and State Parks. And though the trail is a bit far-flung and its path is a bit steep and uneven, the rewards more than justify the effort.

GETTING HERE

Most people access the trail while road-tripping along Hwy 101. If coming from the south, exit onto Humboldt Rd just before Crescent City then make a right on Howland Hill Rd and continue for 2 miles.

If you're approaching on Hwy 101 from the north, exit onto Elk Valley Rd then make a left on Howland Hill Rd. It's also possible to enter the park from the east, turning south off Hwy 199 onto Howland Hill Rd and continuing for 5 miles. Note that Howland Hill Rd is curvy, unpaved and flanked by old-growth forest — an attraction in its own right.

STARTING POINT

The trailhead parking lot is located within a spectacular old-growth grove. There are spots for a couple dozen cars along with a set of restrooms, and the trail begins at the north end of the lot. Consider maximizing your experience by setting out under the morning sun, when slanting beams of light filter through the treetops.

01 You'll wander through **lowland redwoods** shooting some 300ft up from a thick carpet of ferns and sorrel in this first leg of the journey. It's

Stout Grove

If you've gone out of your way to hike the Boy Scout Tree Trail, this famous grove is also more than worth a stop. Perched at the confluence of two rivers, this 44-acre grove is considered by some to be the world's most breathtaking. The understory is a thick mat of sword ferns and sorrel and the densely packed, 300ft redwoods are subject to regular flooding, which has prevented other foliage from encroaching. Defined by its distinctive wavy bark, the Stout Tree is the grove's largest. You can reach it from Howland Hill Rd but also via a half-mile trail departing from the Jedediah Smith campground near the visitor center (open in summer only).

GREG VAUGHN/ALAMY STOCK PHOTO ©

usually very quiet, with a gentle uphill slope with the occasional footbridge or fallen, massive trunk split in half to make way for the trail. After about a mile, you'll also start noticing some **Douglas firs** in the mix.

02 Switchbacks and stairs lead deeper into the forest, where overgrowth isn't as thick, and after crossing **Jordan Creek** you'll start to notice massive redwoods growing in groups, surrounding their mother tree. The canopy is more open here, offering a rare glimpse of the treetops.

03 After descending into a valley of maple trees, you'll come to a turnoff for the **Boy Scout Tree** that's easily missed (look for a small wooden sign). This wondrous redwood got its name for its massive, side-by-side trunks that resemble the Boy Scout salute.

04 The out-and-back trail dead-ends at **Fern Falls**, a small waterfall that feels a bit underwhelming after basking in the glory of the Boy Scout Tree. The good news is the hike back actually offers better views of increasingly larger redwoods.

TAKE A BREAK

Pre- or post-hike roll up to **Sea-Quake Brewing** (📞707-465-4444; www.seaquakebrewing.com; 400 Front St; mains $10-17; 🕐11:30am-9pm Tue-Thu, to 10pm Fri & Sat; 📶), easily the most happening place in Crescent City. We're partial to the inventive pizzas, creative salads and appealing barn-like atmosphere. Oh, and did we mention the 12 taps of home-brewed ales? They're some of the best along the Northern Coast.

08

TALL TREES GROVE LOOP TRAIL

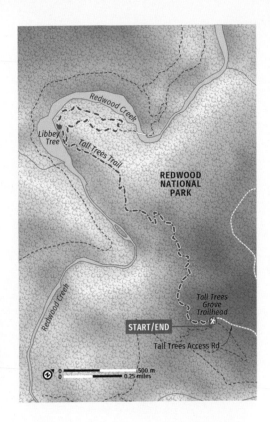

DURATION	DIFFICULTY	DISTANCE	START/END
2-3hr return	Moderate-hard	4 miles	Tall Trees Grove Trailhead

TERRAIN	Forest floor, some parts are steep

Tall Trees Grove Trail is Redwood National Park's most hard-won hike, and the rewards are, well, enormous. At the end of an incredibly serene and winding path hikers come to a sky-high grove, and although its location is secret, the world's tallest tree lives in the vicinity. Also featuring gargantuan ferns, a scenic creek and total isolation, this is one of Redwood National Park's most treasured but seldom-visited attractions.

To protect the Tall Trees Grove, only 50 cars per day are allowed access. Visitors must obtain free permits prior to entry, and at the time of research that meant applying online at least 48 hours in advance. (When the visitor center is open, the permits are available there on the day of your visit.) From there, you'll drive north on Hwy 1010 and take a right on Bald Hills Rd, then continue until you reach the turnoff for the Tall Trees Access Rd. You'll have to enter a code to access the bumpy, 6-mile logging road to the trailhead.

From the trailhead, the path descends 800ft to the floodplain of **Redwood Creek**, where the grove has all the water, soil and protection from wind it needs to thrive. On the way in, you'll actually pass through a **tunneled-out redwood** that's fallen onto the path. It's about 1.5 miles to the loop, where many of the trees soar higher than 350ft, and actually a tree that used to be the world's tallest, the **Libbey Tree**, is found here. (It was demoted when its top broke off in 1994.)

In addition to the redwoods, you'll also notice some large maple trees and moss-covered branches, along with some oversized ferns carpeting the forest. Save some energy for the hike back, as the return trip on the same path ascends those 800ft you dropped earlier.

09

LOST COAST TRAIL: NEEDLE ROCK TO WHALE GULCH

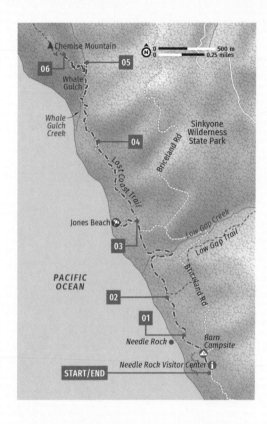

DURATION	DIFFICULTY	DISTANCE	START/END
4-5hr return	Moderate-hard	4.5 miles	Needle Rock Visitor Center

TERRAIN	Coastal bluff, sand, grass

Featuring golden bluffs, majestic wild elk and a rocky, seal-studded sea, this is the most breathtaking hike within Sinkyone Wilderness State Park, a dramatic, 7367-acre stretch of the Lost Coast. The area was named for the native people who once inhabited it, and the lack of development since then means this fog-shrouded coastal wilderness has remained thoroughly pristine, a veritable hiker's dream.

GETTING HERE

From Hwy 101 take one of the Redway exits to the town of Redway, then head west on Briceland Rd toward Shelter Cove. You'll pass some old-growth redwoods before arriving at what's referred to as the 'four corners' intersection. Here the road turns to dirt, becoming bumpy, uneven, narrow and very

steep in some areas. You'll wind your way down to the Needle Rock Visitor Center, where there's a $6 parking fee.

STARTING POINT

Beginning at the Needle Rock Visitor Center, walk up the road toward the barn, an overnight accommodations that's a small step up from outdoor camping. You'll soon see a sign for the Lost Coast Trail.

01 The trail will dip in and out of a gully, and just offshore you'll notice **Needle Rock**, a peculiar arch formed by the surging Pacific. This also happens to be one of the park's loveliest **sunset spots**.

02 Continuing on the grassy bluff you'll pass a couple of primitive campsites before heading inland briefly, then crossing a small creek. **Roosevelt**

OLGA VASYLIEVA/SHUTTERSTOCK ©

elk (pictured) tend to hang out around this area; be sure to keep a safe distance, as they can become aggressive.

03 After reaching a stand of eucalyptus trees you'll see a clearly marked turnoff for **Jones Beach**. Head down the mountainside for an up-close look at the foaming sea, bull-whip kelp and startling rock formations. Don't hesitate to bury your toes in the chocolate-colored sand.

04 Return to the main trail and continue down through a canyon. You'll then cross over a couple of creeks and come upon a pond lined in cat-tails. Climbing, you'll encounter a second pond, and in summer-time there will be **wildflowers** everywhere.

05 Climbing back on the bluff, you'll pass a **postcard-perfect cove** before descending into pebble-filled **Whale Gulch**. Flanked by big-leaf maples and other trees and shrubs, the trail eventually crosses the gulch and heads up Chemise Mountain. The trail at this point is poorly maintained and very steep.

06 Those with the dexterity and the will to climb **Chemise Mountain** will arrive at a dramatic viewpoint overlooking the coastline to the south. You can try to pick out the faraway spot from whence you came from, and to where you'll now return.

 **TAKE A BREAK**

There are no places to buy provisions in the park; the nearest grocery store and restaurants are to the north in Shelter Cove. For a pre-meal bite or a post-hike celebration, **Mi Mochima** (📞707-358-0460; 210 Wave Dr; mains $15-20; 🕐5-9pm Thu-Sun, noon-3pm Sat & Sun) offers authentic and delicious Venezuelan fare.

Also Try...

YAYA ERNST/SHUTTERSTOCK ©

DAMNATION CREEK TRAIL

Within the little-explored Del Norte Coast Redwoods State Park, this stunning trail meanders through old-growth redwoods and Sitka spruce, crossing Damnation Creek and plunging more than 1000ft into a secluded cove.

The trail begins from an unmarked pullout on Hwy 101 about 8 miles south of Crescent City, at mile marker 16. Initially the path is level and flanked by soaring redwoods and huckleberry bushes. After crossing the creek, the trail becomes overgrown, slopes dramatically downward and is sometimes shrouded in fog, offering a bit of a challenge (particularly on the way back). Eventually the terrain levels out again on a bluff with a scenic overlook of Damnation Cove and the crashing Pacific, before dropping down to the rocky shoreline. At high tide there's no beach, and at low tide you can sometimes find tide pools.

DURATION 3-4hr return
DIFFICULTY Moderate-hard
DISTANCE 4.2 miles

LADY BIRD JOHNSON GROVE TRAIL

If the goal is to experience the majesty of the redwoods with minimal effort, please allow us to introduce this accessible, easy loop within Redwood National Park (pictured above). High on a ridgetop, the trail is flat and winds through massive redwoods, gigantic ferns and rhododendrons that bloom in May and early June.

The grove is named for Lyndon Johnson's wife because she was here in 1969 to dedicate the national park, and you'll find many other interesting historical tidbits on trail placards. You'll also notice quite a few 'goose pens,' or hollowed-out redwoods that early settlers used to contain their livestock.

The grove is understandably popular, but maintains a tranquil atmosphere, particularly when the fog has rolled in.

DURATION 1-2hr return
DIFFICULTY Easy
DISTANCE 1.4 miles

SKUNK CABBAGE TRAIL

Tucked into Redwood National Park, this isolated and somewhat overgrown trail features forestland and coastline, and will appeal to hikers seeking solitude, variety and a bit of a challenge.

The low-lying areas of the trail also offer the pod-like and strange-smelling plant for which the trail is named. To reach the trailhead, drive 2 miles north of Orick on Hwy 101 and head west at the sign for the trail.

DURATION 5-6hr return
DIFFICULTY Moderate
DISTANCE 10.4 miles

KING PEAK TRAIL

If a beach hike isn't appealing but the rugged beauty of the Lost Coast beckons, try summiting the area's highest mountain, a 4000ft peak appropriately dubbed King Peak.

The 2½-hour drive on backcountry roads is a knuckle-whitener, but intrepid hikers appreciate the unobstructed views of the entirety of King Range, the sea, the surrounding river valleys and the distant Klamath Mountains.

DURATION 3-4hr return
DIFFICULTY Hard
DISTANCE 5.3 miles

KORTUM TRAIL

Within Sonoma Coast State Park, this unchallenging trail (pictured above) features abundant wildlife, seasonal wildflowers, tide pools, panoramic views of the Pacific and oversized climbable boulders.

With good timing and a bit of luck, you can watch sea birds gliding along the Pacific flyway or whale pods migrating just offshore.

DURATION 4-5hr return
DIFFICULTY Easy-moderate
DISTANCE 9 miles

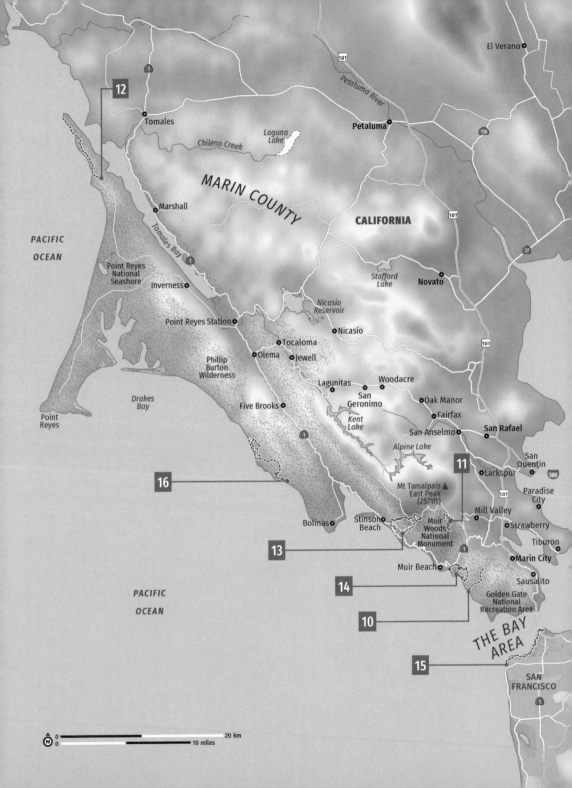

MARIN COUNTY & THE BAY AREA

Explore
MARIN COUNTY & THE BAY AREA

When it comes to natural settings, few places on earth are as lucky as the Bay Area. The untamed landscapes at San Francisco's doorstep offer some of California's most beautiful and dramatic hiking. In Marin County, mountains, redwoods and gorgeous shorelines all converge in a cornucopia of state and national parks. Across the bay, the East Bay boasts its own plethora of green spaces, and makes a sunny escape when summer fog envelops the coast. Even within San Francisco's city limits, great hikes are never far off, thanks to the huge swaths of parkland protected within Golden Gate National Recreation Area. For people who love to walk, it's hard to imagine a dreamier urban backdrop.

SAN FRANCISCO

If you want to mix outdoor adventure with the urban charms of one of America's most walkable cities, San Francisco makes a great base. San Franciscans love the outdoors, and their historic conservation efforts have protected acres of parks, beaches and woodlands for all to enjoy. Beautiful green spaces such as Lands End and Golden Gate Park beckon right within the city limits, and there are scores of great trails within an hour's drive up and down the coast and across the bay.

POINT REYES STATION

Though the railroad stopped coming through in 1933 and the town is small, Point Reyes Station is nevertheless the hub of western Marin County and a pleasant gateway to Point Reyes National Seashore. Dominated by dairies and ranches, the region was invaded by artists in the 1960s. Today Main St is a diverting blend of art galleries and tourist shops. The town has a great bakery, some good restaurants and a rowdy saloon, with the occasional smell of cattle on the afternoon breeze.

MILL VALLEY

It's still hanging on to its bohemian roots, but beautiful Mill Valley, nestled under the redwoods at the base of Mt Tamalpais, is nowadays home to wildly expensive houses, luxury cars and pricey boutiques. It's one of the Bay Area's most picturesque hamlets and is a great place to stay, visit or use as a base for forays up Mt Tamalpais or the southern Marin coast.

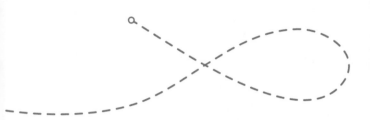

California Department of Parks & Recreation (www.parks. ca.gov) General information on Bay Area state parks.

National Park Service (www. nps.gov/pore, www.nps.gov/ muwo, www.nps.gov/goga) Maps and trail info for Point Reyes, Muir Woods and Golden Gate National Recreational Area.

East Bay Regional Park District (www.ebparks.org) All you need to explore the East Bay's excellent regional park network.

Reserve California (www. reservecalifornia.com) State park camping reservations, including Samuel P Taylor Redwoods SP and the coveted Steep Ravine cabins at Mt Tamalpais SP.

Recreation.gov (www. recreation.gov) National park camping reservations, including backcountry sites at Point Reyes.

WHEN TO GO

Spring and fall are prime time for hiking in the Bay Area. Winter rains turn the hills brilliant green and flowery throughout March and April, while September and October bring some of the area's warmest, driest weather (along with higher fire risk). Wind-lashed storms off the Pacific drench the region with frequent rains between November and March. Thanks to San Francisco's legendary fog, summer days on the coast can be downright frigid, though the situation improves as you move inland.

WHERE TO STAY

When it comes to accommo-dations, the Bay Area offers an embarrassment of riches...for a price. Rates at the region's hotels and B&Bs are notoriously high, but there's a fantastic variety of options. Hikers on a budget will be glad to know that the Bay Area also has some superb hostels and campgrounds, often right at the doorstep of the region's most desirable hiking spots, such as Mt Tamalpais State Park and Point Reyes Na-tional Seashore. Places book up fast, so plan well ahead.

WHAT'S ON

Bay to Breakers (www.capstoneraces .com/bay-to-breakers; ⊘May) Trade your hiking boots for running shoes and break out your favorite costume for San Francisco's offbeat 7.5-mile race, held annually since 1912.

Dipsea Race (www.dipsea.org; ⊘Jun) America's oldest trail race follows the Dipsea Trail up staircases and down creek gorges from Mill Valley to Stinson Beach.

AIDS Walk San Francisco (https:// sf.aidswalk.net; ⊘Jul) Until AIDS takes a hike, this 10km fundrais-er walk through Golden Gate Park will continue its four-decade tradition of raising mon-ey for HIV/AIDS organizations.

Mill Valley Film Festival (www.mvff. com; ⊘Oct) An innovative, inter-nationally regarded program of independent films screened in Mill Valley and San Rafael.

TRANSPORT

San Francisco and Oakland airports are the main gateways to the Bay Area.

Public transport in the region is generally good, with local agencies such as Muni (www. sfmta.com) in San Francisco and Marin Transit (www.marin transit.org) in Marin County offering access to several trailheads. However, it helps to haveyour own wheels to explore further afield, especially if you plan to hike in the outer reaches of Point Reyes National Seashore.

10

TENNESSEE VALLEY

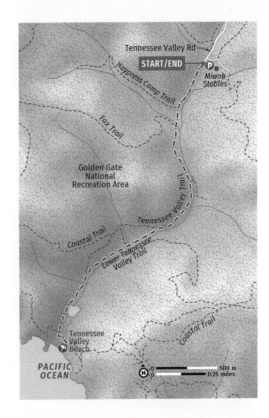

DURATION	DIFFICULTY	DISTANCE	START/END
2hr return	Easy	3.6 miles	Tennessee Valley parking lot

TERRAIN	Level trails & dirt roads

Few hikes in California are as popular as this easy out-and-back jaunt to a splendid black-sand beach only half an hour's drive from downtown San Francisco. It's manageable for hikers of any age, from toddlers on up, and the wild beauty of the landscape is stunning, providing a welcome antidote to the Bay Area's urban sprawl.

From the **Tennessee Valley parking lot**, head south on a broad paved road that shortly turns to dirt. Pass junctions with the Haypress and Fox Trails on your right and follow a long row of eucalyptus trees on your left to a junction with the Coastal Trail at the 0.6-mile mark. Following signs for Tennessee Beach, round a bend toward the coast, where ocean breezes often rush in between the trailside bluffs. You'll soon reach a fork where the wider main road climbs right, while a narrower trail stays left on the valley floor. Take the latter path and continue towards the Pacific. After a blissfully level half mile, rejoin the main road near a trailside outhouse. **Magnificent views** unfold to your left over a **reed-fringed lagoon** (pictured) backed by chaparral-covered hills, and you catch distant glimpses of the ocean as the undulating road contours the base of a hill on your right.

At the 1.8-mile mark, the trail deposits you on **Tennessee Valley Beach**, a vast sweep of dark pebbly sand cradled between rugged headlands. The waters here are usually too cold for a swim, but it's a magical spot to sit and watch the waves, toss a Frisbee, or wander barefoot down the sand. Intrepid souls can tackle the Tennessee Beach Overlook Trail, a short but steep detour that climbs straight up the right-hand headland for riveting views. The parking lot is an easy return jaunt on the same trail you came in on.

11

MUIR WOODS

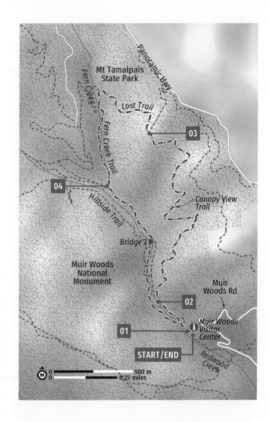

DURATION	DIFFICULTY	DISTANCE	START/END
2½hr return	Moderate	5 miles	Muir Woods Visitor Center

TERRAIN	Boardwalks, wide & narrow paths

Established as a national monument in 1908, Muir Woods is America's oldest federally protected coast redwood grove, offering a majestic glimpse of the Bay Area before large-scale development. It's also one of the most accessible redwood parks in California – both in terms of its proximity to urban areas and its wheelchair-friendly infrastructure of wide, level paths and boardwalks.

GETTING HERE

Muir Woods is a 30-minute drive north of San Francisco. Reserve parking or shuttle bus service ahead at www.gomuirwoods.com.

STARTING POINT

The entrance kiosk has maps, water, restroom facilities, picnic tables, a cafe and a gift shop.

01 Pass beneath the **grand entrance archway** onto a sturdy wooden boardwalk – part of Muir Woods' central loop of broad, flat, wheelchair-accessible paths, which parallel both sides of **Redwood Creek**, interconnected by four **numbered bridges**. The route described here starts and ends on this main loop, but also detours onto narrower, steeper trails that access the park's higher reaches.

02 A short distance upstream, branch right onto the **Canopy View Trail** (pictured), and leave the valley floor behind, snaking up a staircase into the forest. Redwoods crowd the edges of the trail, at times offering only the narrowest of passages, while ferns and wild sorrel abound in the understory. As you climb, the trees grow sparser and more sunlight filters through the canopy. Just past the 2-mile mark, a trailside **bench** offers a chance to contemplate the grandeur and tranquility of the surrounding woods before resuming your loop.

Reservation System

In response to increasing visitation numbers, Muir Woods has recently established a new reservation system. All park visitors – aside from those arriving by bike or on foot – must now reserve a spot, either in the national monument's parking lot (gas/electric vehicle $8.50/11.50) or on one of three convenient shuttle buses from remote lots. All reservations are made via the website www.gomuirwoods.com. As an added bonus, visitors with electric vehicles can now charge them on-site. The net effect is less congested roadways leading to the park, less pollution and less crowded trails when you arrive.

GREGOR CLARK/LONELY PLANET ©

03 Turn left onto the **Lost Trail**, which begins a sustained descent through the forest. Watch for exposed roots on this stretch of trail, especially after rains. Sunlight plays on the redwoods' higher branches as the valley floor gradually returns to view far below. After nearly a mile, drop into a lovely glen at a trail junction. A temptingly **photogenic bridge** straddles a massive fallen log to your right, but your route heads left onto the **Fern Creek Trail**. This narrow path lined by ferns and fence posts plunges through the redwoods within earshot of the creek. Occasional bridges ease your passage, and a massive hollow tree on the right makes an inviting place for kids to play.

04 Around the 4-mile mark, **water fountains** and a **trailside plaque** mark the end of the Fern Creek Trail and your return to Muir Woods' central loop. Turn left and you're soon on the boardwalk again. Half a mile down, turn right to cross **Bridge 3** to the opposite side of Redwood Creek. From here it's a short saunter back to the visitor center. Along the way, interpretive plaques illuminate Muir Woods' long human and natural history.

☕ TAKE A BREAK

No walk on Mt Tamalpais would be complete without a stop for lunch and drinks on the sun deck at the **Mountain Home Inn** (☏ 415-381-9000; www.mtnhomeinn.com; 810 Panoramic Hwy; r $215-400; 🖨 📶), a hillside institution founded by Swiss-German immigrants in 1912. The menu (mains $15 to $29) features everything from vegan burgers and wild mushroom ravioli to bratwurst, Dungeness crab cakes and ribeye steak. If you fancy a sugar fix, look no further than the chocolate lava cake and root beer floats!

12

TOMALES POINT TRAIL

DURATION	DIFFICULTY	DISTANCE	START/END
5hr return	Moderate	9.8 miles	Pierce Point Ranch parking lot

TERRAIN	Undulating dirt roads & trails

Point Reyes' lonesome northern reaches culminate in Tomales Point, a narrow wedge of land jutting up between Tomales Bay and the Pacific Ocean. Vast coastal views combine here with excellent wildlife spotting and perspectives on the prosperous history of the peninsula's 19th-century dairies.

GETTING HERE

The trailhead is a 30-minute drive north of Point Reyes Station, or 90 minutes from San Francisco.

STARTING POINT

You'll find free parking and a public restroom at the trailhead. For other services, the closest town is Inverness, 20 minutes to the south.

01 Set off from **Pierce Point Ranch**, once a prosperous dairy that shipped its butter by schooner across Tomales Bay to supply San Francisco's finest restaurants. Check out the farm buildings and historical plaques, then follow signs for Tomales Point past fences and barns onto a dirt road beneath a cypress windbreak. The broad path climbs through scrub-covered hills, with occasional seductive glimpses of **McClure's Beach** below. Within half a mile, the trail flattens out atop coastal bluffs, revealing the rugged coastline to your north.

02 Curve inland through a gully, enjoying your first views east to the glassy waters of **Tomales Bay**. A brief, steep uphill slog gradually settles into a gentler climb. Near the 2-mile mark the trail levels off in grasslands where **tule elk** (pictured) often graze. Views north to Tomales Point, where the Pacific rounds the bend and meets Tomales Bay, get increasingly impressive as the trail begins trending

Side Trip: McClure's Beach

If you've made it this far north, you simply have to visit McClure's Beach. This long and lovely expanse of sand, bookended by massive headlands, is accessible via a half-mile trail from a parking lot a few hundred feet below Pierce Point Ranch and the Tomales Point trailhead. The sandy trail descends a long gully to the ocean's edge, with bright green vegetation fringing the creek as it flows picturesquely beneath a giant sand dune. All told, a visit to McClure's makes for a 20- to 30-minute detour, plus however much time you spend on the beach.

Best for

WILDLIFE

RADOSLAW LECYK/SHUTTERSTOCK ©

gently downhill. Across the bay, you can make out the dunes above Dillon Beach, while on the far horizon, cliffs extend north to Bodega Head.

03 You soon near the abandoned **Lower Pierce Point Ranch** site, identifiable by a cluster of cypresses. The trail bends east towards an old stock pond, then doubles back north under a eucalyptus windbreak that makes a pleasant rest stop. Beyond the ranch site, a sign announces the end of the maintained trail. Never fear: the remaining 1.7 miles to Tomales Point pose no real challenges and are worth the effort.

04 The trail becomes sandy and less distinct near the 4-mile mark as it weaves through wild lupines, but the point remains clearly visible ahead. The peninsula soon narrows to its **northernmost tip**, where a single gaze encompasses both the mouth of the bay and the sandstone cliffs dropping into the Pacific. As you begin your final descent, pelicans soar past, gulls and cormorants congregate amid seagrass and tidepools on offshore reefs, and boaters dip in and out of the mouth of Tomales Bay. Near the water's edge, sandstone shelves offer enticing spots to enjoy a picnic before retracing your steps to the ranch.

TAKE A BREAK

For a satisfying sense of déjà vu after your Tomales Point ramble, head for the outdoor deck at **Tony's Seafood** (415-663-1107; www. tonysseafoodrestaurant.com; 18863 Shoreline Hwy, Marshall; mains $16-24; 11am-5pm) on the opposite (eastern) shore of Tomales Bay. Owned by the Hog Island Oyster Company, it serves up a half-dozen varieties of the freshest oysters, along with po'boy sandwiches, mussels, fish and chips, and other sea-sourced treats, all served with a dazzling view of sunset over the bay's sparkling waters.

13

DIPSEA, STEEP RAVINE & MATT DAVIS LOOP

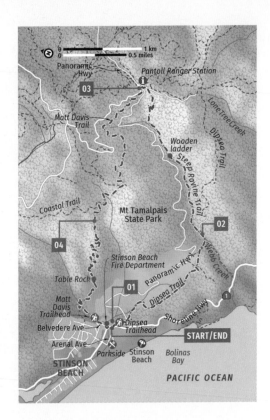

DURATION	DIFFICULTY	DISTANCE	START/END
4hr return	Moderate	8.2 miles	Stinson Beach

TERRAIN	Steep, hard-packed dirt trails

For a varied mix of Bay Area landscapes, you couldn't choose a more satisfying trail than this classic loop through Mt Tamalpais State Park. Starting from Stinson Beach on the Pacific coast, it climbs through lush redwood forest to Mt Tam's upland slopes, returning to the sea by a different, but equally beautiful, route.

GETTING HERE

Marin Transit bus 61 (www.marintransit.org) goes to Stinson Beach; there's free beach parking.

STARTING POINT

Stinson Beach has restaurants, shops and parking.

01 With the ocean roaring at your back, hit the **Dipsea Trail** just south of Stinson Beach's fire station, following signs for Muir Woods. The trail initially climbs, then levels out on exposed bluffs with views up the coast. After crossing two fire roads near the 1-mile mark, the Dipsea briefly merges with the **Steep Ravine Trail**, descending a staircase to the banks of **Webb Creek**. Just upstream, continue straight on the Steep Ravine Trail, as the Dipsea diverges over a bridge towards Muir Woods.

02 You're now clambering up the fern-strewn floor of a deep redwood canyon. Aided by bridges and stone steps, the trail twists up the chasm past **giant mossy boulders**, **trickling waterfalls** and **enormous trees**, some towering overhead, others fallen at haphazard angles. At the 2.7-mile mark, ascend a boulder on the gorge's right bank via a **giant wooden ladder** (pictured) with 14 well-worn rungs. Up top, sunlight increasingly floods the forest floor, proof that you're nearing Mt Tam's higher slopes. The trail leaves the creek and negotiates

Sleeping by the Sea

Some of California's most sought-after lodging is at Steep Ravine, a precipitous coastal bluff in Mt Tamalpais State Park where eight rustic cabins and a half-dozen campsites perch precariously above the Pacific. Snagging a reservation here is a challenge, and takes a mix of serious commitment and luck. New slots are available daily on a six-month rolling basis – so for example if you're trying to book for June 7, you need to be logged in to www.reserve california.com (California's state park reservation website) at 8am sharp on December 7 and hope that the digital gods are smiling on you. Good luck!

GREGOR CLARK/LONELY PLANET ©

several switchbacks framed by wooden fences, finally emerging at the **Pantoll Ranger Station** parking lot (3.7 miles).

03 Cross Panoramic Hwy, following signs for the **Matt Davis Trail** towards Stinson Beach. The new trail ascends ever so slightly over the next mile as it traverses a fragrant forest of bay laurel. At the 5.2-mile mark, emerge onto open, grassy slopes with distant ocean views, hugging the edge of flaxen hillsides for nearly a mile as you dip in and out of laurel canyons high on the mountain's edge. At a junction with the Coastal Trail, bear left to stay on the Matt Da-

vis Trail. The path soon curves decidedly downhill and enters the woods.

04 A series of long, gradual switchbacks sends you down through bright, open forest, with occasional glimpses of the Pacific peeking through far below. Around mile 7, the trail begins descending more steeply and you can hear Table Rock Creek below. Merge with the creek and continue downstream under a canopy of laurels to reach **Table Rock**, a high outcrop overlooking the houses and waterfront of Stinson Beach. Contour the rock's base and cross a pair of bridges as you navigate

the final descent to town. From the Matt Davis trailhead in Stinson Beach (8.1 miles), descend Belvedere Ave to the fire station and turn left 250ft up Hwy 1 to the Dipsea trailhead.

TAKE A BREAK

Smack in the heart of Stinson Beach, the **Parkside** (☎415-868-1272; www. parksidecafe.com; 43 Arenal Ave; restaurant mains $16-30, snack bar $4-9; ⊙7:30am-9pm, coffee bar from 6am;) cafe makes an ideal spot for a pre- or post-trail pick-me-up, serving breakfasts of *gougères* (French cheese puffs) to lunches and dinners featuring wood-fired pizzas and seasonal seafood.

14

GREEN GULCH, PIRATES COVE & MUIR BEACH

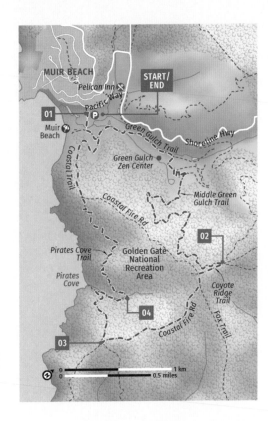

DURATION	DIFFICULTY	DISTANCE	START/END
3hr return	Moderate	5.7 miles	Muir Beach parking lot

TERRAIN	Dirt roads & steep, rocky trail

From the tranquil organic gardens of a Zen center to the imposing cliffs of Marin County's rugged coastline, this moderate loop offers an intriguing mix of experiences – all enhanced by a glorious beach and a popular pub at trail's end.

GETTING HERE

Muir Beach is 18 miles north of San Francisco on Hwy 1; there's free parking in a big beachside lot.

STARTING POINT

Water, restrooms and free parking are available at the trailhead. The nearby Pelican Inn serves food.

01 Cross the long bridge towards the beach, turn left, and head inland, bypassing a junction with the Coastal Fire Rd and continuing straight onto the **Green Gulch Trail**. Within half a mile, cross through a gate into the luxuriant organic gardens of the **Green Gulch Zen Center**, where Buddha statues mingle with farm implements. Middle Green Gulch Trail turns right between cultivated fields and a woodpile (0.7 miles), exiting the farm through another gate. The wide dirt trail climbs chaparral-covered slopes overlooking the Zen center's gardens and yurts. The mostly gradual ascent is broken by a couple of steeper sections near the junction with Coyote Ridge Trail (2.5 miles).

02 Turn right on **Coyote Ridge** and soak in the phenomenal views as you follow the ridge line south, turning left onto the Coastal Fire Rd (2.6 miles), bypassing a left-hand turnoff for the Fox Trail (2.7) and descending to a junction with **Pirates Cove Trail** (3.4). The **all-encompassing panoramas** extend southeast to San Francisco and Sausalito, north to Muir Beach and Bolinas Head, and south to Pacifica, Devil's Slide and the Golden Gate, where

Green Gulch Zen Center

In the hills above Muir Beach, the Zen Buddhist retreat center of Green Gulch is known throughout the Bay Area for its splendid 7-acre expanse of organic orchards and gardens. Produce from the farm is sold at farmers markets in San Francisco and Mill Valley throughout the summer months. **Green Gulch** (☏ 415-383-3134; www. sfzc.org; 1601 Shoreline Hwy; incl all meals s $100-175, d $175-250; **P** ⊜ @ ⧉) also offers contemporary accommodations for personal retreats or those attending the center's workshops (see the website for a calendar of options). Delicious buffet-style vegetarian meals are included.

Best for

POST-HIKE CHEER

occasional freighters chug out into the open Pacific.

03 Grand views continue as you leave the Coastal Fire Rd for the narrower Pirates Cove Trail, following coastal cliffs a stone's throw from the Pacific. The trail steeply descends along a dilapidated fence line, then plummets down a long staircase affording **dizzying views** over the rugged shores of Pirates Cove. Don't miss the right-hand turnoff for Muir Beach at the foot of the steps (3.9). A sign here points straight ahead to Pirates Cove (350ft below via an eroded path), but your perpendicular trail to Muir Beach is

not signposted. Once you turn right, the trail is clear, climbing steadily inland up a gully, with chaparral-covered slopes towering ahead.

04 The trail crosses the creek and climbs onto high bluffs, continuing its undulating course across bridges and boulder-paved sections before passing through a fence line and emerging at a junction with the **Coastal Trail** (5.0). It's all downhill from here. The broad dirt road descends gradually, then more steeply, as it nears the hillside homes and sandy expanses of **Muir Beach**. Back at the Green Gulch Trail junction (5.4), turn

left and retrace your steps across the bridge to the parking lot.

TAKE A BREAK

It's a time-honored Marin County tradition to end a day at Muir Beach with drinks on the lawn at the **Pelican Inn** (☏ 415-383-6000; www.pelicaninn.com; 10 Pacific Way; dinner mains $15-38; ⧖ 8-11am Sat & Sun, 11:30am-3pm & 5:30-9pm Sun-Fri, to 9:30pm Sat), a British-themed pub just a stone's throw from the beachfront. Bring a blanket and sprawl out in the sunshine with a pint or two, accompanied by classic pub fare like bangers and mash, shepherd's pie, Guinness beef stew, or fish and chips.

15

LANDS END TO THE GOLDEN GATE

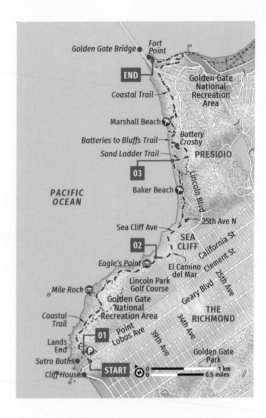

DURATION	DIFFICULTY	DISTANCE	START/END
2hr one way	Moderate	4.3 miles	Cliff House/ Fort Point

TERRAIN	Paths, staircases, beach

Perched at the city's northwestern edge, Lands End epitomizes the grandeur and romance of San Francisco's natural setting. In winter, storms race in off the Pacific, lashing the coast with ferocious winds and rain; on a sunny May afternoon, it's an exuberant green oasis; and when the city's famous fog rolls in, the interplay of mist, trees, foghorns and bridge views is downright iconic.

GETTING HERE

Take Muni bus 38 (www.sfmta.com) to the Cliff House; return from the Golden Gate on bus 28.

STARTING POINT

Restrooms, water, food and drink are all available near the Cliff House parking lot.

01 Follow signs for the **Coastal Trail** and enter the **Golden Gate National Recreation Area**, an 82,000-acre green space at the city's edge. Beyond a turnoff for the Sutro Baths, the broad path traverses a tunnel of cypresses and rounds a bend to reveal your first views of the Golden Gate and the rugged Marin Headlands. A mix of trails and staircases next leads to **Mile Rock Lookout** (0.7 miles), a sweet knoll above a rock-strewn beach where more bridge views come framed by cypress branches. Back on the Coastal Trail, cross through a pretty eucalyptus grove and parallel the Lincoln Park Golf Course (beware of wayward balls!) en route to another scenic overlook at **Eagle's Point** (1.5 miles).

02 Lands End gives way to the mansions, palms and bougainvillea of San Francisco's well-heeled **Sea Cliff neighborhood** for the next half mile. Exit the park on El Camino del Mar, branch left onto Sea Cliff Ave, then turn left on 25th Ave North

The Sutro Baths

It's hard to imagine from the ruins you see today (pictured), but San Francisco's **Sutro Baths** (www.nps.gov/goga/ historyculture/sutro-baths. htm; 680 Point Lobos Ave; ☉sunrise-sunset, visitor center 9am-5pm; P; ☐5, 31, 38) were once a social and recreational hot spot, where Victorian dandies and working stiffs converged for bracing dips in woolen rental swim-suits. In 1896, when the baths were built as the world's larg-est indoor swimming complex, Lands End was a little-trodden wasteland of dunes far from the city center. Former mayor Adolph Sutro set about revi-talizing the spot, and ensured access by building a steam train line to whisk clients here from downtown.

MIGHTYPIX/SHUTTERSTOCK ©

to reach a cul-de-sac opposite a metal gate marked 'GGNRA'. Beyond the gate, the Coastal Trail resumes, descending stairs to **Baker Beach**, one of the city's most delightful urban getaways. The long beach here basks in delirious Golden Gate views, luring joggers, dog-walkers, fishers, kayakers and occasional swimmers. The trail soon runs down a boardwalk to the beach.

03 Continue down the beach to the **Sand Ladder Trail**, a glorified dune climb with a few wooden steps buried in the drifting sand. At a hilltop junction with the Coastal Trail, turn left to briefly parallel traffic

on Lincoln Blvd, then left again onto the **Batteries to Bluffs Trail**. You've just discovered one of San Francisco's best-kept secrets. Leaving behind the whoosh of cars, descend to Battery Crosby, one of several WWII-era bunkers scattered across the coastal bluffs. From here, a long, sinu-ous staircase plunges towards the water; near the bottom, a left turnoff descends to **Marshall Beach**, a hidden cove with amaz-ing close-up views of the Golden Gate. Sitting here, the city feels a world away. After a long steep stair climb, rejoin the Coast-al Trail near the bridge's toll plaza (4.0 miles), then end your journey at **Fort Point** (4.3 miles),

where a Civil War–era fort sits directly beneath America's most beloved bridge.

TAKE A BREAK

Just a mile or so south of the Golden Gate Bridge lies the Richmond dis-trict, a neighborhood whose multi-cultural roots are reflected in its vast diversity of Asian restaurants. One of the best is **Burma Superstar** (☏415-387-2147; www.burmasuperstar. com; 309 Clement St; mains $12-29; ☉11:30am-3pm & 5-9:30pm Sun-Thu, to 10pm Fri & Sat; ☐1, 2, 33, 38, 44), where you can feast on authentic Burmese cuisine, from tea leaf salad to coconut chicken curry noodles to basil chili pork belly.

16

BASS LAKE, WILDCAT & ALAMERE FALLS

Best for

BIG VIEWS

DURATION	DIFFICULTY	DISTANCE	START/END
7hr return	Hard	14 miles	Palomarin trailhead

TERRAIN	Dirt roads, trails, beach

A variety of landscapes awaits you on this delightful out-and-back trail, which encompasses the very best of Point Reyes National Seashore: remote backcountry lakes, endless beaches at the foot of long sandstone bluffs, and a waterfall dropping picturesquely to the ocean's edge.

GETTING HERE

Palomarin trailhead sits at the end of a dead-end dirt road, 5 miles from the nearest town (the notoriously reclusive community of Bolinas). From Hwy 1, take Olema-Bolinas Rd and Mesa Rd 6.5 miles west to the trailhead.

STARTING POINT

Services are rudimentary at the Palomarin Trailhead, with an outhouse, a trail map, and little else.

Bring everything you'll need for the trail, including plenty of water and sunscreen.

01 The parking lot on a dead-end dirt road tells you all you need to know. You've already reached the edge of the wilderness before you begin, and each step today will take you further in.

02 From **Palomarin Trailhead**, the **Coast Trail** starts as a wide, level road through a eucalyptus grove, with dappled sunlight filtering down through the trees. Beyond a left-hand turnoff for Palomarin Beach at 0.2 miles, the trail narrows and begins climbing gently, with glimpses of the ocean peeking through the trees off to the left.

03 After half a mile or so, the trail emerges into coastal scrub. **Wide-open views** of the ocean unfold, and on a clear day you can see the **Farallon Islands** lurking far offshore. Closer at hand, sandstone cliffs drop dramatically into the Pacific.

04 The trail turns inland at the 0.7-mile mark, dropping briefly through clumps of evergreens before ascending again into more open country. The gently curving climb through the chaparral-covered hills is sustained but relatively untaxing – though dust and lack of shade can make this stretch fatiguing on a hot day.

05 A forested stretch starting around the 1.2-mile mark comes as a welcome relief, offering intermittent shade as the trail continues to weave

inland. The trail crosses a bridge after 1.4 miles and narrows again as it passes through a **cool landscape of ferns and overhanging trees** over the next half mile. The banks on either side of the trail grow higher and steeper on a delightful final passage to a junction with the Lake Ranch Trail. You've now come just over 2 miles.

06 Continue straight at the junction, staying on the Coast Trail and paralleling the east bank of a **seasonal pond** (dry in summer and fall) on your left for the next half mile or so. After 2.7 miles, the trail begins descending through a beautiful

grove of evergreens, offering you first glimpses of the contours of Bass Lake along the trail ahead.

07 You reach the northern shore of **Bass Lake** just before the 3-mile mark. Ducks floating on the sparkling waters below set a tranquil scene. The lake is a popular swimming spot in summer, and it merits a detour any time of year for a picnic or a rest stop.

08 After your layover at Bass Lake, resume climbing gently through shady forest on the Coast Trail. A few hundred yards up the hill, the trail levels off at a mini-pass and begins

Illicit Side Trip

Between Palomarin and Wildcat Camp, you may notice a mysterious stone arrow on the trail at the 3.9-mile mark. This not-so-subtle cue points to an unofficial trail to the top of Alamere Falls. Enter the bushes here and in 0.3 miles you'll reach a spectacular overlook encompassing the falls and the cliffs beyond. While it's fairly safe to walk as far as the overlook, the park service discourages use of the trail because some folks invariably try to go further and scramble down the falls to the beach – a practice that causes erosion and can have fatal consequences. So if you do follow the arrow, tread with caution and respect. And for close-up views of the cascading water, visit the base of the falls from Wildcat Beach.

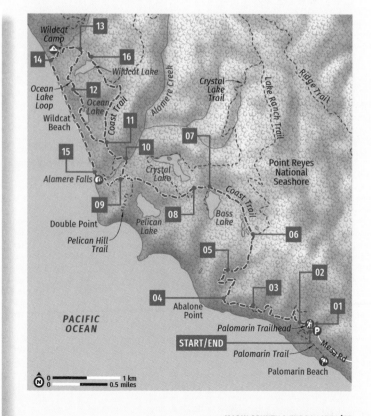

dropping equally gently towards **Pelican Lake**, a breathtaking body of water on your left backed by a coastal ridge and the Pacific Ocean beyond. Views of the lake continue as the trail opens up into scrub-covered hills, with evergreens topping another ridge line to your right.

EDDIE-HERNANDEZ.COM/SHUTTERSTOCK ©

09 **Spellbinding views** of sandstone cliffs backed by the distant arc of Point Reyes greet you as you round a bend to the right around the 4-mile mark. The trail, now narrow and eroded, begins descending, passing through a dead forest illuminated by golden light off the Pacific in late afternoon. Another tenth of a mile down the trail, you cross through an idyllic riparian landscape where a copse of silver-barked alder trees fringes **Alamere Creek**. Just a short distance to your west, these same waters tumble down a cliff face to the beach at Alamere Falls – but there's no easy access to the falls here, so stay on the main trail.

10 Cross the creek on a **wooden bridge** and head back uphill through the coastal scrub. Within two-tenths of a mile, you'll reach a junction with the Ocean Lake Loop on your left. Continuing straight on the Coast Trail here will get you to Wildcat Camp a bit faster (1.3 miles versus 1.4 miles), but the longer loop is recommended for its **divine scenery**.

11 Shortly after branching onto the **Ocean Lake Loop**, the trail emerges onto coastal bluffs that command long views over the ocean, the cliffs, and the distant point. An exhilarating flat stretch of trail bordered by blackberry bushes continues north, with **Ocean Lake** on your right backed by an evergreen-topped ridge. Elk can often be seen grazing on the trailside greenery here.

12 After contouring the bluffs for half a mile, the trail begins climbing a brushy slope, revealing even more stupendous views of the surrounding coastline. To the north, a long sweep of **wave-lapped sand** seems to stretch forever along the base of tall cliffs, while to the south fine views unfold to **Double Point**, the grandiose headland adjoining Pelican Lake. A **trailside meditation bench** invites you to pause and soak it all in.

13 Half a mile further on, the Ocean Lake Loop rejoins the Coast Trail at a signposted junction. You're now only 0.2 miles from **Wildcat Camp**, which spreads out across a grassy bluff just below. The highly sought-after campground has rudimentary facilities, with picnic tables and food storage lockers at each of its eight sites, along with an outhouse and a spigot for drinking water. If you haven't reserved ahead for the campground, turn left here and follow the trail another couple hundred yards down to Wildcat Beach.

14 Here on **Wildcat Beach**, the full drama of Point Reyes' wilderness coastline is palpable. Big waves crash on a sandy shore that stretches north and south along the cliffs for miles

Alternate Route: Point Reyes Coast

If you've got lots of energy, two vehicles and sufficient daylight, you can turn this into a 16-mile one-way hike, running all the way from Limantour Beach in the north to Palomarin Trailhead in the south. Here's how it works: leave one car at Palomarin, then drive the other 50 minutes north and park it at Limantour. From there, you can walk southeast along the beach to join the Coast Trail, then take an exhilarating amble all the way down the coast to Wildcat Camp via Sculptured Beach, Kelham Beach and Arch Rock (the last off-limits since its collapse in 2015). Upon arriving at Wildcat, simply follow our trail directions the rest of the way to Palomarin.

in either direction. If you've had enough hiking for one day, you can always turn around here and double back to the Palomarin Trailhead, but it's well worth pressing on to see **Alamere Falls**, one of the national seashore's quintessential sights.

15 Set off south down the beach, and follow the cliffs for about a mile to the foot of Alamere Falls. You'll see the falls glistening in the distance long before you reach them. As you approach, the full majesty of this spot begins to work its magic, as you catch clearer glimpses of the exuberant greenery sprouting along the cliff face where the water rushes or trickles down from the creek above. Around the 7-mile mark from the Palomarin parking lot,

you've arrived. A heavily eroded trail leads up to the top of the falls from here, but the National Park Service prohibits its use due to unsafe footing and the fragility of this unique natural environment. Do yourself and nature a favor by staying on the beach and retracing your steps the way you came. You'll have a chance to detour to the top of the falls (see p69) on your way back along the Coast Trail.

16 Return north along the beach to Wildcat Camp, then head inland to rejoin the southbound Coast Trail. When you reach the junction of the Coast Trail and the Ocean Lake Loop, stay left to take the Coast Trail (the route you bypassed on the way in) and follow it the rest of the way to Palomarin.

TAKE A BREAK

Just inland from the Point Reyes National Seashore visitor center, the minuscule hamlet of Point Reyes Station boasts one of Marin County's most beloved bakeries, the **Bovine Bakery** (☎ 415-663-9420; www.bovinebakeryptreyes.com; 11315 Hwy 1; most items $2-6; ⏰ 6:30am-5pm Mon-Fri, 7am-5pm Sat, 7am-4pm Sun; 🖋), named (naturally) for the cows that dot the surrounding pastureland. Locals line up early to carbo-load on delectable morning buns, sweet and savory scones, and homemade slices of pizza.

Also Try...

GREGOR CLARK/LONELY PLANET ©

FILBERT STEPS, CHINATOWN & NORTH BEACH

Discover one of San Francisco's prettiest streets and two of its most characteristic neighborhoods.

From Liguria Bakery at Filbert and Stockton Sts, climb up Telegraph Hill to Coit Tower. A fanciful descent follows as Filbert St becomes a steep wooden staircase (pictured above) dropping past colorful houses, flowery gardens and palm trees filled with chattering parrots. Turn right at Levi's Plaza, walking seven blocks south to Washington St. Next, head three blocks west to Portsmouth Sq – San Francisco's original 19th-century town square, now popular for morning tai chi and afternoon playdates. Continue up Washington, turning right on Grant Ave through the heart of Chinatown. Last, jog left up Columbus Ave to City Lights Books, and return to your starting point via Molinari's Deli, Caffè Trieste, Mario's Bohemian Cigar Store or one of North Beach's other historic hang-outs.

DURATION 1hr return
DIFFICULTY Moderate
DISTANCE 1.9 miles

BRIONES LAGOONS LOOP

Explore lagoons and oak-dotted hillsides in one of the East Bay's most popular regional parks.

Discover why Briones Regional Park is such a popular local getaway on this roller-coaster loop through the East Bay's backcountry. It's especially beautiful in springtime, when winter rains have replenished the lagoons and the hills glow green and burst with California poppies.

Start from the Alhambra Staging Area, 6 miles south of Martinez, and head uphill on the Diablo View Trail. Continue climbing on the Spengler Trail, turning left onto Old Briones Rd just beyond the Maricich Lagoons. The route now passes through open rolling grasslands, turning briefly right on the Briones Crest Trail, then right again on the Lagoon Trail, where you enjoy long views across to the Carquinez Strait as you approach Lower Sindicich Lagoon. From here, drop back to your starting point via the Toyon Canyon and Orchard Trails.

DURATION 3hr return
DIFFICULTY Moderate
DISTANCE 5.7 miles

AJ9/SHUTTERSTOCK ©

NIMITZ WAY

Family- and wheelchair-friendly, this paved multiuse trail on a high ridge line commands vast Bay Area views.

Ask anyone in Berkeley to recommend a scenic, accessible trail, and they'll likely mention the Nimitz. Starting at Inspiration Point in Tilden Park, it winds across the summit of San Pablo Ridge, through eucalyptus groves and cow pastures, eventually crossing north into Wildcat Canyon Regional Park. The long views up top extend east to Mt Diablo and west to the Golden Gate Bridge, and it's suitable for all ages and abilities.

DURATION 3hr return
DIFFICULTY Easy
DISTANCE 8.2 miles

SAN PEDRO VALLEY TO GRAY WHALE BEACH

Tackle this strenuous mountain traverse to a dreamy beach south of San Francisco.

From San Pedro County Park in Pacifica, follow Montara Mountain Trail up through eucalyptus trees into the coastal scrub. Bypass a junction with the Brooks Creek Trail and zigzag up Montara Mountain's steep slopes. Turn right on Montara Mountain Rd to begin the long, scenic descent to Gray Whale State Beach (pictured above), a sandy cove backed by sheer cliffs. Make this a one-way hike by parking a vehicle at either end.

DURATION 3½hr one way
DIFFICULTY Hard
DISTANCE 5.3 miles

BEAR VALLEY TRAIL

Shady and well-graded, this out-and-back favorite runs through the heart of Point Reyes National Seashore.

From Point Reyes' Bear Valley Visitor Center, climb gradually through a Douglas fir forest along Bear Valley Creek, pausing to enjoy the grassy expanses of Divide Meadow at the 1.6-mile mark. Continue towards the coast, paralleling Coast Creek on the broad, gently descending trail. Upon arrival at the Pacific Ocean (4.1 miles), retrace your steps or design a longer return loop via your choice of other trails.

DURATION 4hr return
DIFFICULTY Moderate
DISTANCE 8.2 miles

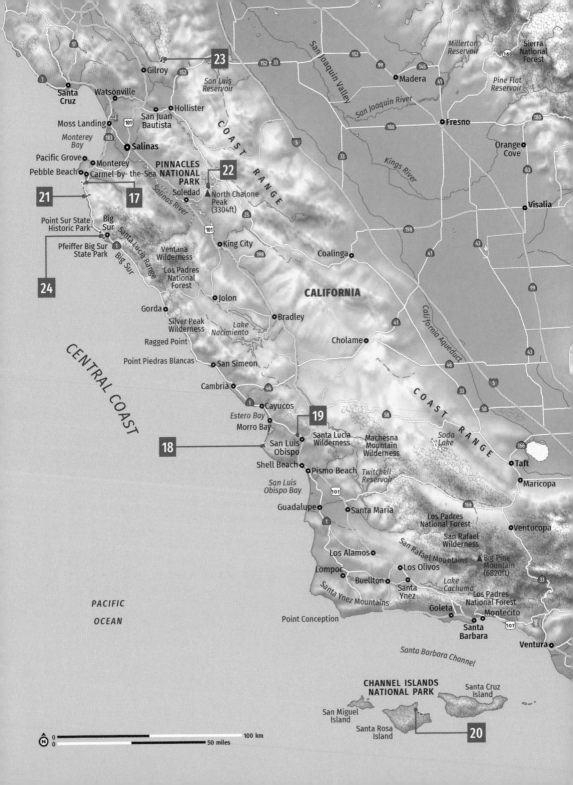

CALIFORNIA'S CENTRAL COAST

Explore
CALIFORNIA'S CENTRAL COAST

At the meeting of north and south, California's Central Coast spans the best of both worlds. As you travel from Santa Cruz to Santa Barbara, cool redwood canyons give way to sunny surfing beaches, while the lower 48's longest contiguous stretch of undeveloped coastline (Big Sur) vies for your attention with the rugged Ventana Wilderness, the windswept Channel Islands, and some of California's most gorgeous oak grasslands. The weather is often blissfully balmy (bring your sunglasses), yet there's barely a whiff of SoCal's urban congestion. In short, if you're looking for a laid-back vibe with exuberant nature always close at hand, you've come to the right place.

BIG SUR

Big Sur is more a state of mind than a place to pinpoint on a map, and when the sun goes down, the moon and the stars are the area's natural streetlights. Raw beauty and an intense maritime energy prevail on this emerald-green edge of the continent shoehorned between the Santa Lucia Range and the Pacific Ocean, and a first glimpse of the craggy, unspoiled coastline is a special moment. The Monterey airport is only 40 minutes north, and there are some dreamy places to stay and eat (book ahead), with the redwoods and the beach always waiting right outside your door.

SAN LUIS OBISPO

San Luis Obispo (SLO) sits smack in the heart of California's Central Coast, at the junction of Hwys 1 and 101. With its small airport, it's a handy arrival point and a convenient launch pad for trips west to coastal state parks, north to Big Sur or south to Santa Barbara and the Channel Islands. SLO's lifestyle is refreshingly low-key, helped along by Cal Poly university students who inject a healthy dose of hubbub. The region has an abundance of restaurants, craft breweries and vineyards, and Thursday's farmers market turns downtown into a party with live music and sidewalk BBQs.

SANTA BARBARA

Perfect coastal weather, Spanish-colonial architecture, an easy-to-stroll downtown, excellent bars and restaurants, and activities for all tastes and budgets make Santa Barbara a great place to live (as the locals will proudly tell you). The city's well-connected airport makes it a logical place to start or end your trip, especially if you're traveling to or from the Channel Islands.

 **WHEN TO GO**

Spring and fall are ideal seasons for hiking in Central California, with sunny days and milder

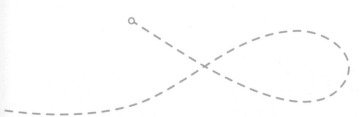

temperatures. Hills glow green, wildflowers bloom, and whales migrate in abundance from March through mid-April, while the wine harvest adds color and zest in September and October. The summer months (June through August) can get torridly hot inland and uncomfortably chilly along the coast when seasonal fogs roll in.

 **WHERE TO STAY**

If coastal camping is your thing, you're in for a treat. California's state parks system abounds in campsites by the water's edge, from New Brighton near Santa Cruz to Refugio, El Capitan and Carpinteria outside Santa Barbara, along with riverside sites in redwood forests (Pfeiffer Big Sur), secluded pack-it-in environmental camps (Montaña de Oro and Julia Pfeiffer Burns), and even more primitive backcountry sites (Ventana Wilderness, Henry Coe State Park). For indoor lodging, Central California's offerings run the gamut from roadside motels to boutique hotels and wine country B&Bs, encompassing everything from the super-cozy (Deetjen's rustic cabins in Big Sur) to the super-quirky (San Luis Obispo's over-the-top, pink-meets-Stone-Age Madonna Inn).

 **WHAT'S ON**

Big Sur International Marathon (www.bigsurmarathon.org; ☺Apr) 'Running on the ragged edge of the western world' since 1986, this supremely scenic spring-time race goes from Big Sur to Carmel.

Pebble Beach Food & Wine (www.pbfw.com; ☺Apr) Excellent four-day gastronomy-focused festival sponsored by the prestigious *Food & Wine* magazine.

Summer Solstice Celebration (www.solsticeparade.com; ☺Jun) Kicking off summer, Santa Barbara's wildly popular parade features floats, dance troupes and inventive miscellany.

Gilroy Garlic Festival (www.gilroygarlicfestival.com; ☺Jul) Show up for garlicky fries, garlic-flavored ice cream and cooking contests under the blazing-hot sun.

Concerts in the Plaza (www.facebook.com/concertsintheplaza; ☺Jun-Sep) San Luis Obispo's Mission Plaza rocks out with local bands and food vendors.

 **TRANSPORT**

For easy access with minimal fuss, the small airports at Monterey, San Luis Obispo and Santa Barbara make ideal gateways

Resources

BigSurKate (www.bigsurkate.blog) Fantastic source for up-to-date info on Big Sur.

California Department of Parks & Recreation (www.parks.ca.gov) Information on the Central Coast's many state parks and beaches.

National Park Service (www.nps.gov/chis, www.nps.gov/pinn) Maps and trail info for Channel Islands and Pinnacles National Parks.

Ventana Wilderness Alliance (www.ventanawild.org) Everything you need to know about the Ventana Wilderness.

The Pine Ridge Association (www.coepark.net) Top advice on Henry Coe State Park from the Pine Ridge Association's dedicated volunteers.

Reserve California (www.reservecalifornia.com) State park camping reservations.

Recreation.gov (www.recreation.gov) National park camping reservations.

to Central California. Once on the ground, having your own wheels is advisable given the lack of public transportation to more remote trailheads. Island Packers (www.islandpackers.com) runs excellent year-round ferries to the Channel Islands, while regional transport systems such as Monterey-Salinas Transit (www.mst.org) offer dependable if limited local bus service.

17

POINT LOBOS

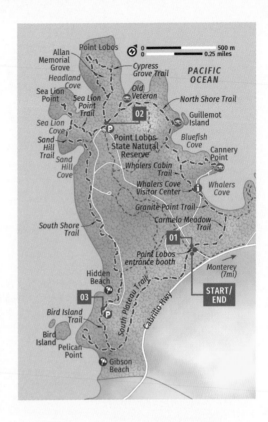

DURATION	DIFFICULTY	DISTANCE	START/END
3hr return	Easy	6 miles	Point Lobos entrance booth
TERRAIN	Flat wide paths & narrower trails		

Sea lions, wind-sculpted Monterey cypresses and dramatic rocky coastlines are the star attractions at this legendary park south of Carmel. The reserve is laced with trails, many wheelchair-accessible and most skirting the ocean's edge. The hike described here circumnavigates the entire peninsula, but even a short walk here is rewarding.

GETTING HERE

Point Lobos is 7 miles south of Monterey. Park in the reserve's lot or on the shoulder of Hwy 1 (heed posted signs carefully). Monterey-Salinas Transit bus 22 (www.mst.org) stops out front.

STARTING POINT

The park has water and restrooms; other services are in Carmel, 2.5 miles north.

01 From the entrance, follow the **Carmelo Meadow** and **Granite Point Trails** to **Whalers Cove Visitor Center**, a historic cabin at the foot of a venerable Monterey cypress. Inside the cabin, a museum traces the history of the region's Chinese, Japanese and Portuguese settlers. Behind the museum, follow **Whalers Cabin Trail** through the pines to the **North Shore Trail**, which grants access to several overlooks where you can admire Point Lobos' fabled coastline. Among the best are **Cannery Point** (just beyond Whalers Cove), **Guillemot Island** (bleached white with seabirds' prodigious droppings) and **Old Veteran**, a 200-year-old Monterey cypress clinging to the cliffs above Cypress Cove.

02 Two miles into the hike, the North Shore Trail dead-ends at the Sea Lion Point parking lot. Turn right here onto the renowned **Cypress Grove Trail** (pictured above right) and branch either direction at a Y intersection to loop through **Allan Memorial Grove**,

Accessible Trails at Point Lobos

Point Lobos offers an excellent network of wheelchair-accessible trails, including the scenic Granite Point Trail, which follows the peninsula's splendid northern coastline from Whalers Cove to Coal Chute Point, as well as a pair of trails to the popular wildlife-watching destinations of Sea Lion Point and Bird Island. For full details on accessibility within the state reserve, see www.pointlobos.org.

GREGOR CLARK/LONELY PLANET ©

one of the world's only remaining native stands of Monterey cypress. There's an exquisite beauty to these wind-sculpted trees, which frame rocky coves around the point's perimeter. Return to the parking lot and cross south to the **Sea Lion Point Trail**, which takes you around a west-facing peninsula with **fabulous open views** onto a rocky point where barking sea lions congregate. Return via the **Sand Hill Trail** along the peninsula's southern edge and branch right down steps onto the **South Shore Trail** (3.3 miles). This mile-long trail parallels Point Lobos' main vehicle road past a series of coves facing the open Pacific,

where waves crash over reefs and explode through blowholes.

03 Just beyond **Hidden Beach** on your right, cross through a parking lot and continue south on the **Bird Island Trail**. The by-now-familiar scents of pine needles and salt spray fill the air as you veer right towards the aptly named **Pelican Point** and **Bird Island**, where hundreds of pelicans and other shorebirds huddle on rocky headlands. Retrace your steps and turn right onto the **South Plateau Trail**. Before leaving the coast, descend the nearby steps to **Gibson Beach**, one of the reserve's loveliest and most expansive stretches of

sand, then climb back to the trail and loop through the woods to the park entrance.

TAKE A BREAK

Start your morning off right with scrumptious French pastries and espresso drinks at the **Lafayette Bakery** (☎831-915-6286; www. lafayette-bakery.com; 3672 The Barnyard, suite E22; pastries from $3; ☺7am-3pm Wed-Mon), just up the road from Point Lobos in the town of Carmel Valley. The display case is packed with enticing trail snacks, including quiches and miniature sandwiches stuffed with veggies, smoked salmon, turkey, salami and more.

18

MONTAÑA DE ORO

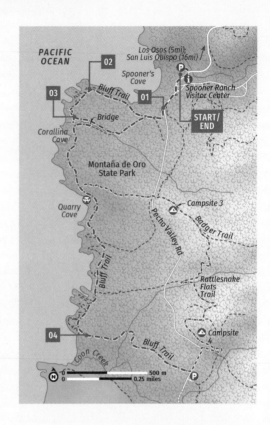

DURATION	DIFFICULTY	DISTANCE	START/END
2hr return	Easy	5 miles	Spooner's Cove parking lot

TERRAIN	Wide flat paths

Built around a historic ranch on a dead-end coastal road, Montaña de Oro State Park preserves a beautifully rugged shoreline, with two great trail networks: one wheelchair-accessible along the coast, and a second that goes higher into the hills. The park is among the best spots in Central California to spot otters, seabirds, seals, dolphins and whales. It's an easy detour off Hwy 101 from San Luis Obispo or Hwy 1 from Morro Bay.

GETTING HERE

The Spooner Ranch Visitor Center sits on a dead-end road, 16 miles west of San Luis Obispo.

STARTING POINT

The trailhead offers restrooms, water and a campground. Other services are at Los Osos (5 miles).

01 The wheelchair-accessible **Bluff Trail** starts south of the parking lot as a wide, lightly graveled path heading west through the coastal scrub toward the point separating Spooner's Cove and Corallina Cove. **Beautiful views of golden cliffs and sandy beach** soon unfold to the north, with cormorants congregating on an arched rock offshore and the hulking form of **Morro Rock** rising in the distance.

02 The trail soon rounds a bend at the bluff's western edge, and you begin walking south beside the open Pacific. Continue to enjoy **magnificent views of Montaña de Oro's striated shoreline**, where ancient marine layers have been tilted and contorted by tectonic forces. The main trail remains wide and accessible to wheelchairs and strollers, while narrower side trails loop off to explore the surrounding cliffs and coves. Detour down steps to reach the beach at **Corallina Cove** (0.6 miles),

Side Trip: Up into the Hills

For a glimpse of Montaña de Oro's high country and its remote environmental campsites, expand this hike into a slightly longer loop. From Coon Creek parking area, take the paved road 0.1 mile north and turn inland on the **Rattlesnake Flats Trail**, a wide dirt road that winds uphill to **campsite 4**, perched on a solitary ocean-facing bluff. From here, the trail narrows, continuing north to a junction with the **Badger Trail**. Turn left and head downhill past **campsite 3** – beautifully sited in a eucalyptus grove – to rejoin the Bluff Trail, your original coastal route. Total distance for this alternative loop is about 5.5 miles, including return to the Spooner's Cove parking lot.

Best for

POST-HIKE CHEER

where signs encourage you to get to know the octopi, sea stars, abalone and other creatures in the tide pools below. Corallina's attractive expanse of small, pebbly sand sits at the mouth of a narrow inlet, framed by stratified cliffs of gold, white and gray rock and pounded by crashing waves.

03 Turn inland along the deep inlet coming off Corallina Cove, cross a **bridge** to the opposite bank, and turn right again to follow the shoreline towards **Quarry Cove** (pictured). Soon after bypassing a junction with the Badger Trail on your left, two **picnic tables**

on your right – one adjacent to the trail, the other further out on the coastal cliffs – invite you to break for lunch. The **superb coastal scenery** continues for another half mile, as you pass long, sheer-walled inlets and photogenic coves with amazing sandstone rock formations, some pierced with holes and tunnels where the waves break through.

04 Around the 2-mile mark, the trail (still accessible) curves definitively inland through the coastal scrub and climbs gently to the **Coon Creek** parking lot in another half mile. From here, you can retrace

your steps to Spooner's Cove or extend your hike on the Rattlesnake Flats/Badger Trail loop.

TAKE A BREAK

The international comfort food at San Luis Obispo's **Big Sky Café** (📞805-545-5401; www.bigskycafe.com; 1121 Broad St; dinner mains $11-26; 🕖7am-9pm Mon-Thu, to 10pm Fri, 8am-10pm Sat, to 9pm Sun; 🅿♿) runs the gamut from New Orleans–style beignets to Spanish paella to a mean chile verde (served in omelets at breakfast time and on tostadas for lunch and dinner).

19

BISHOP PEAK

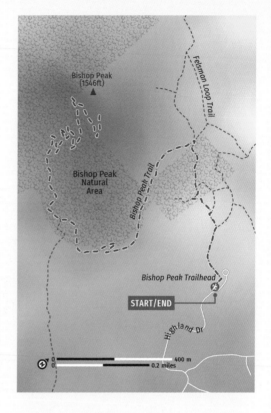

DURATION	DIFFICULTY	DISTANCE	START/END
2hr return	Moderate	3.3 miles	Highland Dr trailhead

TERRAIN	Steep rocky trails & wider paths

Outside the laid-back college town of San Luis Obispo ('SLO' for short) one of California's most unique landscapes unfolds. From Morro Rock on the Pacific coast, a set of nine photogenic volcanic plugs stretches east to SLO's city limits. The highest of these 'Nine Sisters,' Bishop Peak (1546ft), makes a short, supremely scenic out-and-back jaunt, extremely popular with hikers and climbers alike.

From the trailhead, pass through a green metal barrier and start climbing, following signs for the Summit Trail. After 0.4 miles the trail narrows, entering the welcome shade of **oaks and laurels** and passing a **rock wall** on the right where climbers hone their skills. From here, a brief descent follows, skirting the outcrops along the base of Bishop Peak.

Emerge from the forest and begin switchbacking up the mountain around the 0.7-mile mark. Jumbles of boulders litter the hillside above, while **views over the neighboring volcanic plugs** open up to your left. The trail, now fully exposed to the sun, begins scrambling over boulders, as the view improves with every step. Climbers on the adjacent rocky spires provide an inspirational backdrop, as the nicely graded trail traces the mountain's contours steadily uphill. Despite the lack of shade, breezes pick up as you climb, carrying the scent of wild sage.

Around the 1.5-mile mark you get heartening glimpses of hikers standing atop the **summit**, and a few hundred feet later you arrive at a pair of benches where you can stop to absorb the **amazing panoramic views**. A scramble up the boulders to the left or right takes you even higher. Wherever you decide to stop, your return route involves simply retracing your steps to the parking lot.

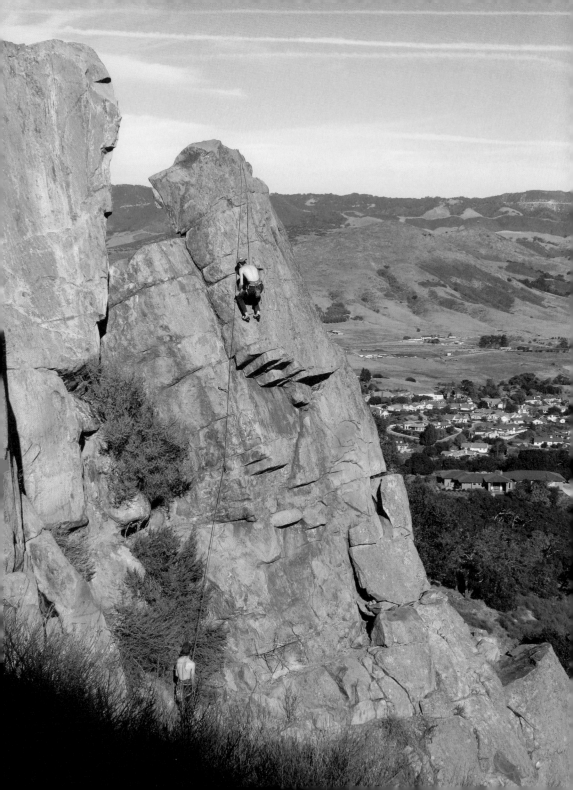

20

TORREY PINES LOOP

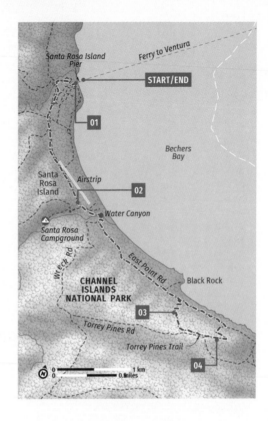

DURATION	DIFFICULTY	DISTANCE	START/END
3hr return	Moderate	6.8 miles	Santa Rosa Island Pier

TERRAIN	Hard-packed dirt trails, dirt roads

The critically endangered Torrey pine (*Pinus torreyana*) is found only two places on earth: San Diego and Santa Rosa Island. This loop leads to a lonely grove on a remote island hilltop, giving you a taste of Channel Islands National Park's raw, windswept beauty. It's a manageable day trip, but you'll feel less constrained by return ferry schedules if you camp overnight on Santa Rosa.

GETTING HERE

Island Packers (www.islandpackers.com) runs two to three ferries weekly from Ventura to Santa Rosa.

STARTING POINT

There's only a restroom near the dock. Bringing your own water in adequate amounts is essential.

01 From the **Santa Rosa pier**, follow signs for the campground onto a dirt path between wooden fences. The trail curves past a red barn, a white farmhouse and several outbuildings, soon crossing through a gate onto a level dirt road running east along the coastal bluffs. Santa Rosa's primitive airstrip (note the wind socks) is just to your left, as Santa Cruz Island appears across the channel.

02 Continue straight at the 1.3-mile mark, ignoring a right-hand turnoff for the campground. The road abruptly drops into reed-filled **Water Canyon**, crossing a plank bridge and climbing steeply out the other side. Bypass a junction with Wreck Rd and resume your level course along the bluffs, following signs for Torrey Pines. The pines soon appear on the hillside ahead, backed by Skunk Point and Santa Cruz Island. After passing a turnoff for Black Rock, branch right onto the **Torrey Pines Trail** and start climbing. Switchbacks quickly ascend to

Whales, Dolphins & Island Foxes

Wildlife watching is one of the great joys of any Channel Islands visit. The ferry ride across from Ventura is a prime opportunity to spot the channel's abundant whales and dolphins, aided by Island Packers' expert crew, who will slow the boat down to share spontaneous sightings such as a shark devouring a giant sea bass. Once on the islands, watch for island foxes, the cute-as-a-button miniature foxes (about the size of house cats) that roam the backcountry with their distinctive colorful markings and bushy tails.

GREGOR CLARK/LONELY PLANET ©

the forest's edge, affording close-up views of the long needles of this rare endemic species.

03 After a steady half-mile ascent, arrive at a **hilltop bench with breathtaking views**. A long sweep of coastline stretches west to the pier, with the dirt road you walked in on and a pair of beaches visible in the foreground. Scores of Torrey pines cling to the sandy hills below, with **Santa Cruz Island** floating on the horizon just beyond. Above the bench, another short climb brings you to the ridge, where the trail levels out for half a mile, dipping in and out of the forest, with needles carpeting

the path, a divine piney scent filling the air, and occasional glimpses of the ocean peeking through the trees. At a right-hand junction with Torrey Pines Rd (3.2 miles), your narrower trail continues straight.

04 The trail soon turns downhill, but before you descend, step into the grassland just beyond the forest's edge. From this wide-open vantage point, seductive **views** stretch far southeast into the island's interior and northeast to **Skunk Point**, a sprawling peninsula that's worth a visit if you're camping overnight on the island. From here, a dizzying series of

switchbacks and stairs deposits you back on the coastal road, where it's a straightforward 3-mile walk back to the pier.

 **TAKE A BREAK**

You won't find a better fish taco anywhere in coastal California than at **Spencer Makenzie's** (805-643-8226; www.spencermakenzies.com; 806 E Thompson Blvd; mains $5-10; 11am-8pm Sun-Thu, to 8:30pm Fri & Sat), about 10 minutes inland from the Channel Islands ferry dock in downtown Ventura. Fish and shrimp come either grilled or tempura battered, supplemented with cabbage, cilantro and fresh avocado from the surrounding hills.

21

GARRAPATA GETAWAY

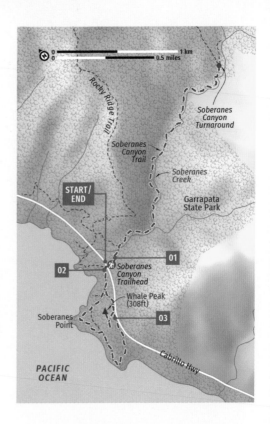

DURATION	DIFFICULTY	DISTANCE	START/END
2½hr return	Moderate	4.6 miles	Soberanes Canyon trailhead

TERRAIN	Narrow dirt paths & steps

Getting off the beaten track isn't easy in Big Sur, but Garrapata State Park offers an opportunity to do just that. Most drivers zip on past on their way down Hwy 1 to Big Sur, yet the less-trodden trails in this lovely state park are well worth exploring. This sampler combines two separate hikes with a common starting point: the Soberanes Canyon Trail to a lush redwood forest, and the Soberanes Point loop along the park's rugged coastline.

GETTING HERE

The trailhead is 4.7 miles south of Point Lobos, at a gate marked 'Fire Road/No Parking' in a cypress windbreak east of Hwy 1. Monterey-Salinas Transit bus 22 (www.mst.org) can drop you here on request.

STARTING POINT

There are no services whatsoever in Garrapata State Park. Bring water, snacks and sunscreen.

01 Walk through the gate and head inland, following a dirt road past a corrugated metal barn to a junction with the Rocky Ridge Trail. Go straight here on **Soberanes Canyon Trail**, which is initially exposed and sun-parched, with prickly pear cactuses dotting the valley floor and adjacent slopes. Continuing inland, the trail weaves through thickets of willow, crisscrossing the creek as the canyon narrows. Half a mile upstream, you're immersed in a full-fledged **redwood forest**, enlivened by the rushing creek and a lush understory of ferns and wild sorrel. A mile in, the trail steepens and climbs a staircase, affording **dazzling views** over the canyon floor, where fallen redwoods serve as 'nurse logs' for offshoot trees springing vertically from their decaying bark. Visible fire damage marks some of the taller trees, though a feeling of lushness prevails. The trail's final stretch abruptly zigzags down steps to a **tranquil glen** backed by a massive rock face – a suitable spot for a picnic. From here, retrace your steps and cross to the west side of Hwy 1.

Whale Watching at Garrapata

From December to mid-May, Garrapata State Park is a prime whale-watching destination. California gray whales (*Eschrichtius robustus*) swim just offshore during their annual winter migration to breeding grounds in Baja California, returning north again every spring en route to their summer feeding grounds in Alaska's Bering and Chukchi Seas. These massive marine mammals, which can grow to nearly 50ft in length, are large enough to spot from land even with the naked eye. A good – and aptly named – lookout point is Whale Peak on the park's coastal loop.

Best for

ESCAPING THE CROWDS

02 Head south through the cypresses on the west side of Hwy 1, with the ocean roaring to your right and the highway roaring to your left. At a fork, turn left onto the coastal loop, climbing through scrub towards diminutive **Whale Peak** (308ft). At the top of a staircase, detour right on an unmarked trail to the summit. Views northwest directly overlook the sea and **Soberanes Point**, making this a prime vantage point for spotting whales. South lie bird's-eye views of Hwy 1 undulating through misty coves down the Big Sur coast.

03 Rejoining the loop trail below, turn right down steps and veer back towards the coast, where **south-facing overlooks** offer spellbinding views of chiseled coves, ice-plant-covered slopes, and deep blue-green waters. The trail soon bears hard right, returning north along the seaward side of Whale Peak. Scrub-covered bluffs slope down to cliffs of golden sandstone and gray volcanic rock on your left. For a closer look, take a side trail across the headland to the coves and sea caves of **Soberanes Point**. Back on the main trail, curve gently round Whale Peak's northern slopes to close the coastal loop, then return to the cypress windbreak on Hwy 1.

TAKE A BREAK

You couldn't ask for a cozier dinner spot than **Deetjen's** (📞831-667-2378; www.deetjens.com; 48865 Hwy 1, Deetjen's Big Sur Inn; mains breakfast $12-18, dinner $24-42; ⏱breakfast 8am-noon, dinner 6-9pm; P👤), a rustic restaurant that regularly gets ranked as one of the area's finest. The menu features exquisite salads and a range of main courses, from paella to grilled rack of lamb, all served in an intimate candlelit dining room.

22

PINNACLES HIGH PEAKS LOOP

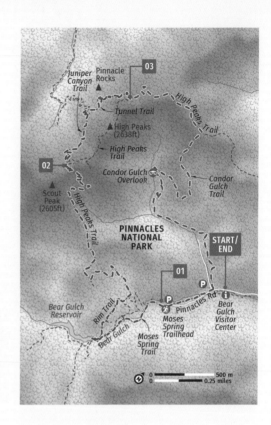

DURATION	DIFFICULTY	DISTANCE	START/END
4hr return	Moderate	6.6 miles	Bear Gulch Visitor Center

TERRAIN	Narrow, steep & rocky trails

Even if you're mainly here to hike California's Central Coast, you've got to venture inland to Pinnacles. This remnant of an ancient volcano, displaced nearly 200 miles north from Southern California by the San Andreas Fault and now jutting incongruously above chaparral-covered slopes and lonely oak grasslands, is the centerpiece of one of America's less-visited national parks. Pinnacles draws campers, hikers and climbers – and hardly anyone else. The High Peaks Loop offers a quintessential Pinnacles experience in just half a day.

GETTING HERE

You'll need your own wheels to get to Pinnacles' eastern entrance at Bear Gulch; it's 90 minutes from Monterey, Santa Cruz or San Jose via sleepy Hwy 25.

STARTING POINT

There are restrooms at the trailhead, and a camp store at nearby Pinnacles Campground. All other services are 30 miles away in King City or Hollister.

01 From the **Bear Gulch Visitor Center** follow signs for 'Reservoir/High Peaks Trail,' then join the **Moses Spring Trail** (pictured) at the upper parking lot. This engaging roller coaster of a path skirts the base of sheer rock walls, scrambles beneath a series of overhangs and climbs a precipitous staircase through a narrow gorge to reach a **rock-fringed reservoir** (1 mile). From the reservoir, double back hard right onto the **Rim Trail**, then turn left onto the **High Peaks Trail** at the next junction. Rock pillars on the horizon above offer hints of the landscape ahead. Below, the chaparral is dotted with red-berried manzanita bushes (*Arctostaphylos glauca*) and gray pines (*Pinus sabiniana*), California natives that thrive in these dry, rocky conditions.

California Condors

When it comes to endangered species, one of California's biggest success stories is the California condor (*Gymnogyps californianus*). These gigantic, prehistoric birds weigh more than 20lb with a wingspan of up to 10ft, letting them fly great distances in search of carrion. They're easily recognized by their naked pink head and large white patches on the underside of each wing. Condors became so rare that in 1987 there were only 27 left in the world, forcing their removal from the wild to captive-breeding facilities. Today more than 500 condors fly free in California's skies; Pinnacles National Park and the Big Sur coast both offer excellent opportunities to spot them.

GREGOR CLARK/LONELY PLANET ©

Best for

WILDLIFE

02 Around the 3-mile mark, the trail emerges on a windy ridge at the foot of Scout Peak (2605ft), yielding **stunning close-up views of rocky spires** and fresh perspectives on the park's northern and western reaches, where cars glint in a distant parking lot. Leaving the ridge, bear left at a fork towards the Tunnel Trail and descend through a beautiful landscape of stratified rocks to a junction with the Juniper Canyon Trail. Turn hard right onto the **Tunnel Trail**, crossing beneath enormous rock spires to reach a tunnel within five minutes. Beyond the tunnel, cross a bridge and ascend the rugged slopes above,

keeping your eyes peeled for **California condors** riding the updrafts. Pause near the top for **splendid perspectives over the trail** you've just climbed, with the bridge spanning the gorge far below and a fluted ridge of pinnacles directly opposite.

03 Merge with the **High Peaks Trail** coming in from the right and follow the ridge line, where boundless views encompass waves of foothills cloaked in chaparral and oak savanna. Begin a long descent on the **Condor Gulch Trail** near the 5-mile mark. Part way down, a right-hand detour leads to the **Condor Gulch Overlook**,

where an intermittent waterfall flows in springtime. From here it's another mile downhill to the Bear Gulch parking lot.

 **TAKE A BREAK**

Let's face it: Pinnacles sits in the middle of nowhere, so grabbing a bite after your hike requires a bit of a trek. For Mexican food and margaritas in a delightful garden setting, head about 55 minutes north towards San Francisco and stop in at **Jardines de San Juan** (☏ 831-623-4466; www.jardinesrestaurant.com; 115 3rd St; mains $13-19; ☉ 11am-7pm Sun-Thu, to 8pm Fri & Sat) in San Juan Bautista.

23

HUNTING HOLLOW TO WILLSON PEAK

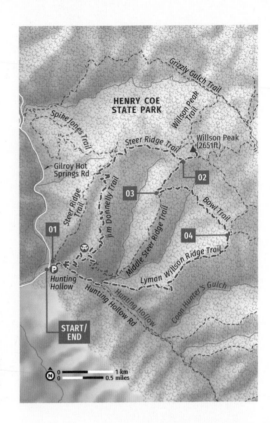

DURATION	DIFFICULTY	DISTANCE	START/END
5hr return	Moderate	10.1 miles	Hunting Hollow parking lot

TERRAIN	Undulating dirt roads & trails

Henry Coe State Park is a rare treasure. Encompassing 89,000 acres of oak grasslands, gray pine uplands and remote valleys, California's second-largest state park boasts an extensive trail network that rewards intrepid hikers willing to devote a few days to exploring its sprawling backcountry. The park also abounds in fantastic day hikes that can be combined into loops of varying lengths.

GETTING HERE

The Hunting Hollow entrance is 10 miles east of Gilroy off Hwy 101; you'll need your own wheels.

STARTING POINT

The closest services are at Gilroy. Bring water, snacks and sunscreen.

01 Follow Hunting Hollow Rd east, soon turning left on the **Jim Donnelly Trail**. The trail climbs in lazy curves above the valley floor, passing through **moss-draped oak forest** and gradually emerging onto open grassy slopes. A **trailside picnic table** (1.4 miles) invites you to pause and appreciate the increasingly unfettered views. Turn right onto **Steer Ridge Trail** near the 3.2-mile mark. After passing another picnic table, the broad dirt road steepens considerably, but the **expansive views** of oak-dotted hillsides and wide-open skies help compensate. Beyond a left-hand junction with the Spike Jones Trail, the gradient eases and the oak trees get sparser. New perspectives open north over Grizzly Gulch and the sprawling hill country beyond, offering a tantalizing taste of the park's vast dimensions.

02 Forge on towards the summit, bypassing a right-hand turnoff at 4.6 miles for the Middle Steer Ridge Trail, your eventual return route. Near

Discovering Henry Coe's Backcountry

To really get away from it all, consider a longer camping trip in Henry Coe State Park's sprawling backcountry. The helpful folks at the nonprofit **Pine Ridge Association** (www.coepark.net) know every nook and cranny of the park and can help you put together some fantastic overnight or multiday itineraries. They also sponsor several annual events, including the ever-popular Tarantula Fest, in which volunteer naturalists help visitors track down the park's charismatic furry spiders!

GREGOR CLARK/LONELY PLANET ©

Best for

ESCAPING
THE CROWDS

the 5-mile mark, after a final left turn on **Willson Peak Trail**, alight on the grassy summit of **Willson Peak** (2651ft; pictured), where views on a clear day extend all the way from the Sierra Nevada to Monterey Bay.

03 Retrace your steps to **Middle Steer Ridge Trail**, turn left and begin descending. About half a mile down, turn left again onto the **Bowl Trail**, following signs for Willson Camp. Undulate across oak-clad hillsides for the next mile and a half, dipping in and out of mini canyons where sycamores and bay laurels offer welcome shade on the fringes of small rocky

creeks. At the 7.2-mile mark, turn right onto the **Lyman Willson Ridge Trail**.

04 **Views from the ridge line are spectacular**, with steep drop-offs left into Coon Hunter's Gulch. About half a mile along, a long, glorious flat stretch cruises towards lone oaks crowning huge, grassy slopes. Beyond the 8-mile mark, begin descending towards Hunting Hollow, curving broadly left through a fence line, swooping back right, and eventually dropping steeply towards the valley. At 9.3 miles, Middle Steer Ridge Trail enters from the right, and at 9.4 miles you reach a

T intersection with Hunting Hollow Rd. Turn right here, fording a wide, rocky creek and proceeding back to the parking lot.

 **TAKE A BREAK**

Gilroy is California's self-proclaimed garlic capital, and the **Garlic City Cafe** (408-847-7744; www.garliccitycafe.com; 7461 Monterey Rd; mains $10-27; 8am-9pm Tue-Sun) in the heart of downtown will gladly give you a taste, even if you're not here during the city's annual festival (p77). You can't go wrong with the garlic fries (available with any item from its extensive sandwich menu) or local artichokes with roasted garlic aioli.

24

BIG SUR BLUFFS & BEACHES

DURATION	DIFFICULTY	DISTANCE	START/END
5hr return	Hard	9 miles	Andrew Molera State Park parking

TERRAIN	Flat to steep roads & trails

In Big Sur, the meeting of land and sea is abrupt. In many places, precipitous cliffs plunge directly into the Pacific, leaving precious little room for walking trails; in others, private land holdings preclude coastal access. But in Andrew Molera State Park, a different world awaits. At the mouth of the Big Sur River, a broad coastal plain stretches from California State Hwy 1 out to the sea, offering up an enticing network of hiking trails that take in high bluffs and secluded beaches, along with a remnant of hilltop redwood forest.

GETTING HERE

Andrew Molera State Park is on California Hwy 1, 26 miles south of Monterey and 5 miles north of Big Sur. Monterey-Salinas Transit bus 22 (www.mst.org) stops out front.

STARTING POINT

There are restrooms and running water at the trailhead. For other services, head to Big Sur.

01 Leave the Andrew Molera State Park parking lot behind and hit the signposted trail to the beach, just left of the park entrance booth. The trail starts as a wide, shady, level dirt road running through farmland. After passing an old white barn on the left, you'll soon reach a right-hand turn for the Creamery Meadow Trail. The trail immediately crosses the Big Sur River. If you're lucky, a **seasonal bridge** makes for easier passage; otherwise, it's quick and easy to ford the ankle- to knee-deep waters.

02 The **Creamery Meadow Trail** resumes as a wide, shady dirt road on the opposite riverbank, proceeding 0.7 miles through fragrant coastal vegetation and occasional big-leaf maples to reach a signposted junction with the Bluff Trail

(0.9 miles). If you want a sneak preview of the beach, you can continue straight ahead for 0.3 miles on the Creamery Meadow Trail, but the main loop heads left here.

03 The hard-packed **Bluff Trail** climbs 0.1 mile through a canopy of trees and bushes to reach a second junction with the Ridge Trail, where you turn left again (the continuation of the Bluff Trail straight ahead of you will be your return route). A quick glance inland immediately lets you know you're in for a hefty climb. The good news? You're getting done with the hard part first, making for a blissfully scenic return on the second half of today's loop.

04 The **Ridge Trail** (pictured) begins as a steep, erosion-scarred dirt road, charting a punishing uphill course for the first half mile. While this section can feel brutal, especially on a warm day, the **views** unfolding behind you to the north are vast and dramatic, stretching way up the coast past **Andrew Molera's large eucalyptus grove** (a popular waystation for migrating monarch butterflies) and across open fields towards the Point Sur lighthouse. As you continue climbing, you begin to get nice perspectives on **Cone Peak** (5155ft); only 3 miles inland as the crow flies, it's one of the tallest mountains so close to the coast in the lower 48 states. Flame-scarred from California's 2020 wildfires, its pyramid-shaped summit is one of the most majestic in Central California.

05 After a brief, delightful flat stretch around the 1.5-mile mark, the road resumes its relentless ascent, but half a mile further on it settles into a more rolling up-and-down pattern along the ridgetop, revealing **new vistas** southeast into

Big Sur's Hinterland

Straddling the rugged Santa Lucia Range, the 240,000-acre Ventana Wilderness is Big Sur's wild backcountry. Still slowly regenerating after devastating wildfires in 2008 and 2020, Ventana is a beloved destination for adventurous backpackers. A popular overnight hike goes to **Sykes Hot Springs**, natural 100°F (35°C) mineral pools framed by redwoods. It's a moderately strenuous 10-mile, one-way hike along the **Pine Ridge Trail**, starting from Big Sur Station on Hwy 1, where you can get free campfire permits and pay for overnight parking ($5). Don't expect solitude during peak season (April through September) and always follow Leave No Trace (www.lnt.org) principles.

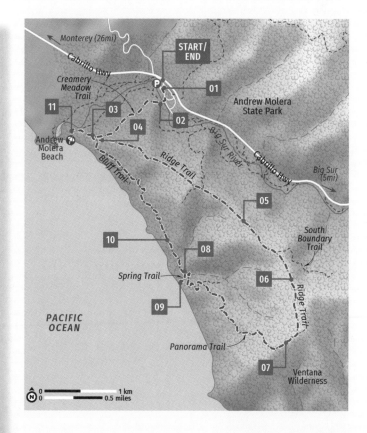

the rugged hills of Pfeiffer Big Sur State Park and the Ventana Wilderness. While the overall trend remains generally uphill for the next mile or so, the going gets far less grueling, and the scenery rewards your efforts. Along the way, you'll pass a couple of junctions with lesser-used trails on your left; stay on the main road, following the ridge line south.

06 Forested sections begin creeping in to replace the chaparral as you climb. A few scraggly oaks and baby redwoods provide welcome shade just past the 3-mile mark; moments later, you find yourself walking through a full-fledged **mountaintop redwood grove**. Pause to appreciate this rare remnant of forest before resuming your ascent on the Ridge Trail, which presents a few more short, steep sections in the remaining half mile before a summit junction with the Panorama Trail at Andrew Molera's southern boundary (3.8 miles).

07 OK, relax, breathe deep, and prepare to enjoy the fruits of your labors. As your route turns west towards the ocean, the **Panorama Trail** immediately lives up to its name. The **miraculous views** north and east span the entire sweep from Cone Peak to Point Sur Lighthouse, while an overlook on the left 0.2 miles past the trail junction yields the walk's best south-facing **coastal panoramas**, featuring the distinctive pierced rocks of **Pfeiffer Beach** in the mid-distance.

PAOLO TRALLI/SHUTTERSTOCK ©

08 The journey back to the coast along the Panorama Trail is slow and steady, with a healthy dose of flat and gently downhill sections, intermingled with switchbacks and steeper terrain. The one constant is the **stupendous views**, which are with you most of the way. At the 5.2-mile mark, as the trail begins a final, precipitous descent toward the Pacific, a beautiful sandy beach comes into view directly below. Half a mile later, after dipping into a cool creek valley, you arrive at the signposted junction of the Spring and Panorama Trails.

09 Whatever your energy level, don't miss the 0.15-mile detour to the beach along the **Spring Trail** – one of the hike's most memorable highlights. The trail winds down the bluff back to the creek gully you just crossed, then deposits you on an **exceptionally gorgeous expanse of sand**, flecked and streaked with purple-hued sediments and wedged between imposing headlands. Watch your step on the transition from trail to beach, which involves clambering over picturesque piles of driftwood logs.

10 Back at the signpost along the main trail, turn left (north). You're now on the aptly named **Bluff Trail**, which skirts the edge of the coastline for the next mile and a half, staying mostly level as it crosses

Wildfires are a natural part of California's ecosystems, but climate change has recently amped up their ferocity and scope. In 2020 a particularly intense fire season devastated several of Central California's iconic natural areas, including Big Basin State Park north of Santa Cruz and Los Padres National Forest south of Big Sur. At the time of research, dozens of trails remained closed indefinitely, including classics like Skyline-to-the-Sea and Berry Creek Falls in Big Basin and the Kirk Creek–Vicente Flat–Cone Peak trail system in the Ventana Wilderness. By the time you read this, some trails will have doubtless reopened; for up-to-date info, consult the web resources listed at the start of this chapter or inquire locally with rangers.

coastal scrubland, dips briefly in and out of gullies and offers intermittent vistas of cliffs, dunes and beaches. Just past the last viewpoint, around the 7.4-mile mark, the trail swoops right (inland) and shortly reaches the familiar junction with the Ridge Trail that you passed earlier in the hike.

11 From here, retrace your steps downhill 0.1 mile to the Creamery Meadow Trail, turning left at the bottom to head for **Andrew Molera Beach** (pictured). This vast driftwood-littered strand is one of Central California's finest wild beaches, and a spectacular place to celebrate the sunset at the end of a long hike. If you've still got the stamina, you can take an exploratory wander quite a ways both north and south. Whenever you're ready to head back, simply retrace your steps down the Creamery Meadow Trail 1.3 miles to the parking lot.

A parting note: the trail as described here is a California classic, offering all the advantages of a loop trail and some stupendous coastal views. However, if you lack the stomach for steep hills, the route can easily be adapted into an easy or moderate there-and-back hike by bypassing the Ridge and Panorama Trails, or by simply walking the Creamery Meadow Trail from the parking lot to the beach.

 TAKE A BREAK

After a day on the trail, nothing compares to the sunset magic of **Nepenthe** (☏ 831-667-2345; www.nepenthebigsur.com; 48510 Hwy 1; mains lunch $18-25, dinner $18-53; ⏱ 11:30am-10pm; 🛜 🖋 👪). Perched high above Hwy 1, the lantern-lit, open-air dining area commands eagle-eye views of the Pacific, with fire pits lit on the terrace at sunset. The steep menu prices reflect Nepenthe's dreamy mountaintop location, but you won't find a more perfect spot to soak in the Big Sur vibe, and budget-minded diners can always opt for the delicious Ambrosia burger at 'only' $19.95!

Also Try...

DELLA HUFF/ALAMY STOCK PHOTO ©

LOVER'S LOOP

This off-the-beaten-track loop rambles through lovely oak grasslands and a shady creek bed in Santa Barbara County.

From the town of Los Olivos, drive 6.9 miles north on Figueroa Mountain Rd, parking at a hairpin bend where a sign reads, 'This land is protected forever.' Walk 100ft north and turn hard right at the 'Lover's Loop' signpost.

The trail zigzags 0.8 miles south up a forested slope, then turns north and emerges into wide-open oak foothills. Views of the Santa Ynez Valley and surrounding mountains get vaster as you climb through the oak-dotted grasslands, emerging at a summit after 2.2 miles. From here it's a long, gradual descent through sloping meadows and gray pine forest towards Birabent Canyon, where you ford the creek at 3.5 miles, then return downstream under the shade of sycamores to your starting point.

DURATION 2hr return
DIFFICULTY Moderate
DISTANCE 4.3 miles

BUCKEYE TRAIL

For dazzling bird's-eye views over Big Sur's southern coastline, this rugged trail in the Silver Peak Wilderness can't be beat.

Spared from the 2020 fire damage that devastated trails further north, the Buckeye Trail is a strenuous out-and-back trip to a wilderness campsite, meaning you can tackle it as a day hike or an overnight.

Start from the abandoned Salmon Creek ranger station on Hwy 1 (near the must-see waterfall of the same name, 8 miles south of Gorda). Hike straight uphill on the Buckeye Trail, reaching a junction with the Soda Springs Trail after a mile or so and crossing into the Silver Peak Wilderness (pictured above). The trail meanders in and out of forested creek gullies for the next mile or so, then emerges into blissfully open high coastal bluffs with mesmerizing views south towards Hearst Castle and Morro Bay. From the trail's high point around 2240ft, descend more gradually into Buckeye Flat Camp.

DURATION 5hr return
DIFFICULTY Hard
DISTANCE 6.8 miles

MYWP/SHUTTERSTOCK ©

POTATO HARBOR

For phenomenal coastal scenery and abundant wildlife, try this relaxed half-day jaunt in Channel Islands National Park.

From the Scorpion Cove dock on Santa Cruz Island, head west, following Potato Harbor Rd to the North Bluff Trail. Just past the 2-mile mark you'll arrive at a bluff-top overlook above Potato Harbor (pictured above), a stunning cove encircled by rugged headlands. Fine coastal views continue on your return to the dock via the North Bluff and Cavern Point Trails. Watch for whales, dolphins and diminutive island foxes as you walk.

DURATION 2½hr return
DIFFICULTY Moderate
DISTANCE 5 miles

BERRY CREEK FALLS

California's oldest state park, Big Basin, is home to this iconic circuit through the redwoods to an idyllic 70ft waterfall.

Start from Big Basin park headquarters, 21 miles north of Santa Cruz, and follow the Sunset Trail 5 miles west through the mountains. Turn left on Berry Creek Falls Trail, descending to discover the gracefully cascading falls in a deep green glen. Return through old-growth redwoods via the Skyline to the Sea Trail. (Note that Big Basin suffered major damage in California's 2020 wildfires; check trail conditions before setting out.)

DURATION 5hr return
DIFFICULTY Hard
DISTANCE 10.2 miles

SOUTH MARSH LOOP

Birdwatchers will love this languid loop through the wetlands just inland from Monterey Bay.

Start from the Elkhorn Slough Visitor Center, 6 miles east of Moss Landing off Hwy 1; upon request, you can borrow a free pair of binoculars before setting out. The trail descends directly to the edge of a vast estuary bordered by the Moss Landing State Wildlife Area. More than 300 bird species can be seen here, including egrets, herons and pelicans. The mostly level, clearly marked loop meanders past old barns out to Hummingbird Island and back to the visitor center.

DURATION 1½hr return
DIFFICULTY Easy
DISTANCE 3.6 miles

SOUTHERN CALIFORNIA COAST

Explore
SOUTHERN
CALIFORNIA COAST

The coastal cities of Southern California are iconic in their own rights, and these trails offer a diverse mix that will take you high up to majestic vistas or plop you at the coast as the sun plunges into the Pacific. Some are so popular that the peak will be a party; others may have you wondering if you're the only one to hike the trail. They all highlight how unique, varied, and just plain gorgeous Southern California is.

LOS ANGELES

One of the United States' greatest hub cities, Los Angeles and its surrounding urban sprawl encompasses everything from the tourist-laden beaches to the gentle hills east of San Bernadino. While technically different urban centers, the traffic, strip malls and palm trees make it all blend. You'll find one of America's most-used international airports here, a host of hotels and motels ranging from the budget-friendly to the budget-busting, and places to eat from mouthwatering food trucks to fancy Michelin-starred establishments where you'll need to dine in a suit and tie, as well as sizable Asian food and shopping areas. And oh, yeah, there's that Hollywood place that you might have heard of. That's here too. Though the size and the traffic make some folks avoid LA, you can't deny that it's the area's biggest (and some would say best!) city, and it certainly makes a useful hiking hub for the surrounding trails.

SAN DIEGO

Los Angeles' sister city to the south, San Diego is a quirky mix of surf-boys and babes, Silicon Valley types, fraternity and sorority members, and artsy gurus. The Gaslamp district is where you'll go to party (assuming you're not sore from the day's hike!), with a core of packed bars, restaurants and clubs. The city is large and spread out, yet somehow seems small, thanks to well-designed public transportation. If you're looking to visit Mexico while on your visit, this is the place – you can take a trolley all the way to San Ysidro and walk the rest of the way. Hiking shops, department stores and, of course, a variety of restaurants make SD a great hub.

LAS VEGAS

Las Vegas is not exactly a 'hub city' for these Southern California coastal hikes, but don't discount it: it's a good entry or exit point for the area, and whether you love it or hate it, you can't deny that it's a unique city that has far more flair for tourists than either of the coastal hubs listed above. Driving or flying, you could make it one corner of a giant triangle. Or an entry or exit point for a one-way journey that includes not just the coastal hikes but the desert ones as well. Be aware that many hotels here (if they are part casino) will tack on a hefty 'resort fee' to the room charge.

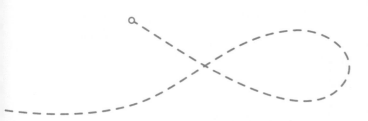

Resources

Discover Las Angeles (www.discoverlosangeles.com) A tourist-friendly searchable list of events and festivals going on in the LA area.

LA Weekly (www.laweekly.com) Great all-around spot for things to do, see, eat, etc in Los Angeles. Separate sections for food, music, even cannabis make it a great tool for planning your non-hike activities.

City of San Diego (www.sandiego.gov/events/calendar) Though a bit dry and info-heavy, this is a comprehensive spot for info about what's going on in San Diego.

WHEN TO GO

Some would call temperatures in Southern California sublime, especially in San Diego: the coolest days rarely drop below 65°F (18°C), the warmest range into the 90s (30s) but without oppressive humidity, and there are those breezes off the ocean to make things feel more pleasant. Los Angeles can be a bit more iffy, hotter in July and August, but not unbearable.

WHERE TO STAY

The Southern California coastal cities have everything you could imagine in terms of sleeping options, from campsites up to five-star resorts where you'll be hobnobbing with celebs. Plan on simpler, more rustic options the closer you get to the trailheads, which can be worth it to avoid the risk of the parking being full by the time you get there.

WHAT'S ON

California Science Center (www.californiasciencecenter.org) This multilevel, large science museum in LA is a great option for a rainy day or for something to do when you're tired of hiking. The Space Shuttle Endeavour is on display here, among a bunch of other cool things to see, explore and do.

Hollywood Walk of Fame (www.walkoffame.com) You can walk for miles following the stars – no, not the ones in the sky, the ones at your feet. Over 2600 celebrities and entertainment icons are immortalized here on over 15 blocks of sidewalk. Look for a particular person or just walk for a block or two and see what names you recognize.

Festival of Colors (www.festivalofcolorsusa.com; ☻Mar) In early March, this grand celebration of the Hindu holiday of Holi welcomes all, where participants dance and revel and paint each other with different colors to mark the passing of winter and the beginning of spring. Performers and events and hourly 'color throws' make it a unique experience and a lot of fun.

San Diego Pride (www.sdpride.org; ☻Jul) It doesn't get more flamboyant (or more fun!) than this massive celebration of the rainbow, usually in mid-July, which closes streets and often involves outfits that run from eye-opening to nearly not there. By some measures it's the city's largest event, with more than 200 floats, and attended by over 200,000 people.

TRANSPORT

It's easy to get from airports to major parts of these hub cities using public transportation, either buses or trams, but that's about all you'll be able to do without renting or using a private vehicle. Some of these hikes may be too off the grid for the rideshare services, so if you're not visiting friends or fellow hikers, you'll need to rent a car. Rental at a downtown office can be cheaper than at the airport, as you will save on the airport surcharge fees.

25

SUNSET CLIFFS

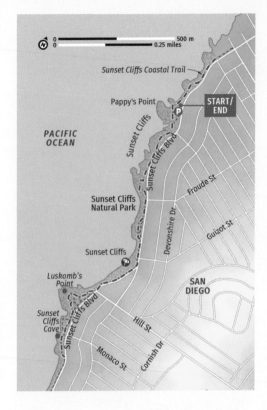

DURATION	DIFFICULTY	DISTANCE	START/END
1-2hr return	Easy	2.5 miles	Sunset Cliffs parking lot

TERRAIN	Dirt, sandstone, rock

Sunset Cliffs is exactly what it sounds: a rugged, wave-washed series of scarps and cliffs and tide pools that's the last land until you reach Hawai'i. The sun vanishes into the sea every 24 hours, drawing out lovers, families, fishers, snorkelers, yogis, meditators, photographers, and – if you're lucky – a sun-yodeler or self-proclaimed guru or someone wearing a pyramidal tinfoil hat. The people-watching is often better than the sunset. On clear evenings it's possible to reliably see the green ray: that good-luck flash of green light before the sun fully vanishes.

This is more of an amble than a hike, though there are some spots where you can clamber down to the water's edge if you like, investigating tide pools and nooks and crannies. Some people even snorkel around in the waves. It's possible to walk for several miles along the busy, traffic-clogged **Sunset Cliffs Blvd**, paying no attention to what's behind you as you marvel at the pretty sunset. Rock caves, atmospheric cliff faces, waves, even the occasional pelican flock or two – it all makes for a very picturesque stroll. The reality hits about five minutes after sunset, when a flood of people leave en masse and the streets come to a honk-filled standstill. Highlights include **Luskomb's Point** and **Sunset Cliffs Cave**.

Parking can be a crazy hassle, as there's really only a few official lots and they're small lots. But assuming you can find a spot (rideshare is another option) you'll be able to walk in either direction, either high up near Sunset Cliffs Blvd, or (in certain places) down at the water's edge, such as **Pappy's Point**.

26

BLUE SKY ECOLOGICAL RESERVE & LAKE POWAY LOOP

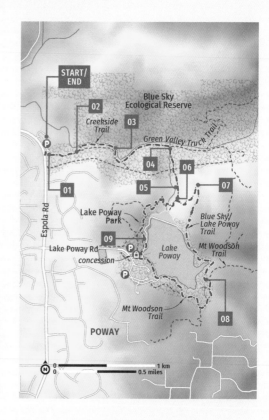

DURATION	DIFFICULTY	DISTANCE	START/END
2-3hr return	Easy	5.3 miles	Blue Sky Eco Reserve parking lot

TERRAIN	Trail, dirt road

This easy hike is great value, as it affords sightings of a variety of plants, animals and birds, and excellent scenery, while never being too challenging or remote. This is a wake-up-and-go-do-it hike; however, bring plenty of water.

GETTING HERE

Poway does not have good public transportation, so you'll want to drive, especially if you'll be arriving in the wee hours of the morning.

STARTING POINT

There is a clearly marked parking area where the trail begins. Alternatively, you could start (and end) at the Lake Poway Recreation Area and do the walk in reverse.

01 From the parking lot, head down the dirt road (officially known as the Green Valley Truck Trail) to where it levels off at the bottom of the hill. This is a great spot to see **acorn woodpeckers**: look for a medium-sized black-and-white bird with a crimson spot on its head.

02 After just 0.2 miles you can either keep going straight, or turn left onto the **Creekside Trail**, a narrow path that runs parallel to (you guessed it!) the creek bed that, during rainy times, can see a decent bit of water rushing through.

03 The Creekside Trail runs about half a mile and then rejoins the **Green Valley Truck Trail**. In the wider dirt road you'll again see large cottonwoods and have a good chance of spotting acorn woodpeckers.

Woody Woodpecker

If you've grown up with Saturday morning cartoons you may be more familiar with the acorn woodpecker than you think, as it was the original inspiration for the Universal Studios character, which famously kept its creator and his wife awake on their honeymoon. Look up into the cottonwood trees on the Blue Sky Ecological Reserve hike and you'll likely see a few of these brightly colored birdies, identified by a red cap on their head, and black and white on their bodies and wings.

B CRUZ/SHUTTERSTOCK ©

04 Just 0.5 miles further is a T intersection, where you'll see signs for Lake Poway. Turn right here, following the signs. When you pass through a chain-link fence you'll officially be in **mountain lion territory**. Avoid hiking solo in the early morning or late evening, and heed the cautions on the sign.

05 Just before you reach the base of the dam that forms one side of Lake Poway, you'll see a **large covered picnic area** and restrooms.

06 At **Lake Poway** (pictured), you have a choice of going either left or right. The steeper incline is on the left: either get it over with now or leave it for your descent.

07 Going left, clockwise around the lake, you'll ascend in a route that almost looks like you'll head towards the dam for Lake Ramona, but don't worry: it makes a sharp hairpin turn at the top and you'll head back to Lake Poway again.

08 Keep going clockwise, following signs for the Blue Sky/Lake Poway Trail, which will become the **Mt Woodson Trail** as you get closer to the recreation area and parking lot.

09 Pass the **small docks** and rental kayaks, and head back to the dam. Descend to where you meet up with your original path and follow it home.

TAKE A BREAK

Want to rest your weary feet for a bit? You can grab a bite and eat it at the various lakeside picnic tables, or even rent boats from the **concession** (☎858-668-4400; www.poway. org/412/Boating; 14644 Lake Poway Rd, Poway; per hr $15; ⏱6am to 30min before sunset Wed-Sun) stand and either fish or pedal around in the sunshine.

27

POTATO CHIP ROCK TRAIL & MT WOODSON

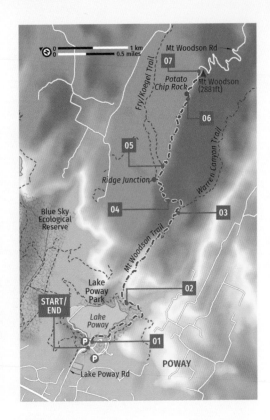

DURATION	DIFFICULTY	DISTANCE	START/END
4hr return	Moderate	6.8 miles	Lake Poway Recreation Area

TERRAIN	Dirt, gravel, steps, rocks

Potato Chip Rock is what it sounds like: a giant, thin slab of rock that sticks out over a hillside and makes, yes, one of the world's most perfect spots for selfies and general goofing around. People do yoga poses, pretend to be falling off it, even jump into the air for that photo op. But the trail is more than just a giant potato chip. It's a beautiful meander through gneiss- and conifer-strewn mountainsides, with some excellent birding and (be alert!) the chance to see mountain lions.

GETTING HERE

Unfortunately there aren't many public transportation options for getting out here. Either hail a rideshare to the starting point or drive there yourself.

STARTING POINT

There are two entry points for trails heading up to the summit, but this route assumes you're starting at Lake Poway Recreation Area parking lot, following the signs for the Mt Woodson Trailhead. (The other route does offer the spectacularly named 'Butt Cheek Rock' vista along the way, but it's a winding, mostly paved route that's not as scenic.)

01 The trailhead begins at the right side of the recreation area, so keep the **lake** on your left as you follow the wide gravel road. You will want to veer right at the (clearly marked) **Mt Woodson Trail** sign, about one-third of the way around the lake.

02 After leaving the lake, the trail gets steeper and a bit more rock-strewn, with lovely gneiss ('nice,' get it?) boulders that peek out of chaparral and scrub oak.

⚠ Mountain Lion Safety

While it's far more likely that the worst predator you'll meet on a hike will be a mosquito, in some areas mountain lions have become accustomed to human hikers, bikers and runners, and every so often their paths cross – when that happens, the human usually gets the worse end of the stick. To be safe in mountain lion territory, you should never flee, but back away, keeping your eyes on the lion at all times. If possible, throw rocks, sticks, even a water bottle or cellphone to scare it away. Never crouch down, as you want to look as large, imposing and dangerous as possible.

RAY BARTLETT/LONELY PLANET ©

03 If you haven't broken at least a little bit of sweat by the time you reach the **stairs**, you're going too slowly. The trail narrows from a road to a footpath, with a gazillion stairs. Early risers may be treated to the spectacular sight of a **'cloud ocean'** below them made of morning fog.

04 Imposing gneiss boulders are mammoth at certain points, making for **dramatic photographs** or selfies. You will be able to see the peak by now, too: just look for the pincushion of radio and cellphone antennas.

05 You'll reach **Ridge Junction** and, shortly after, the Mt Woodson Trail crosses the Fry/Koegel Trail. It's hard to get confused, but make sure you don't, as you'll end up miles away.

06 The moment you've been waiting for: **Potato Chip Rock**! Depending on how busy it is, you may find that this is basically a party, with people offering to take photos of others on the rock and sharing their contact info for photo sends. There's often a line for time atop the 'Chip' (pictured).

07 You've finally reached the **summit**. And after all that, it's disappointing, with views that can only sort of be seen through chain link and radio towers.

 **TAKE A BREAK**

If the hike has gotten you worried that you're going to lose too much weight, consider an emergency visit to **Phil's BBQ** (☎858-312-6161; www.philsbbq.com; 17051 W Bernardo Dr, Poway; mains $9-35; ⏰11am-9pm; P ❋ 🛜), where you can replenish all those calories...and then some. Phil's is a casual, come-one-come-all joint with rough-hewn walls, counter ordering, and tasty drink specials, such as the pineapple whiskey sour.

28

TEMESCAL CANYON

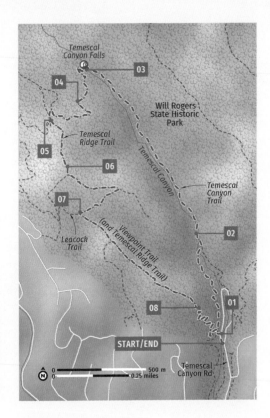

DURATION	DIFFICULTY	DISTANCE	START/END
2hr return	Moderate	3 miles	Temescal Canyon trailhead

TERRAIN	Dirt trail, hills, switchbacks, rocks

Temescal Canyon Trail is one of those magical 'good value' spots where you get great views, a decent workout and some varied terrain, all without having to drive too far or plan a whole day. It's easily done in two hours, less for active hikers, and with the pretty waterfall and the unbroken vistas from the peaks, it's really worth it.

GETTING HERE

Unlike so many other trails, this one can be accessed by bus: take the No 9 from Santa Monica and get off at the Sunset WB and Temescal Cnyn TS stop. From there, walk six minutes up Temescal Canyon Rd to the trailhead. Note there's a fee for entry.

STARTING POINT

The trail begins and ends at the Temescal Canyon trailhead.

01 From the trailhead, you can either go counterclockwise or clockwise; the latter is much steeper initially but takes you quickly to the best views. Going counterclockwise, you'll ascend sharply up a hillside and then level out, rising much more gradually until you reach the waterfall.

02 After the initial steep bit, the path follows the (often dry) **stream bed** for about the first mile and a half, rising much more gradually as it takes you through rocky bluffs and brush so dense it often hides the riverbed completely.

Will Rogers State Beach

Chances are that much of the water that passes through the Temescal Canyon and goes over its scenic falls ends up traveling down to the Pacific Ocean at Will Rogers State Beach.

Parking can be a challenge but if you're lucky you'll find a spot and can sunbathe, people watch, swim, or even surf to your heart's content at one of the area's most prized beaches.

Best for

POST-HIKE CHEER

03 At **Temescal Canyon Falls** there's a nice bridge that offers excellent views of the waterfall. Fluffy stalks of foxtails and yuccas line the stream bed, and even if no water is flowing, it's a pretty spot.

04 Turning sharply, the trail heads uphill once again, entering a series of gentle switchbacks. Here and there it's a bit rough, with loose dirt and rocks making it important to choose one's footing with care.

05 The **viewpoint** at the top of the switchbacks is where you'll understand why

this is such a popular hike: the **360-degree views** of greater Los Angeles.

06 There's a network of trails up here, all well traveled. You'll want to keep going due south to stay on track. It will take you to a series of **lovely lookout spots**, some that offer good glimpses of the mega-mansions that LA is famous for.

07 Make a hard, 90-degree left turn at the intersection of Leacock Trail and Temescal Ridge or you'll head down to the Leacock trailhead.

08 A few more **viewpoints** and then you'll descend back to the parking lot via a steep series of switchbacks. Voilà, you're done.

TAKE A BREAK

Since you'll be burning calories anyway on the hike, why not stop off at iconic Randy's Donuts for a bite (or box!) of sweet, pillowy-soft, caloric goodness? This shop has been in business for over 60 years, and is open 24/7, meaning you're never deprived of an epic doughnut fix when you need one.

29

CORTE MADERA TRAIL

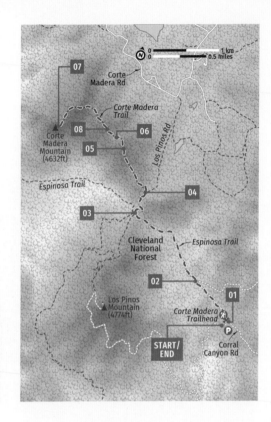

DURATION	DIFFICULTY	DISTANCE	START/END
5-6hr return	Hard	7 miles	Corte Madera trailhead

TERRAIN	Rocky trail, gravel road, boulders

Corte Madera Trail is a bit out of the way, but those that get here will be rewarded: it's a fantastic hike, though on the harder and longer side. Get out early to beat the late-morning heat, and, unlike at Potato Chip, come at an off time and you may have the entire trail to yourself. It's got excellent birding, fantastic photo ops with great views, and a host of different microclimates as you climb. Be sure to bring plenty of water and sunscreen though, as it's a long, pretty challenging trek up to the peak.

GETTING HERE

You will need a car to reach the trailhead parking. It's a good ways out of San Diego, so check with a rideshare service first before planning on being dropped off or picked up. You'll also need to make sure to pick up a park usage pass or risk a ticket.

STARTING POINT

Start and end at the Corte Madera trailhead parking lot. There's only space for a few vehicles, so it's good to arrive as early as possible.

01 From the parking lot, head across the street to a small hill and a gate where the trail begins. Clamber up, through the gate, and then down to a closed-off dirt road that meanders along a creek bed and is shaded by tall cottonwood trees.

02 Leaving the road, you'll climb up narrow **Espinosa Trail** that's overgrown in places by scrubby underbrush, goosethorn, and asters.

03 You'll rejoin the dirt road again for a brief bit after about 30 minutes of hiking uphill.

Ho, Ho, Jojoba!

Jojoba (pronounced *ho-ho-ba*) is a sturdy bush recognizable by its deep maroon stems and tough, thick, grayish leaves that escape the sun's punishing heat by orienting vertically rather than broadside. It's the same plant that jojoba oil is made from, still used today in applications that require extra-fine oil that won't break down or degrade over time, even at high temperatures. In fact, it was preferred during WWII for machine guns, which have parts that can overheat quickly and cause jams in the firing. Though far more expensive than regular petroleum-based oil, it has been considered for a variety of uses as an oil substitute.

RAY BARTLETT/LONELY PLANET ©

A 'CM' sign marks the way.

04 Once you leave the road for the final time, you'll be on the true **Corte Madera Trail**, ascending a steep hillside and getting your first really **impressive valley views**. Large gneiss boulders make imposing scenery, and the scrub changes from rabbit brush to jojoba.

05 What you think is the top is actually a false summit. Keep pushing on, reaching a **gorgeous peak** that gives great views of where you came from as well as into the valley on the other side, where you'll see fields and a reservoir glimmering below.

06 After that, the trail curves around the peak and drops down a bit into a saddle. When you come out again, you're onward to the real summit, which is still 30 minutes away.

07 The **summit** (pictured) is a collection of gneiss boulders that seem like a giant's set of building blocks. **Vultures** wheel lazily in the sky as you sip water, chow on a snack, and marvel at it all.

08 As soothing as the view is, at some point you'll have to head back down. Sections of the trail are more slippery on the descent, so take care. It's slightly faster going down, and just as beautiful.

 TAKE A BREAK

If you're heading back into San Diego rather than off towards Anzo-Borrega, you'll be driving for 30 minutes before you're in a spot with decent food. Keep going and if you're hankering for Mexican, you'll do yourself right by hitting tasty, authentic, **Carnitas Uruapan** (☎ 619-337-2448; www.mexican restaurantlamesa.com; 4233 Spring St, La Mesa; mains $6-21; ⏰ 9am-9pm; P ✳), with carnitas, *birria* (goat stew), and more usual options like tostadas and tacos.

30

HOGBACK LOOP TRAIL

DURATION	DIFFICULTY	DISTANCE	START/END
6hr return	Hard	10 miles	Commonwealth Nursery

TERRAIN	Trail, pavement, cliffs

Assuming you're up for the challenge, and it really is challenging, this is a fun adventure with some great views of Los Angeles, Hollywood, Inglewood, Burbank and Glendale, and even a chance to detour for a peek at the famous Hollywood sign. Prepare for well-traveled dirt or paved roads with sharp veers into nearly vertical ascents up root-tangled cliffside runoff channels, or rocky one-lane trails. You'll need to have GPS to stay on track (and a phone that can last all day), and to be able not just to walk but to climb a few steep scrambles up and down.

GETTING HERE

Buses do run, infrequently, close to Commonwealth Nursery. Take the Metro to Vermont/Sunset Station, walk to the Vermont/Prospect bus stop and catch the 180/181 bus north to the intersection of Los Feliz and Commonwealth Canyon Dr. Walk the rest of the way, about 20 minutes, to reach Commonwealth Nursery and the trailhead. Street parking is possible.

STARTING POINT

The trailhead is outside the Commonwealth Nursery grounds on the right side, through a split rail fence. An eroded hillside leads steeply up... Enjoy!

01 Once you've crossed over the low split rail fence, ascend the bare, eroded cliff in front of you. It's steep, dusty, and in places easy to lose your footing, but doable even in sneakers or normal shoes. (Leave the high heels at home for this one.)

02 At the top of the cliff, things flatten and you'll pass through a thick, dense, fragrant

grove of tall conifer trees, with a few benches and even picnic tables. This is a popular spot for families and picnickers, and the occasional group of slouching teenagers.

03 You'll then merge onto Vista Del Valle Dr, a paved road, for the next section, which heads uphill and makes a very sharp hairpin turn. Joggers, folks pushing strollers, walkers, rollerbladers, you name it will be trucking up and down this road. Going around the hairpin, among the landmarks you'll see is a large water tower with a pretty silhouette painted on it,

a helicopter landing area, and, going a bit further, some nice **views of Glendale and Burbank**, already far below.

04 Don't miss the sign for the **Hogback Trail**, next to a small green shed (officially labeled Pumphouse 13) beyond the helicopter landing area. The route leaves the road at this point and becomes an actual trail for a bit. It's (still) well traveled, with some nice **views** and a bridge along the way. The sign post indicates that you're 1 mile to Dante's View and 1.2 miles away from the Hollywood sign.

05 Cross the small foot-bridge and eventually you'll reach **Dante's View**, a pretty lookout spot that's one of the highest points of the trail. There's a post that alerts you that you're only 0.3 miles from the Hollywood sign.

06 Keep following the trail and you'll come to **North Trail**, a section of well-trodden, wide dirt path. At one point you'll be walking parallel to some high tension wires that crackle and hum from the electricity, with vistas of Glendale and Burbank below. Across the valley you'll see La Tuna

Commonwealth Nursery

Not many know that Commonwealth Nursery, nestled into the dell below Vista Del Valle Dr, was an ambitious plan to offer the plants, shrubs and trees the city needed locally, without importing them from other places. Run from 1928 to the 1970s, when disastrous Prop 13 cut heavily into budgets, the nursery offered sustainably grown plants, horticulture lessons, and a chance for residents to enjoy horticulture that they would not normally have.

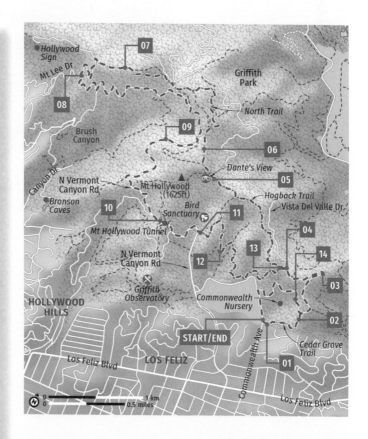

Canyon park, and even further, the mountains of the Angeles National Forest, some of it burned in the 2020 wildfires.

07 Shortly after that, you'll reach the third-most challenging section of trail: a narrow, rocky path that connects North Trail with the road to the Hollywood sign. It's easy to trip or lose your footing, so be cautious here, even though the route isn't particularly exposed.

08 Pretty soon, you'll see the radio tower above the iconic **Hollywood sign**. It was originally built in 1923 as a temporary advertisement for the nearby development, but it quickly became so famous and popular that removing it no longer made sense. The **Hollywood Sign Trail** will bring you right to it, but the two routes do overlap and it's possible to add a little detour to get a close-up view if you wish. You can go down and back in about 30 minutes round-trip.

RAY BARTLETT/LONELY PLANET ©

09 If you stick to the route as described, you'll get some solid views of the sign from afar, along a paved section of road that takes you downhill and eventually deposits you at the **Mt Hollywood tunnel**, on Mt Hollywood Dr.

10 Use extreme care going through the tunnel, as it is dark and there are no sidewalks, and vehicle traffic is heavy. If you have reflective gear or a flashlight, this is a good time to use it. Luckily, most traffic is not going by at

highway speed, but in the dark tunnel it may be difficult to see a hiker, especially if drivers aren't expecting them to be there. Once you're on the other side of the tunnel, walk downhill until you reach the **bird sanctuary**, via N Vermont Canyon Rd.

11 Just after the bird sanctuary, the trail heads up a crazy hard cliff to a path atop a bluff that's got some **gorgeous views**. Find it by passing the sanctuary and looking for a rain-washed gully that cuts through the hillside (there are several;

you can use whichever seems the easiest). Whichever you take, it will be the second steepest spot in the climb. Ascending is tough, and you'll need to haul yourself up over some roots and dig into soft sand to make it. Once you're at the top, go left, gradually uphill, and curve around at the corner until you're going downhill again.

12 This beautiful view leads you to a **20ft cliff** that you'll have to scale to get to the dirt road below. It's not particularly high, just 15 or 20

Save Griffith Park

There's talk (and proposals) to run an aerial tram up through here, allowing the less ambulatory to get a bird's-eye view of the park from the comfort of a cable car. Not surprisingly, this is mired in controversy and (at least for now) you'll see plenty of 'Save the Park!' signs. No less than four proposals have the cable car originating from various places, among them Universal Studios, Griffith Park's Commonwealth Nursery, and several locations with good highway access. The optimistic hiker hopes for options that have public transportation access. Or perhaps for the plan to fall through completely, as an aerial tram would certainly affect the vistas and sense of being in nature, what little LA has left.

feet, but a slip here could mean a twisted ankle. The good news is that this is the last really hard thing you'll do on this hike, but this little section is closer to rock climbing than hiking. If this seems too daunting, you can skip sections 11 and 12 by following N Vermont Canyon Rd downhill past the bird sanctuary and looking for the Riverside Trail entrance on your left, across from the Glendale Peak Trailhead parking lot.

13 Follow **Riverside Trail** all the way until it ends near the helipad at Pumphouse 13, which you'll recognize because you passed it at the beginning of the hike when you first got on Hogback Trail.

14 You're nearly home. Return the way you came until you see the Commonwealth Nursery, then head to the right (rather than through the Cedar Grove, unless you want to go back that way) and down to the street where you parked. Pat yourself on the back: this was a long one.

TAKE A BREAK

Griffith Observatory (📞 213-473-0890; www.griffithobservatory.org; 2800 E Observatory Rd; admission free, planetarium shows adult/student & senior/child $7/5/3; ⏱noon-10pm Tue-Fri, 10am-10pm Sat & Sun; P ♿; 🚌 DASH Observatory/Los Feliz Route), with its rotundas and white exterior, is impossible to miss as you contemplate Los Angeles vistas from Hogback Loop Trail. Stop here for a peek at the cosmos, or even join a monthly 'star party' and meet other amateur astronomers. The Observatory also has weekly Sky Reports that list what's possible to see up there.

Also Try...

WALTER CICCHETTI/SHUTTERSTOCK ©

BRONSON CAVES

The hike to Bronson Caves, abandoned quarry holes at the foot of Griffith Park near the much harder Hollywood Sign Trail, is a great option for anyone with mobility issues or families with strollers: it's a quick, well-traveled dirt road leading to some caves, rocky cliffs, and (from the right angle) a peek at the distant Hollywood sign.

The caves (pictured above) are nothing grand, but are mildly interesting, with low-hanging ceilings and a disgruntled bat or two. Currently a rock labyrinth lies outside. They are most loved as movie set locations, as they are easy to access yet (with proper camera placement) seem to be in the middle of nowhere. You can easily tack this on to the end of the Hollywood Sign Trail, since parking for both is the same.

DURATION 30min return
DIFFICULTY Easy
DISTANCE 0.4 miles

WISDOM TREE

This meandering loop hike will bring you behind the Hollywood sign and also to the eponymous, iconic Wisdom Tree. It's a pine that survived the 2007 forest fire and looks out over some stunning views of the city and reservoir below.

One may or may not become wiser by reaching this beloved tree, but it's certainly a nice destination, and on a sunny California day many would say it doesn't get better than this. If you're not up for the meandering and rock-scrambling of the much harder Hogback Loop option, this may be a fun substitute. Though oft touted as a 'lonely' pine, it's certainly got plenty of company these days: throngs of people make this trek daily, so don't expect to be out here by yourself. As with Potato Chip, you may find yourself needing to wait in line for those 'lonely-looking' selfies.

DURATION 2-3hr return
DIFFICULTY Moderate
DISTANCE 3.5 miles

RAY BARTLETT/LONELY PLANET ©

MALIBU LAGOON STATE BEACH

Malibu Lagoon State Beach is a mix of primarily flat walking that skirts a shorebird- and duck-frequented tidal estuary, a point break popular with surfers, and some sandy coastline that's fun for meandering.

You won't find too many shells and you may have trouble parking, but it's a lovely spot to watch the sunset from or enjoy a morning jog.

DURATION 1hr return
DIFFICULTY Easy
DISTANCE 1-2 miles

SAN DIEGO SEA TO SEA TRAIL VIA CAMINO RUIZ PARK

There's a steep section at the beginning and end but mostly this is a flat, shady walk beside a river that – in season – has a waterfall at the end.

If you keep going you can reach the ocean, but as described here it's a 5-mile round trip to the waterfall and back.

DURATION 3hr return
DIFFICULTY Easy
DISTANCE 5 miles

IRON MOUNTAIN TRAIL

Iron Mountain is a hugely popular hike that will take you up a peak near Mt Woodson.

If you liked Potato Chip and want more of the same, or don't need to brave the crowds for the chip rock selfie, this trail (pictured above) is a great option, with a much nicer view from the summit.

DURATION 3hr return
DIFFICULTY Moderate
DISTANCE 5.5 miles

SOUTHERN DESERTS

Explore
SOUTHERN DESERTS

Hiking in the Southern California deserts brings you to vistas as foreign as the moon at times, and the chance to see plants and animals that exist nowhere else in the world. Even the easy trails offer unparalleled beauty. Incredible adaptations allow life to flourish despite the heat and lack of water. To hike safely here means heeding the warnings of rangers, obeying signs and closures, and bringing far more water than you think you will possibly need. Don't mess around: temperatures in certain places can reach 121°F (49.4°C). Paradoxically, in the shoulder seasons and winter, temperatures can be low enough to cause hypothermia, especially at night.

LAS VEGAS

The glitter and glam of the Vegas Strip, the ubiquitous gambling and casinos (even the airport has abundant video slot machines!), and the shows and entertainment are why most people come here. But the proximity to your hiking destinations may make this your best option as a fly-in, fly-out spot with which to bookend your trip. You'll find plenty of restaurants and hotel options (often with a hefty resort fee), hiking and shoe stores, and places to rent vehicles.

LOS ANGELES

Los Angeles offers anything you could need to plan, prep, or provision for a hike in the deserts

(as well as some decent walks in the city itself). It's a great place for Mexican and international foods, and there's all styles of accommodations (from hostels to B&Bs to five-star resorts), so you will definitely find a spot that suits your needs...and hopefully your budget. Hollywood and Disneyland are key reasons to choose LA, particularly if you're starstruck or have kids in tow.

TWENTYNINE PALMS

This small town is a good hub for Joshua Tree National Park excursions, with a variety of small to midrange hotels and some B&Bs, restaurants that lean towards the American chains (though with a few exceptions),

and a laid-back, sleepy atmosphere that's a refreshing change from LA or Las Vegas, where everything is go-go-go.

BORREGO SPRINGS

Tiny Borrego Springs lacks almost everything, and that's exactly why people come: it's a Dark Sky preserve, meaning the stargazing here is second to none, and businesses are held to strict night illumination rules. A handful of hotels serve the visitors, as do a few restaurants.

JOSHUA TREE NATIONAL PARK

One of the top destinations for travelers in this region, in part because of the eponymous 1987

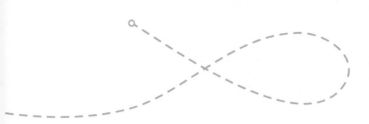

Resources

Joshua Tree National Park
(www.nps.gov/jotr) Information on hiking, safety, where to stay and other resources.

Anzo-Borrego Desert State Park (www.parks.ca.gov/?page_id=638) Official web page from the state of California.

Borrego Springs (www.borregospringschamber.com) Borrego Springs' chamber of commerce's site, with an event calendar and resources for places to eat and stay.

29 Palms (www.visit29.org) This small-but-useful site has 29 Palms information, such as events, camping and lodging suggestions.

album by rock megastars U2. It's got three visitor centers, and a fee to enter that's paid per vehicle: at the time of writing, $30 for seven days of in-out visiting. Many choose to camp at the various sites around the park – these spots can fill up months in advance.

 WHEN TO GO

Avoid hiking between April and October, as daytime temperatures may exceed 110°F (43.3°C). By starting in the early pre-dawn when temps are a 'chilly' 90°F (32°C) or so, you can often do the hikes before the sun turns the canyons into kilns. Ideal hiking is October to March, though between December and February may be cold, with the higher hikes even having snow.

 WHERE TO STAY

This region has a solid variety of hotels in the biggest cities, but for many hikes, you'll need to pick a spot in a smaller town where a cheap motel or no-name B&B are the only options.

👍 WHAT'S ON

Coachella (www.coachella.com; ⏱Apr) This mega music festival is held in Indio, CA, and draws thousands to hear, see, and experience a variety of rock, pop and indie performances. Recent years have seen it expand from just one day to multiple weekends, with attendees that include big-name celebs, movie stars, billionaires and music legends.

Milky Way Photography (www.joshua treeworkshops.com/milkyway) Held in Joshua Tree National Park, these outings (private, not park run) teach amateur stargazers how to best capture the night panoply on film. Options vary depending on the program, with some running camping trips in the park, others simply gathering at night, but the big requirement is always up to the heavens: a clear, bright night filled with stars.

Mule Days (www.muledays.org; ⏱May) A typical rodeo this isn't, but if you're in Bishop, CA, on Memorial Day weekend you can see this unique take on Western heritage, where mules and riders compete in rodeo-style events and festivities. There's even the world's longest non-motorized parade. Some may find this (or any) rodeo-like event problematic due to animal treatment issues; others may find this an interesting tribute to one of the West's most valuable animals.

 TRANSPORT

You will need to access these hikes with a vehicle. Rental agencies are in all the main cities. Rideshares may not be viable for some of the remoter trailheads, particularly since wi-fi and cell service is often unavailable in the remoter regions.

31

BORREGO PALM CANYON LOOP

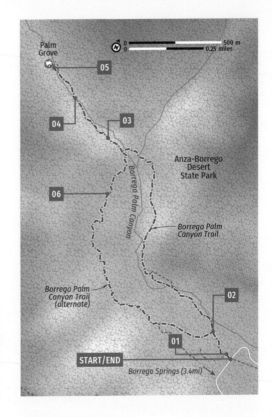

DURATION	DIFFICULTY	DISTANCE	START/END
2hr return	Easy	3 miles	Borrego Palm Canyon Trailhead

TERRAIN	Rocks, gravel, dirt path

Borrego Palm Canyon Loop gets you into the desert without being overwhelming. As such, you'll see more hikers here than on the nearby Hellhole Canyon Trail, but it's still a great hike with a lot to see. You'll begin in a desertscape of rocky boulders, cacti and ocotillo trees, then work into the canyon where (if you're lucky) you might see bighorn sheep. The oasis at the end was damaged in 2020 by arson, but the trees are rebounding. Currently hikers are not permitted in the oasis itself, but it's possible to hike to its perimeters and enjoy some great views of the recovering palms.

GETTING HERE

Borrego Springs is accessible by bus, but the Borrego Palm Canyon Trailhead isn't. You can camp in the park or drive/rideshare from town, five minutes away.

STARTING POINT

Borrego Palm Canyon trailhead is a large parking lot with toilets, some campsites and a few billboards with information about the trail. A pool with reeds in it houses some desert pupfish, though you'll need heron-sharp eyesight to catch a glimpse of them.

01 Head towards the canyon, passing beautiful sections of rock-strewn chaparral, a variety of cacti, ocotillo and acacia. Keep an eye out for jackrabbits, as well as snakes and lizards.

02 As you near the canyon, the trail splits into two options (the loop). One is a more direct route to the oasis at the end, and most people follow this on their ascent and take the more circuitous section when they're returning. Whichever route

The Mighty Minnow

You don't expect a superhero to be less than 3in long, but the desert pupfish is pretty darn mighty. Evolved to endure in even the harshest of climates, the pupfish can live in waters as high as 108°F (32°C) and salinity up to twice that of a normal ocean. It's found in unassuming puddles and streams, and can evade predators by burrowing into the mud or sand. Alas, even this 'mighty minnow' can't survive the toll of habitat loss and invasive species. It's now found in only the barest shadow of its range and remains endangered.

RAY BARTLETT/LONELY PLANET ©

you choose, continue towards the canyon. As you approach, keep an eye out for **bighorn sheep**, which can be sighted anywhere but are most often seen in the lower hills.

03 Once in the **canyon**, you'll follow the dry wash, and unless you're into cliff climbing, there's really no other way to go (besides back towards your vehicle). The coppery cliffs rise up on either side, and every so often there's a boulder you'll need to scramble over or around.

04 A few **palms** become visible as a harbinger of the oasis to come. Keep going.

05 You'll know you're at the **oasis** (pictured) when you see a large stand of lush, wavy palms – about 70 in all, though some are spread out further up the canyon. Amazingly, the palms have recovered from the fire and, while the black bark is still visible, lush fronds have already returned.

06 On the return, you can opt for the 'loop,' which takes you circuitously through a **picturesque landscape** of cholla cactus, ocotillo trees, various brush and rock piles, and with an increased chance of seeing snakes, jackrabbits, lizards and birds.

 **TAKE A BREAK**

While you can't claim to be south of the border per se, you'll find surprisingly decent Mexican food at **Carmelita's** (760-767-5666; www.facebook.com/carmelitasborrego; The Mall, 575 Palm Canyon Dr, Borrego Springs; mains $6-17; 10am-9pm; P), a cute and colorful taco and more joint that's tucked into the rear of the only mall in Borrego Springs. There's tables with Mexican decor but it's not a bad spot to grab takeout for a trailside picnic in the nearby canyons.

32

SPLIT ROCK LOOP

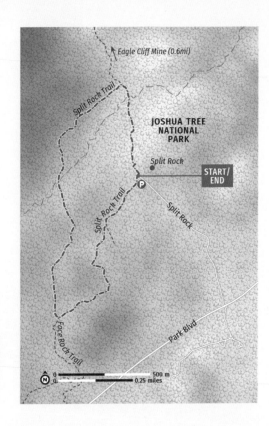

DURATION	DIFFICULTY	DISTANCE	START/END
2hr return	Easy	2 miles	Split Rock Loop trailhead

TERRAIN	Rock, path, sand, gravel

This Joshua Tree National Park top spot is a great way to get out into the gneiss fields and see the otherworldly rock formations, including the eponymous 'Split Rock' which, yeah, is unmistakably split top to bottom. The rounded metamorphic boulders take all sorts of shapes, and with the dotting of cacti and Joshua trees, it's a hike that's unforgettable. You will not be the only ones on the trail, however. If you plan to combine it with the Eagle Cliff Mine hike, be sure to leave plenty of time before sunset so as to not get stuck after dark.

The **trailhead** is easy to spot from the parking lot. Going counterclockwise, you'll soon be surrounded by giant gneiss formations, dotted with cacti and rabbitbrush.

Visible 200yd after you begin hiking is *the* **Split Rock** (pictured). Look for the distinct notch at the top and a straight split perpendicular to the ground. This is the iconic one. Antelope ground squirrels frolic beneath the shelter of bristly teddy-bear cholla cactus, and hawks and turkey vultures soar overhead.

The trail heads northwest for the first third, following a clearly marked path that's up and down but without any great rise in elevation. It then turns and heads nearly directly south, following a bone-dry (most of the time) wash.

About three-quarters of the way along, the trail again turns, going around an impressively large set of gneiss formations to the left. Once you're around that, you will start to see the parking lot in the distance.

33

GOLDEN CANYON TO RED CATHEDRAL TRAIL

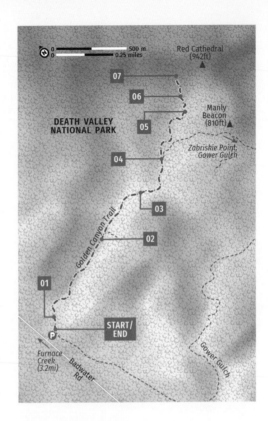

DURATION	DIFFICULTY	DISTANCE	START/END
3hr return	Easy	3 miles	Golden Canyon parking lot

TERRAIN	Sand, rock

Golden Canyon to Red Cathedral Trail is in many ways the perfect Death Valley in-out hike, with stunning, otherworldly vistas and a glimpse, up close and personal, at one of the area's biggest attractions: Red Cathedral, a massive bluff that overlooks the area, visible from Zabriskie Point and many parts nearby. The surrounding grays, yellows, and ochre eroded hills of Death Valley contrast sharply with the deep rust of Red Cathedral. Bring plenty of water and hike as early as possible to ensure that temperatures are not life-threatening.

GETTING HERE

You'll need a car to get yourself to the trailhead. Furnace Creek is the nearest outpost of civilization, about 5 miles away.

STARTING POINT

Golden Canyon parking lot has room for about 20 cars, and there are toilets here. The trail begins and ends here, and is the easily visible chasm into the rocks in front of you.

01 From the parking lot, head straight into **Golden Canyon** rather than going off to the side as you would for the Gower Gulch loop. It's clearly signed with distances, making it easy to choose which path you'll take.

02 The going is pretty easy for much of this walk, with flat, sandy and even once-paved sections that make it possible to come here for a bit even with a stroller or wheelchair.

03 Within a half mile, however, the trail becomes just that: trail. The eroded wash bed has been hard-packed by millennia of flash

Artist's Drive

This twisty drive is one way for a reason: in places, it's so narrow that only one vehicle can get between the rocks, and that excludes campers and pickups with trailers in tow. The road is almost like a roller-coaster ride, twisting and turning and going up and down – with a parking area overlooking some hills that are striated with gorgeous reds, golds and even greens. It's not copper, as many assume, but chlorite that gives the greenish tint, but regardless, it's a striking and very picture-worthy stop if you're doing hikes in Golden Canyon or Gower Gulch.

TOM FENSKE/SHUTTERSTOCK ©

flooding. The greenish-blue rock colors you'll see in places are not turquoise or copper, but rather green chlorite.

04 Exactly at the 1-mile mark you'll find a trail on the right that will take you past Manly Beacon and to Zabriskie Point or Gower Gulch. Don't take that. Keep going straight, up the canyon.

05 Near Red Cathedral, walls get narrow; you'll have to scramble over hefty rocks or squeeze through passages.

06 Photographers may want to plan their shots

carefully because as you get close to the end, there's less and less visibility of the entire Red Cathedral, which looms ever larger above you. The **pillars of rock** are very photogenic, but it's a challenge to get a perfect shot.

07 You'll know you've reached the end when the only way you can go is up. Straight up. Sheer cliffs rise above you that would make a rock climber drool and most of the rest of us cringe. When you're done with the 'ooh!'s and 'aah!'s, turn around and head back the way you came.

TAKE A BREAK

There's only one place for miles to get any kind of vittles in ya, and it's the **Last Kind Words Saloon** (☏760-786-3335; www.oasisatdeathvalley. com; Town Sq, Ranch at Death Valley; mains lunch $19-25, dinner $24-105; P✳🛜), inside the Ranch at Death Valley and open to the public. It's a quirky spot that seems pulled from a Western movie, with swinging doors and wood floors. You expect to see a piano player stop the music when you walk in and have to reach for your revolver. But the food is surprisingly good, if a bit on the pricey side. Service is super: friendly and fast, and there's outdoor seating on the patio.

34

HELLHOLE CANYON & MAIDENHAIR FALLS

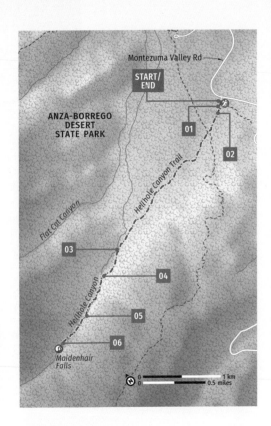

DURATION	DIFFICULTY	DISTANCE	START/END
3-4hr return	Moderate	5 miles	Hellhole Canyon Trailhead

TERRAIN	Rocky trail, rocks, gravel

Hellhole Canyon and Maidenhair Falls is such a treat that it's a shame the name may lead you to think otherwise. You'll gradually ascend up an alluvial plain into a rocky canyon that's got bighorn sheep, a host of reptiles, and even mountain lions to see. At the end is a lush oasis with a waterfall (or watertrickle), depending on the season. The water attracts thousands of bees, so be aware if you're allergic.

GETTING HERE

The trail is best reached by car from nearby Borrego Springs. There is no public transportation around town, but you can (very circuitously) arrive in Borrego Springs by bus from Los Angeles.

STARTING POINT

The trailhead is at a small parking area off Montezuma Valley Rd (S22). It's a fee area, so be prepared to put some cash in an envelope to avoid a ticket.

01 The trail is clearly marked at the entrance and posts a few warnings, primarily about heat, snakes and mountain lions. Be sure to have plenty of water, and to check current conditions beforehand.

02 From the parking area, the trail heads gradually up to the canyon you'll see in the distance. There's also a (hopefully just for show!) **gravesite** made of stones and a sign reminding you to be sure to bring enough water. Did you?

03 After about 15 minutes of walking, the trail begins to follow a dry creek bed, crisscross-

The Magical Ocotillo

You may notice a strange bush (it's actually a tree!) that looks like someone took five to 10 pieces of old bent wire and stuck them into the ground. Brown, twisted, and often thought of as dead, the ocotillo tree (pronounced 'oak-oh-tee-yo'; pictured in bloom) is one of the hardiest survivors of these harsh deserts. It is also a magician of sorts: after a rain, even a short sprinkle, the tree will sprout leaves that appear in less than 24 hours, literally overnight. Most trees take weeks to develop their leaves, but the ocotillo is a master of opportunity. The moment there's moisture, it readies its leaves and takes as much advantage as it can before they quickly dry up again.

Best for

ESCAPING THE CROWDS

ing from one side to the other as you ascend. It's a **beautiful landscape** of rocks and cholla cacti, prickly pear and beavertail, with an occasional fishhook barrel cactus among the stones.

04 Reaching the mouth of the canyon, the trail narrows, with **copper-colored cliffs** on either side. Bighorn sheep are around, though often hard to spot even for the experts.

05 You'll see your first views of the **palms** from a long way away. The trail brings you right to them, and it's a marvel to see them there, lush and green, after crossing such a parched plain. Don't be fooled though: these are not the palms you're looking for.

06 When you push onward, you get to the **waterfall**, which seeps, drips, dribbles or pours over a cliff face, offering grapes and other vegetation a chance to grow in what is literally nowhere. Tall **palms** shade the pools of water; there are frogs hopping, and lots of bees. Enjoy the greenery and relax, and when you're ready to head back, return the way you came.

TAKE A BREAK

Named for the ocotillo trees you'll see sprouting in the desert here, the **Red Ocotillo** (760-767-7400; www.redocotillo.com; 721 Avenida Sureste, Borrego Springs; breakfast $8-17, mains $13-21; 7am-8:30pm;) restaurant is a great spot for breakfast, lunch or dinner, with vegetarian options and a tasty variety of fusion entrees that range from eggs and bacon to Asian noodles slathered with tasty peanut sauce. A patio area makes for nice alfresco dining if you prefer the open air. It's conveniently just off the Borrego Springs rotary, making it easy to find.

35

GOLDEN CANYON & GOWER GULCH LOOP

DURATION	DIFFICULTY	DISTANCE	START/END
4-5hr return	Moderate	6 miles	Golden Canyon parking lot

TERRAIN	Sand, gravel, rock

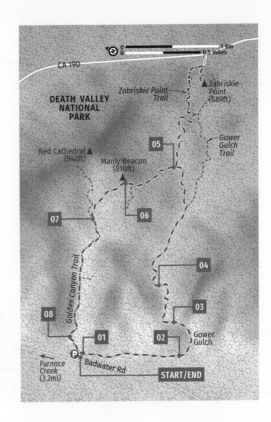

Gower Gulch and Golden Canyon is, for some, the perfect Death Valley hike. It's long enough for you to really experience these arroyos and eroded hills, it's visually stunning – especially in the morning and late afternoon – there's a detour possible to Red Cathedral, and fewer people do the loop. As with most of these hikes, the heat can be beastly or even deadly, so take appropriate precautions and bring plenty of water. This area has no cell service, so if an emergency happens you'll need to deal with it old-school, by finding help...or sending smoke signals.

GETTING HERE

You'll need to arrange for a ride from Furnace Creek to the trailhead, or drive.

STARTING POINT

The Golden Canyon trailhead has room for 20 or so cars, and toilets.

01 From the parking lot, you can go counterclockwise and enter Gower Gulch first, or you can head straight into Golden Canyon and do the loop clockwise. The counterclockwise route starts with a bit more incline, but allows a long, gradual descent at the end when you will likely be tuckered out.

02 The first part of the counterclockwise loop parallels the hillside and is just a well-traveled path in the dirt. It runs for about 15 minutes before turning at a wash. This is the **mouth of Gower Gulch**.

03 **Gower Gulch** is an impressive canyon that rises up narrowly on both sides. A slot canyon, it can become treacherous in heavy rains, so

Not so Boring Borax

You may or may not have grown up with borax, an unassuming (yes, boring) salt that's uses around the home include cleaning, scrubbing, insect control, and (as any kid will tell you) making that oh-so-popular slime. Vast deposits are found in Death Valley and several borax mines are visible today. The most famous is perhaps the 20 Mule Team brand, named for the teams of up to 20 mules that would carry the heavy mineral from the mine to the nearest trains. Anyone hiking in the heat can sympathize with what it must have been like to be one of those 20 mules.

RAY BARTLETT/LONELY PLANET ©

be cautious if thunderstorms are predicted. You will need to climb and clamber a bit, but nothing too strenuous.

04 An **old borax mine shaft** is visible on your left, and is interesting to journey to even if it's been closed off.

05 You will keep gradually ascending the wash, eventually crossing a section where you can do a 2-mile side trip to **Zabriskie Point**, a high lookout spot that has great surrounding **views**.

06 Turning north, you'll walk along the edge of some pretty steep embankments as you head towards **Red Cathedral**, the rust-colored pillar formation in the distance. **Manly Beacon** is the landmark the trail passes beneath.

07 Once you've crossed to the other side of Manly Beacon, you'll be in **Golden Canyon** (pictured). You can either go right, up the wash, which will eventually lead to Red Cathedral, or you can go down to the left and follow Golden Canyon Trail back to the parking area.

08 Another 30 or so minutes' walk and you'll be back at your car.

 TAKE A BREAK

If you think you'll get a few rounds in you've come to the wrong place, and not just because there's something obscene about a lush fairway green in the middle of a parched land where so many plants and animals perish of thirst. No, the **Devil's Golf-course** is a vast expanse of unique salt formations (once a landlocked sea) that are so gnarled and twisted that, as some visitor put it, 'Only the Devil could play golf here.' They aren't exactly beautiful, but they are an interesting spot to check out while you're in the area. Just leave the clubs at home.

36

LOST PALMS OASIS

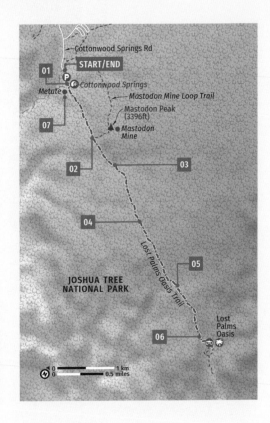

DURATION	DIFFICULTY	DISTANCE	START/END
4hr return	Moderate	7 miles	Cottonwood Springs parking lot

TERRAIN	Desert path, sand, rock

Lost Palms Oasis is an in-out trail that offers gorgeous glimpses of a desertscape unlike anywhere else in the world, though not (due to its low elevation) the iconic Joshua trees. There's an option to duck off to an old mine (ahem, the one that's contaminated the arroyo bed at Cottonwood Springs). Lizards, snakes, and a host of birds are easy to spot. The hardest part is at the end, as the palms lie far below at the canyon floor. Many opt for just getting an eagle's-eye view of the oasis and the vastness of the desert surrounding them from above, where the trail ends.

GETTING HERE

You'll need to have your own transportation for getting to and from the Cottonwood Springs parking

area, and the lot fills up fairly quickly, so you'll want to plan for an early start to ensure a space.

STARTING POINT

The trailhead is at the Cottonwood Springs parking area.

01 Begin the trail at the Cottonwood Springs parking lot, which goes down sharply to the **Cottonwood Springs** proper, an oasis of lush palms that unfortunately has soil contaminated by runoff from the nearby mine. There are numerous signs requiring visitors to stay on marked paths.

02 Not far along, before the 1-mile marker, you'll see signs for a turnoff that leads 1.4 miles to **Mastodon Mine**. If you plan to keep going to Lost Palms then this is either skippable or should be done as an in-out detour so you're back on the same point of the trail.

California Fan Palms

The palms you'll find at Lost Palm Oasis and many other desert hikes are the California fan palm *(Washingtonia filifera)*. These beautiful trees are also called 'petticoat palms' because the dead leaves often hang down, surrounding the trunk in a kind of petticoat. In all but the most intense wildfires, the outer leaves will burn but the trunk and heart of the tree remain unscathed, and in a few months new leaves will sprout to replace those lost in the fire.

CHRISTIAN_B/SHUTTERSTOCK ©

03 The trail, which has been primarily above the wash, now descends into one for a short bit. Note the tamarisk and other vegetation that's able to grow here thanks to the infrequent deluges and flash floods that scour the low canyon.

04 Soon, you'll clamber up and onto another ridge then down again, then back up. In all but a few places you're unlikely to slip, but here and there you'll want to choose your footing carefully.

05 Less than half a mile from the end you'll descend down the steepest arroyo and wind through it a bit before clambering up to the final crest that will, after another 15 or 20 minutes of hiking, bring you to the **Lost Palm Oasis overlook**.

06 A sign at the overlook notes that there are no trails that lead further, so the remaining trek down the canyon wall to the palms is something you'll do on your own. It's much more challenging than any of the trail, so be careful.

07 On the way back, be sure to stop at Cottonwood Springs and veer to the left to see some prehistoric **metate** (mortars made of stone used for grinding grain such as corn) that were used by Mesoamerican inhabitants to the area. It's easy to miss.

TAKE A BREAK

The only place to take a break for miles around is the **Cottonwood Visitor Center**, which you'll need to pass right by on your way to the Lost Palms Oasis trailhead. It's more of a gift shop than museum, but there are some displays and lots of information that the rangers can offer about sights, history and the unique desert ecology. It's also a good place to get a weather update before heading out on hikes that can be dangerous in extreme conditions.

37

RYAN MOUNTAIN TRAIL

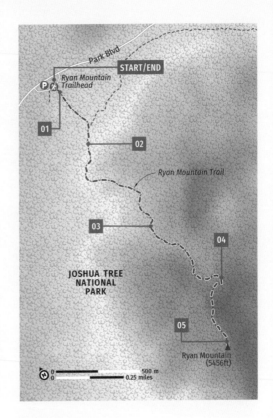

DURATION	DIFFICULTY	DISTANCE	START/END
2hr return	Moderate	3 miles	Ryan Mountain trailhead

TERRAIN	Steep gravel path, steps

Ryan Mountain is a great-value hike, as it's short and sweet and yet offers unparalleled 360-degree views of Joshua Tree National Park's majesty. Save for a few twisty parts and one actual switchback, it's nearly straight, too, though steeper in parts than it could be. It's also a heavily trafficked trail, with tour groups and a constant stream of hikers in varying degrees of fitness. But if you come early in the morning you may find the ascent, at least, is yours and yours alone. As with any of these desert hikes, proper attire, attention to the weather, and plenty of water is crucial.

GETTING HERE

You'll need a vehicle to reach the trailhead.

STARTING POINT

Ryan Mountain trailhead has a small parking area and pit toilets.

01 Starting off at the trailhead, you'll pass between some **impressive gneiss formations** that are very atmospheric and selfie-worthy. Some people veer off the trail and simply perch somewhere in the crags and have breakfast or a picnic lunch. But the view gets better if you venture on.

02 Going further, the trail's incline steepens, but **steps** here and there make it easier. If you find it too strenuous, simply rest and take it slowly, as it's going to be up, up, and more up the rest of the way. Stopping is easy, as the **views are already spectacular**.

Jumping Jackrabbits

Of the wildlife you'll likely see in Joshua Tree National Park or the Mojave Desert in general, none is more common than the black-tailed jackrabbit. These incredible animals not only survive in this harsh, parched landscape but thrive, reaching weights of up to 6lb. You can distinguish them from (also commonly seen) rabbits by the long ears and ungainly, loping gait, which looks awkward until they reach cruising speed of 30mph with jumps as long as 20ft. That's a tough catch for coyotes and other predators who have to also avoid getting impaled on cacti as they chase their dinner.

RAY BARTLETT/LONELY PLANET ©

03 Further on, another large **gneiss formation** looms on your right side. There's a chance (though slim) to see **bighorn sheep** hanging out on the hillsides.

04 Passing the large rocks on the right, you'll reach the one significant switchback. Pass it and you're already three-quarters of the way to the summit.

05 At the **summit**, there's a cairn of rocks marking the very top, and some piñon pine and rabbitbrush. It's very exposed, so use care to avoid snack wrappers, gloves or hats being blown away. Marvel at the **view** that stretches over vast flat desert plains to ridges of mountains that meet the horizon. Head back the way you came. If you've gotten an early start, you'll be glad you did: you'll be going down when lots of people are heading up.

 TAKE A BREAK

The **Jelly Donut** (☎760-367-4202; 73570 29 Palms Hwy; phở $8-13, doughnuts $2; ⏰6am-9pm; Ⓟ❄) in Palm Springs is a bizarre spot to dine but well worth finding if you're into doughnuts or Vietnamese noodles. Yes, you got that right. The morning doughnuts are made fresh daily and often sell out by noon, and by lunchtime there's already people lining up for the piping hot phở that (despite the desert heat!) goes down perfectly after time spent on the trail. That it's in an old gas station (complete with a Norman Rockwell–era pump) only adds to the fun.

38

TEUTONIA PEAK TRAIL

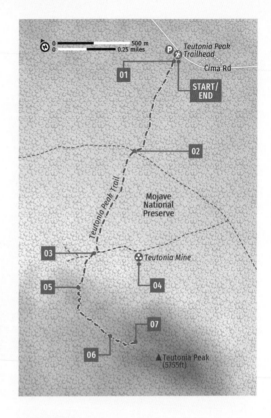

DURATION	DIFFICULTY	DISTANCE	START/END
3hr return	Moderate	3.3 miles	Teutonia Peak Trailhead

TERRAIN	Sand, gravel, rock

Teutonia Peak rises up out of the middle of the Mojave and offers hikers great views of the surrounding desert. Alas, the entire area was burned in a 2020 wildfire that raged through this area leaving charred wasteland in its wake. Miraculously, here and there pockets of desert remained untouched. While it will take years for this area to recover and decades for it to return to its original pristine state, the hike is a fascinating look at what wildfires do to a desert...and how the desert bounces back after they've gone.

GETTING HERE

You will need a car to reach the trailhead parking lot, which is in the middle of the Mojave on Cima Rd, a paved, two-lane road that runs north–south through the park.

STARTING POINT

The Teutonia Peak Trailhead parking lot is just a billboard. No facilities are nearby.

01 Grab plenty of water and sunscreen and head out from the parking lot, keeping an eye out for **bighorn sheep**, which are sometimes seen along the trail or across the road on the other side of the parking lot. The peak is visible ahead at the horizon.

02 About half a mile into the trail, you'll come to a crossing – just keep on going straight. No need to turn. The fire's devastation is mitigated by pockets of **beautiful untouched desert**. Only pockets though.

The 2020 Dome Fire

Teutonia Peak Trail has been described as walking through a natural botanical garden, but unfortunately a naturally caused fire in August 2020 raged through this entire area and reduced nearly 45,000 acres to cinder and ash. Though caused by lightning, and thus part of the region's natural cycles of loss and renewal, it was in the very heart of the Mojave Desert and destroyed some of the region's most iconic landscapes. They will recover, but it's likely to be visible for years.

WILDNERDPIX/SHUTTERSTOCK ©

03 Just under the 1-mile mark, the trail jogs a bit to the right, and on either side there are the remains of **mine shafts**. Be cautious about getting too close even though they're closed off.

04 You can detour, if you like, to the **Teutonia Mine ruin**, which is about 0.2 miles due south of this intersection. It's been closed off, but exercise caution about getting too close as shaft walls could conceivably crumble at any time.

05 Returning to the trail proper, head towards the mountain, which will now be unmissable. A big ridge is right ahead of you.

06 The approach up to the summit is via a trail on the opposite side of the ridge. Again, you'll notice how the fire torched some parts of the area and left others unharmed.

07 The **summit** is actually atop some rocks you'll need to boulder to if you wish to reach the true peak. Most hikers stay at the rock caves below. Be cautious to not leave any trash... or better, take some with you as you head down. You should be able to see your car waiting for you in the parking lot, far below. Return the way you came, stopping off at the mine if you skipped it on the way up.

TAKE A BREAK

Taking a break usually means ducking away from the hike to a cozy spot for a bite to eat. In this case, however, you're smack dab in the middle of of the Mojave and 'civilization' is not just around the corner. If you plan on having some cucumber sandwiches and high tea, you'll need to pack it along with your hiking boots. The upside is that you couldn't ask for a prettier spot to spread out that picnic blanket, surrounded by desert beauty as far as you can see.

39

WILDROSE PEAK TRAIL

DURATION	DIFFICULTY	DISTANCE	START/END
5-6hr return	Hard	8 miles	Wildrose Peak Trailhead

TERRAIN	Steep incline, dirt & rocks

Wildrose Peak Trail is a gem, but it's hard uphill with over 2000ft of elevation gain. Due to its height above sea level, it's a bit cooler than other Death Valley hikes and a good option even for summer hiking, but in the winter it can even have snow. Because it's remote and mostly outside cell signal range, you'll want to plan carefully, bring plenty of water, and be prepared for emergencies. The rewards, however, are many: gorgeous valley views, a trail that's unlikely to be crowded, beautiful wildflowers, a great workout, and the bizarre kilns to explore after you're done.

GETTING HERE

Wildrose Peak is only accessible by car via a remote, lonely road off Hwy 190. You will need to arrange transportation or have a rental vehicle.

STARTING POINT

The trailhead is to the left side of the Wildrose Charcoal Kilns.

01 Start the hike by heading to the left of the **beehive-shaped kilns**, which are in a row opposite the trail's small parking lot. This is a long hike, so skip investigating these structures until you return, as you'll want to maximize your time on the trail, especially if you're hiking when it's hot. Because it's at a higher elevation you can hike this one even in August, but wise hikers will start at daybreak to avoid the punishing peak-of-day heat, and also to reduce the risk of sudden weather changes causing hazardous conditions on the trail. Wildrose Peak is one of the area's highest mountains and, as such, requires more preparation than many of the other hikes in this book. It's long enough (about three to four hours up and at least two, possibly three, down) that you could experience changes of

weather or other such emergencies, not to mention the extreme heat if you hike during the summer months. Footwear needs to fit properly or you may find it especially painful on the descent.

02 The trail leads up and gradually away from the road where the kilns are, then at about 0.4 miles turns sharply to the right, about a 90-degree angle, and levels off for a bit, following a hillside and a ravine. It's peaceful and quiet, narrow but without any exposure or risk of falling. There are lots of **pretty wildflowers** along this stretch

after a rainfall. It's deceptively flat during this section, but don't worry, you'll be getting your workout soon enough.

03 Don't get too comfy with the level terrain, because soon you'll turn again and head much more sharply uphill on what once was a logging road, possibly for the very trees they used in the charcoal kilns at the trailhead. It's steep and there are lots of loose gravel sections, but nothing impossible. **Beautiful piñon pine forest** surrounds you on either side. **Bobcat** and even **mountain lion** sightings are possible, as well as plenty of **birds**.

Though extremely unlikely, if you do see a mountain lion, do not approach it and do not lie down. Instead, make yourself as large and as threatening as possible, and ideally throw rocks or even a water bottle to scare it away. Mountain lions are an apex predator in California, and they do occasionally attack – and sometimes eat – human prey. Minimize risks by hiking in groups, being alert on the trail, and having a plan in mind should a lion suddenly appear.

04 At about the 2-mile mark the trail will curve gradually to the left and you'll finally

Charcoal Kilns

Wildrose Charcoal Kilns are an interesting spot to visit even if you don't plan to hike the relatively challenging trail that's behind them. Shaped like giant beehives, the 10 structures were completed in 1877 to provide fuel for smelting lead and silver ore. The Modock Consolidated Mining Company ran them only for a few years, however. The beautifully shaped kilns were made with a mix of Native American, Mexican and Chinese labor, as was typical for mining projects in the area at the time. Though in good condition (perhaps due to lack of heavy use after being made), they were restored to their current condition in 1971 by Navajo stonemasons.

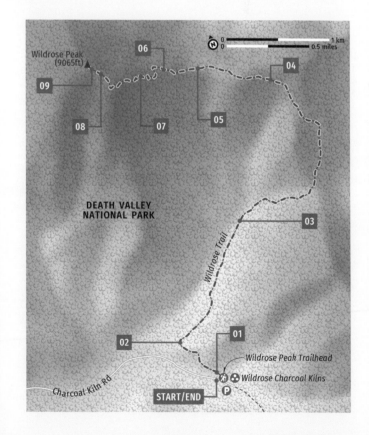

see the peak ahead of you, visible here and there through gaps in the forest. It's a **lovely landscape**, with wind-gnarled conifers and patches of wildflowers and grasses that catch the sunshine perfectly. The ground will be almost entirely covered with loose rocks and shale. Creosote bush is another holdout, unique for its tiny oil-covered leaves that lock in moisture. It's a bit humbling to think that even these spindly, scrawny trees and bushes have likely lived on these slopes for many human lifetimes.

05 Go another mile and you'll have a **stunning vista** to the right of Death Valley sprawling out below you for miles and miles. It's useful to have a pair of binoculars to spot places like **Devil's Golfcourse**, visible in the center of the dry lake bed below, or **Mt Perry** and **Dante's View**, approximately due east on the opposite side. **Telescope Peak**, to the south of you, is the highest point in Death Valley, with an altitude of 11,054ft, as high as a low-flying airplane. On this trail you'll 'only' hike up to 9065ft. It's not so high that you'll experience any breathing trouble, but it's high enough that you should take it slow and steady. When you're ready, keep going.

06 A grueling series of switchbacks begins at about 3.3 miles, which are especially punishing after the steepness of the earlier parts of the trail. The reward is additional **valley views**, better and better as you ascend, and lots of cool critters (lizards, mostly) hiding out

in rocks along the trail. Attentive hikers will eat their hard-earned snacks here, in the shelter of the trees, rather than risk their trash and wrappers blowing away at the windswept summit.

07 Keep going up those switchbacks. It's pretty... and pretty hard.

08 Go another half a mile up and you'll be nearly there: a **saddle** is all that separates you from the official summit. It's **alpine meadow**, with totally different flowers and plants than what you saw on the way up. Wind may be fierce, and for those hiking in the fall or winter, it can be chilly or downright cold. It's not unheard of for snow to cover the peak, so be careful to bring additional wind- and waterproof layers to wear.

09 You've arrived: 9065ft, 4 miles, 2300ft of elevation. At the top there's a **cairn of stones** and a military ammo box that contains a log book you can sign if you're so inclined. Guess what, you may even find that you have cell reception, depending on your plan. Relax, reapply that sunscreen, and eat your snacks, being careful to prevent wrappers from blowing away in the winds, then ready yourself for the long return. It's downhill, yes, but some find going down is more challenging than going up, due to the steep grade that's punishing on the knees. The kilns, when you reach them, are worth poking around in and certainly make for good picture-taking. A few signboards detail some of their history: they

Dante's View

If the thought of hiking six hours for a good view of the valley is a bit daunting, there's good news: you can drive to Dante's View, on the opposite side of the valley, for impressive eagle's-eye panoramas of Death Valley, Badwater Basin, Furnace Brook, and Wildrose and Telescope Peaks (the mountains you'll see to the west, on the other side of the valley). It's very popular at sunset, though shadows darken the valley by then and the best photos are an hour or two before.

were used for making charcoal for nearby mine and smelting operations. The kilns ceased to be used more than a century ago and yet still have a fragrant smoke smell if you poke your head inside.

TAKE A BREAK

There's not a lot nearby but as the crow – or flying saucer – flies, you're not that far from a funky little roadside attraction called **Alien Mailbox**, near the ghost town of Ballarat. A bright shiny green mailbox with an antenna on it sits there awaiting your mail, next to a yellow road sign warning of alien activity. You may get there and be disappointed. Or you may never be seen again. Regardless, if you're looking for quirky weirdness in the middle of nowhere, you (and perhaps the aliens) are in the right place.

Also Try...

HANNATOR/SHUTTERSTOCK ©

BARKER DAM NATURE TRAIL

This easy hike (a walk, really) is popular, even crowded. But it's gorgeous, meandering through giant gneiss boulders that have evocative, otherworldly shapes, cacti, and desert flora and fauna. It's a great way to see a bit of what Joshua Tree's unique landscape has to offer without risking heatstroke or being too far from civilization. It does require some ups and downs over rocky terrain.

The wildlife (such as antelope ground squirrels) are very accustomed to people, so it's fun to see some of these shy critters close up. (Note: do not feed them!) Among the highlights are some ancient petroglyphs, and a reservoir (pictured above), often dry, that attracts birds like herons and ducks that you normally don't see in the desert.

DURATION 1hr return
DIFFICULTY Easy
DISTANCE 2 miles

AMBOY CRATER

Amboy Crater is a near-perfect cinder cone that rises out of the desert near the eponymous town of Amboy. It is a great place to spot reptiles – especially snakes and a species of desert iguana.

It would be an easy hike but for one factor: the heat. It can reach up to 110°F (43°C) between 10am and 5pm, so bring crazy amounts of drinking water and be prepared to turn around if you feel ill. Once atop the crater (pictured above right), it's a nice view of the surrounding desert but there's not much else here other than the vistas. A few trails crisscross through the crater and one goes around the rim. In places the rocks are knife-sharp, so tread carefully and make sure you have good footwear. This is not a spot for flip-flips or thongs.

DURATION 2hr return
DIFFICULTY Moderate
DISTANCE 3.5 miles

HANK SHIFFMAN/SHUTTERSTOCK ©

SURPRISE CANYON TRAIL

If you want punishing, but gorgeous, check out Surprise Canyon Trail, a long, all-day hike that starts at a spring ('surprise!') and follows a winding canyon up to the gorgeous ghost town of Panamint in Death Valley.

This is not for beginners: expect a long, challenging trail that goes unrelentingly up. It's beautiful, though.

DURATION 13hr return
DIFFICULTY Hard
DISTANCE 10 miles

EAGLE CLIFF MINE

This Joshue Tree hike is on the tricky side of moderate with some loose gravel and steep spots, but the rewards are a cool mine shaft, the 'boulder house' (which is well-preserved and very atmospheric), and a nice workout in and out.

It is best accessed off Split Rock Trail, and best done in the morning so that there's plenty of time for exploring and finding the trail.

DURATION 3hr return
DIFFICULTY Moderate
DISTANCE 2.5 miles

BAT CAVES BUTTE

Bat Caves Butte is a lowish, unimposing bluff that overlooks the Salton Sea. For amateur geologists, this is a gold mine: the buttes were once underwater, and the surrounding dusty plain holds a host of interesting rocks and discoveries, such as volcanic pumice.

The caves are worthy of a peek, though it's a multiuse, unprotected area and you may find trash, cans, and so on. Once atop the butte you'll have a nice view of the Salton Sea.

DURATION 1½hr return
DIFFICULTY Easy
DISTANCE 3 miles

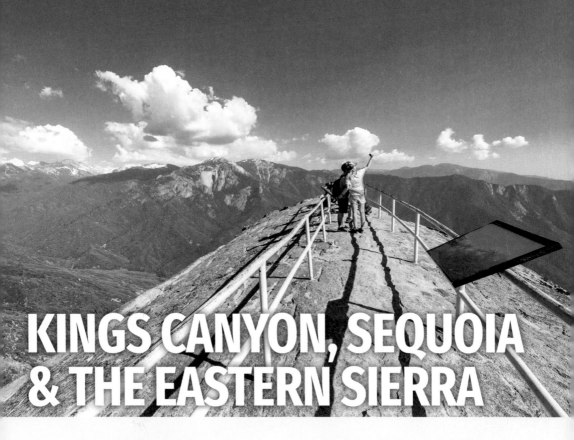

KINGS CANYON, SEQUOIA & THE EASTERN SIERRA

Explore
KINGS CANYON, SEQUOIA & THE EASTERN SIERRA

There's an invigorating sense of adventure that accompanies even the simplest day hike in Kings Canyon and Sequoia National Parks. A stroll in the Giant Forest carries you past towering giant sequoias that are among the largest trees in the world. Anticipation builds as you hike through thick woods beside a wild river to an exuberant waterfall. It's all a great frolic, with colorful wildflowers, lush meadows, granite domes and abundant wildlife adding to the fun. The Eastern Sierra has its own treasures, from easy-to-access alpine lakes to 14,505ft Mt Whitney – the tallest peak in the lower 48 states. With this scenic diversity, you have all the ingredients for some of the best hiking in California.

FRESNO

Smack in the arid center of the state, Fresno is the Central Valley's biggest city. It's hardly scenic, but beautifully situated, just an hour and a half from three national parks (Yosemite, Kings Canyon and Sequoia), making it the ideal last stop for expeditions. Trendy eateries and breweries are in the Tower District and hidden among abandoned storefronts downtown, while farm-fresh restaurants and wineries dot the countryside right outside the city limits. For fantastic raw ingredients, Fresno's excellent farmers markets are abundant all year round.

THREE RIVERS & VISALIA

Named for the nearby convergence of three Kaweah River forks, Three Rivers is a friendly small town just outside the park. The town's main drag, Sierra Dr (Hwy 198), is sparsely lined with small motels, eateries and shops. Day-trippers in need of supplies should fill up here before entering the park. There are also cozy lodgings, campsites, showers and plenty of wi-fi options. Visalia, 30 miles southwest of Three Rivers, is also a convenient stop en route to the national parks. You'll find old-town charm and restaurants and shops downtown, and plenty of chain hotels, most along CA 198.

MAMMOTH LAKES

Mammoth Lakes is a famous mountain-resort town endowed with larger-than-life scenery – active outdoorsy folks worship at the base of its imposing 11,053ft Mammoth Mountain. The Eastern Sierra's commercial hub and a four-season resort, Mammoth is backed by a ridge line of jutting peaks, ringed by clusters of crystalline alpine lakes and enshrouded by the dense Inyo National Forest. Restaurants, from no-frills pizzerias to upscale bistros, are mostly located in drab strip malls scattered around town. The Village, Main St and Old Mammoth Rd have the highest concentration. It's the best dining scene in the region.

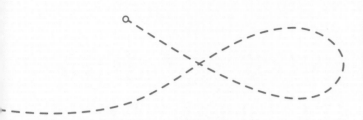

WHEN TO GO

You can hike in the foothills year-round, but wildflowers display kaleidoscopic colors in the lower elevations of both parks in April and May. Hwy 180 through Kings Canyon to Cedar Grove and Roads End is typically open from late April through mid-November. Waterfalls are at full strength in spring and sometimes into early summer. The Mineral King's backcountry-trail network opens and the snow melts in June and July.

WHERE TO STAY

Camping is the most affordable way to experience the parks, though sites fill up fast in high season (May to October). In Kings Canyon National Park, accommodations are offered in Grant Grove and Cedar Grove Villages. Facilities in Cedar Grove Village typically don't start operating until mid-May. Wilderness camping is free (permits required in quota season). Sequoia has one official in-park lodging option. The town of Three Rivers, just outside the Ash Mountain entrance, offers the most nearby accommo-

dations. Those using Fresno as a launchpad have plenty of options in the cluster of chains near the airport or a couple of high-rise offerings downtown. For a luxury hike-in camping experience, consider **Sequoia High Sierra Camp** (☎866-654-2877; www.sequoiahighsierracamp.com; tent cabins with shared bath incl all meals $500; ☺early Jun–mid-Sep) in Sequoia National Forest. In the Eastern Sierra you'll find a vast range of accommodation options in Mammoth Lakes.

WHAT'S ON

The road to Cedar Grove Village
Along the eastern end of the Kings Canyon Scenic Byway/Hwy 180; only open from around April or May until the first snowfall.

Mineral King Rd Generally open late May through late October.

Waterfalls Peak in late spring.

Dark Sky Festival Observe the heavens during this late-summer festival.

Trek to the Tree (🕒2nd Sat in Dec) Holiday carolers and a wreath laying for the Armed Forces.

TRANSPORT

From Fresno, it's 57 miles east on Hwy 180 to Kings Canyon. It's 46 miles east on Hwy 198 from Visalia into Sequoia National Park – you'll pass through the gateway town of Three Rivers before entering the park. Hwy 180 and Hwy 198 are connected by the Generals Hwy, inside Sequoia. There is no access to either park from the east.

There are no shuttle buses in Kings Canyon, but Sequoia National Park has four free shuttle routes within the park (late May to early September).

40

GENERAL SHERMAN TREE & CONGRESS TRAIL

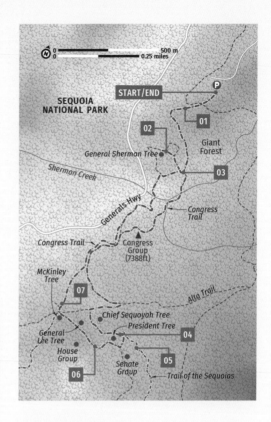

DURATION	DIFFICULTY	DISTANCE	START/END
2hr return	Easy	3.2 miles	Sherman Tree parking area

TERRAIN	Paved forest trail

The world's largest tree by volume anchors this storybook stroll through the Giant Forest in Sequoia National Park, home to the world's most awe-inspiring grove of giant sequoia trees.

GETTING HERE

From Visalia, follow Hwy 198 north past the Ash Mountain Entrance Station and the Foothills Visitor Center. From the visitor center continue north 18 miles on the Generals Hwy. Turn right on Wolverton Rd and follow it just over a half mile to a right turn that leads to the parking lot. The trailhead can be accessed by a free park shuttle in summer on the green route and the orange route. For those with mobility issues, there is an accessible parking lot on the Generals Hwy. A short paved trail leads to the General Sherman Tree from this lot.

STARTING POINT

A small plaza and a wooden A-frame shelter mark the start of the trail to the Sherman Tree. This spot starts getting busy – really busy – after 8:30am in summer.

01 A concrete path with stairs drops from the shelter then switchbacks lazily down into the **Giant Forest**. The trail cleverly starts at the height of the tree's tip (27 stories high) and descends 0.5 miles to its base, passing the trailhead to the Congress Trail.

02 It's hard to get a satisfying photo of the **General Sherman Tree** – it's just too darn monstrous! By volume the largest living tree on earth, the massive General Sherman Tree rockets into the sky and waaay out of the camera frame. Pay your respects to this giant (which measures more than 103ft around at its base and 276ft tall). The tree is 2300 to 2700 years old.

Tunnel Log

Visitors can drive through a 2000-year-old tree, which fell naturally in 1937. It once stood 275ft high with a base measuring 21ft in diameter. Regular sedans and small cars fit through the gap, or it's just as fun to walk through the 17ft-wide, 8ft-high arch cut into the tree by the Civilian Conservation Corps (CCC). In winter the road may be closed due to snowfall, but those with the winter gear can hike to it from the Giant Forest Museum. Tunnel Log is a half mile past Moro Rock.

AMY BALFOUR/LONELY PLANET ©

03 Return to the **Congress Trail**, which unfurls in a 2-mile loop through the Giant Forest. Named by John Muir, this 2312-acre grove protects more than 2000 giant sequoias, including the park's most gargantuan tree specimens.

04 Walk south 0.9-miles from the start of the Congress Trail to the **Chief Sequoyah Tree** and the giant **President Tree** (pictured), the third-largest tree in the world. The Chief Sequoyah Tree is named for a Cherokee tribe member who lived from the 1770s until 1843. Although Sequoyah was never a chief, he created an 85-letter alphabet, or syllabary, for the Cherokee people, which led to mass literacy for the tribe.

05 Next up is the trail junction for the unpaved **Trail of the Sequoias**. To escape the crowds and extend your time in the Giant Forest, turn left on this trail for an at-your-leisure out-and-back or complete a 5.1-mile loop back to the Congress Trail (connecting with the Log Meadow and Crescent Meadow Trails).

06 Continuing on the Congress Trail, you'll pass the imposing **Senate Group**, the equally impressive **House Group** and the **General Lee Tree**, which is just off the Alta Trail, which cuts across the Congress Trail Loop.

07 Turn north at the **McKinley Tree** and continue 0.7 miles to the parking lot.

TAKE A BREAK

Your best bet for picnic sandwiches or a post-hike meal is the town of **Three Rivers**, which is about 25 miles south of the General Sherman Tree via Hwy 198. Several good deli-style options and the town's best markets are congregated near one another on Sierra Dr. Otherwise, there are a few restaurants offering burgers and sandwiches.

41

MORO ROCK

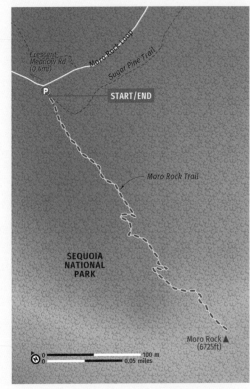

DURATION	DIFFICULTY	DISTANCE	START/END
40min return	Easy	0.5 miles	Moro Rock parking lot

TERRAIN	Concrete & stone stairway

After a quick ascent to the tippy-top of this granite dome, panoramic views are worth every ounce of effort. On clear days, enjoy views up to 150 miles to the Coast Range, plus other skyscraping peaks and the foothills ever-so-far below.

Built by the Civilian Conservation Corps (CCC) in the 1930s, this trail features more than 350 steps, which shoot up over a quarter mile to a railed-in **viewpoint corridor** atop Sequoia's iconic granite dome. Warning – you do not want to be anywhere on this trail during a lightning storm.

From the summit, you can stare down at the Kaweah River's Middle Fork, across to Sawtooth Peak south in the Mineral King region and toward the peaks of the Great Western Divide to the east, including the spike of Black Kaweah, Lawson Peak, Kaweah Queen and Mt Stewart. It's sometimes possible to spot Sugarbowl Dome and Little Blue Dome, near Bearpaw Meadow in the distance. Near dusk, the monolith-like crags of Castle Rocks cast dramatic shadows over the dizzyingly deep river canyon. Beware that on hazy days (most common in summer), air pollution obscures the views.

The road to Moro Rock (Crescent Meadow Rd) is closed from late October until late May, but the hike is still accessible on foot. Walk the 1.7 miles from Giant Forest Museum along Crescent Meadow Rd (conditions may be snowy).

42

TOKOPAH FALLS

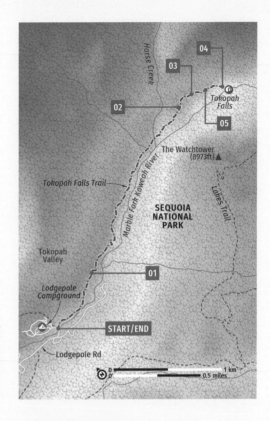

DURATION	DIFFICULTY	DISTANCE	START/END
2hr return	Easy	3.6 miles	Lodgepole Campground

TERRAIN	Dirt trail & forest

Gradually rising over 500ft in elevation, this riverside stroll in Sequoia National Park reaches one of the parks' most scenic waterfalls, tumbling down a boulder-lined canyon.

GETTING HERE

Hwy 198 runs north from Visalia through Three Rivers past Mineral King Rd to the Ash Mountain Entrance. Beyond here, the road continues as the narrow and winding Generals Hwy. From the Foothills Visitor Center just north of the Ash Entrance Station, it's a 21-mile drive to Lodgepole Campground. Sequoia National Park's green shuttle route runs between the General Sherman Tree parking areas and Lodgepole Village every 15 minutes. The purple route links Lodgepole, Wuksachi Lodge and Dorst Creek Campground every 20 minutes. All routes are free and operate 9am to about 6pm from late May to early September.

STARTING POINT

From the trailhead parking area next to the shuttle-bus stop inside Lodgepole Campground (open late May to late September), walk east along the access road. Cross the bridge to the north side of the Marble Fork of the Kaweah River, where you'll spot a trailhead sign.

01 A long stretch of this trail runs through a **sun-dappled forest** beside the river, with **exceptional views** of the glacier-carved canyon and opportunities to watch mule deer, black bears and tiny pika. This hike starts from the campground, making it a popular hike for families with children who are camped nearby. Lots of fun boulders for scrambling.

02 As you walk through the forest and approach the falls, the severe 1800ft granite face of the **Watchtower** looms to the south.

👓 Pikas & Marmots

That odd 'bleating' coming from jumbles of rocks and boulders is likely a pika. A careful search will reveal the hamster-like vocalist peering from under a rock with small beady eyes. Pikas typically live on talus slopes above 8000ft, especially in the alpine realm of mountain hemlock, white-bark pine and heather plants. Yellow-bellied marmots inhabit rocky outcrops and boulder fields at or above 7500ft. Sprawled lazily on sun-warmed rocks, marmots will jolt upright and shriek a warning to their marmot neighborhood when closely approached. Ravenous creatures, marmots spend four to five months putting on weight before a long, deep winter hibernation.

03 The trail becomes fully exposed to the sun, with the rocky path ascending through granite boulders and slabs before arriving at a viewing area. Don't be surprised to see **yellow-bellied marmots** sunning and scampering on the rocks.

04 At 1200ft high, **Tokopah Falls** (pictured) doesn't free fall but rather bounces off the granite canyon cliffs with all the noise it can muster, especially when snowmelt gushes in late spring and possibly early summer. **Wildflowers** are also abloom at this time. The waterfall itself can be a bit disappointing in late summer and fall.

05 Return along the same route. With the gob-smacking views of the Watch-tower behind you, it's time to scan for **ferns** and **wildflowers**! Be careful if you're thinking about swimming. Drownings in the Kings and Kaweah Rivers are the leading cause of death in the parks. Swift currents can be deadly, especially when rivers are swollen with snowmelt runoff in late spring and early summer. Never go in if you see any white water. Always get advice about current swimming conditions at park visitor centers and ranger stations.

☕ **TAKE A BREAK**

The dining room at the **Peaks Restaurant** (📞559-565-4070; www.visitsequoia.com; Wuksachi Lodge, 64740 Wuksachi Way; breakfast buffet $8-13, mains $11-35; ⏰breakfast 7-10am, lunch 11:30am-3pm, dinner 5-10pm, lounge 3-10pm, shorter hours low season; 📶👫) at Wuksachi Lodge has an excellent breakfast buffet and soup-and-salad lunch fare. Dinner is more gourmet. In the lounge, nosh on appetizers and swill cocktails, beer and wine. Non-hotel-guests are welcome.

43

MIST FALLS

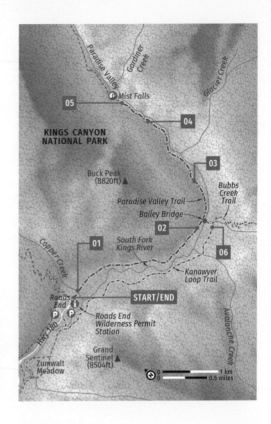

DURATION	DIFFICULTY	DISTANCE	START/END
4-5hr return	Moderate	9.2 miles	Roads End

TERRAIN	Level sandy path, dirt trail

Named for the remarkable plume of mist that rises like a spectre from its base, Mist Falls in Kings Canyon National Park is one of the canyon's largest and most impressive cascades.

GETTING HERE

Take Hwy 180/Kings Canyon Hwy east 34.5 miles from the Kings Canyon Visitor Center in Grant Grove. The parking area is at the end of the road.

STARTING POINT

The trail begins beside the permit station at Roads End, which is the head of Kings Canyon. It's also a staging point for outdoor adventure and a wilderness permit center. You can fill water bottles at the pump here. Bring more water than you'd usually need for a half-day hike. Walking the final mile through the canyon under a hot sun is akin to slow-

ly roasting in a giant Easy-Bake Oven, and dehydration is a concern.

01 From Roads End the trail rolls east, crossing a **footbridge over Copper Creek** and continuing on level, sandy ground through stands of open pine and cedar forest. The **South Fork Kings River** runs parallel to the trail.

02 A **shaded fern-filled area** is a pleasant respite from the sun. Up next is the junction of the Paradise Valley and Bubbs Creek Trails 1.9 miles from the trailhead. Veer left onto the **Paradise Valley Trail** to ascend to Mist Falls along the South Fork Kings River.

03 Climbing through the forest, the trail passes a talus pile then meets the river's edge in 20 minutes. Keep an eye out for **bears**. We saw a mama bear and cub relaxing on the trail in early Septem-

- Although administered as a single unit by the National Park Service (NPS; www.nps. gov/seki), Sequoia and Kings Canyon are actually two national parks.

- The two parks together are commonly referred to as 'SEKI.'

- The seven-day entrance fee ($30 per vehicle) covers both national parks and the Hume Lake District of the Sequoia National Forest.

- The national parks' free seasonal newspaper, the *Visitor Guide*, is offered at either entrance station (Big Stump or Ash Mountain).

- For 24-hour recorded info, including road conditions, call 📞559-565-3341.

AMY BALFOUR/LONELY PLANET ©

ber. The trek up-valley continues. In another 20 minutes, you'll see the river surging down a series of **dramatic cataracts**. This lower series of cataracts, though formidable, should not be mistaken for Mist Falls.

04 As you huff and puff around a narrow switchback on a granite hillside, an **epic view of Avalanche Peak and the Sphinx** smashes into your sightline. You'll want to take photos here.

05 The trail continues through the forest to a grand view of **Mist Falls** (5663ft; pictured) at 2.7 miles.

06 On your return, turn left at the **Bubbs Creek Trail** junction and walk a few steps to the steel **Bailey Bridge**. Pause for a pretty view of the river. Return to the junction and retrace your steps 1.9 miles to the trailhead. For an alternate but longer route to the trailhead, continue beyond Bailey Bridge and turn right onto the trail heading west. Part of the **Kanawyer Loop Trail**, it unfurls along the south bank of the river toward Zumwalt Meadow. The trail eventually crosses the river then leads to the day-use parking lot at Roads End, reaching the trailhead after 2.6 miles.

 TAKE A BREAK

Enjoy lunch on the riverside deck at **Cedar Grove Grill** (Hwy 180, Cedar Grove Village; breakfast $6-11, lunch & dinner mains $7-19; ⏰7am-9pm mid-May–mid-Oct; 📶🚻), where options include grass-fed burger, a mountain trout sandwich and a tofu rice bowl.

44

GEM LAKES

DURATION	DIFFICULTY	DISTANCE	START/END
5hr return	Moderate	7.8 miles	Little Lakes Valley Trailhead

TERRAIN	Dirt trail

A series of blue lakes sparkle in pine-dotted granite bowls in the Little Lakes Valley, with lush meadows, blooming wildflowers, soaring lodgepole pines and snow-capped peaks adding a near-overkill of beauty to the absolutely enthralling high-alpine scene.

GETTING HERE

From US 395, 41 miles southeast of Lee Vining and 14.6 miles southeast of Mammoth Lakes, turn right (south) onto Rock Creek Rd at Tom's Place. Hikes start from the Little Lakes Valley Trailhead (10,230ft) at Mosquito Flat Campground, which is at the end of Rock Creek Rd, 10.2 miles from US 395.

STARTING POINT

Rock Creek and the walk-in Mosquito Flat Campground border the trailhead, which is located at the southern end of the parking lot. As the highest elevation trailhead in the Sierra Nevada easily accessed by a paved road, it shoots you into alpine splendor almost from the get-go – which makes it a very popular trail. The hiking season is from July through September.

Rock Creek Rd is a two-lane, paved road for 9 miles to Rock Creek Pack Station then it becomes one-lane with turnouts. The trailhead fills early and fast. If you arrive after 10am, you'll most likely need to park in one of the overflow lots at the picnic areas dotting the road between the stables and the main parking area, which could add a mile or so to your overall hiking mileage.

01 If you get an early start, and you should, you'll see backpackers waking up and getting ready for the day beside the creek. Permits are not required for day use on the Little Lakes Valley Trail, but if you plan to camp in the John Muir Wilderness, you'll need a wilderness permit. Visit www.fs.usda.gov or www.recreation.gov for more information about obtaining a permit.

02 The broad trail parallels the west bank of Rock Creek, whose cool waters are favored by anglers in pursuit of trout. Ahead, **Bear Creek Spire**

(13,720ft) and **Mt Abbot** (13,704ft) dominate the horizon. These two peaks, along with Mt Dade (13,600ft), Mt Mills (13451ft) and other peaks, passes and ridges, ring the valley in alpine splendor.

03 Passing the **John Muir Wilderness Boundary** sign a scant five minutes from the trailhead, walk up a series of gradual widely spaced **steps** to reach the signed junction with Mono Pass.

04 Continue straight on the trail through the glacier-carved **Little Lakes Valley**,

which heads south to Gem Lakes and Morgan Pass. Near the end of the incline you can swing slightly off the trail to peer down into the ravine holding **Mack Lake** to the east.

05 Descend slightly into the green and well-watered valley passing close to the meadow-fringed southern end of Mack Lake and then grass-filled **Marsh Lake**.

06 Stepping across an inlet to **Heart Lake**, 20 minutes from the Mono Pass junction, the trail crosses a small wooden footbridge over a second inlet

Bighorn Sheep

A high-elevation dweller, although rarely seen, is the endangered Sierra Nevada bighorn sheep. Although they once numbered in the thousands, their wild population declined to around 100 by the year 2000 due to hunting and exposure to diseases from domesticated livestock. Interagency conservation efforts, especially from the Sierra Nevada Bighorn Sheep Foundation (www.sierrabighorn.org), have boosted that number to about 400 – gains, however, have slowed for several years. Your best chance of spotting bighorns is during summer as they scale granite slopes and peaks above 10,000ft in the Eastern Sierra to graze on alpine plants and escape predators.

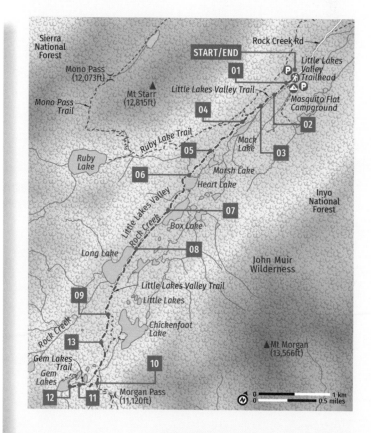

two minutes later and passes along the open western lakeshore.

07 Heading into stands of mixed lodgepole and whitebark pines, ascend easily out of the bowl to emerge well above the west shore of beautiful **Box Lake**. Most of the trees here are whitebark pines, whose red pollen-bearing clusters decorate its branch tips in the summer.

08 The trail crosses an almost imperceptible rise and continues to the northern edge of **Long Lake** (pictured), the largest of the little lakes along the trail. This is a nice spot to catch your breath and take a photo of the shoreline peaks reflected perfectly on the water. As you hike 10 minutes along the lake's east shore, with a rocky cliff alongside the trail, Bear Creek Spire and Mt Abbot seem to fill the entire view upvalley.

09 Beyond Long Lake the trail pushes up through whitebark pines, passing a signed spur trail to Chickenfoot Lake 3 miles from the trailhead.

10 In another 15 minutes you'll reach the outlet from Gem Lakes. Hop rocks to the opposite bank and continue upstream. At 3.7 miles look for a Gem Lakes trail sign – which may not always be there – at a junction with a well-defined use trail on your right. Bear right and follow the use trail south-

west. The main trail continues southeast to Morgan Pass and Morgan Lake.

11 The **Gem Lakes Trail** soon turns south and three minutes ahead is the **first of the three Gem Lakes**. Pass through a pretty little **meadow** along the stream and the set-back second lake. In another five minutes you'll reach upper Gem Lake (10,920ft), 0.3 miles from the main trail.

12 The **largest of the Gem Lakes**, it lies beneath the dramatic Bear Creek Spire and has a talus slope on its south end and whitebark pines along its northern edge. The water is fetchingly green, and you might see snow lingering on the steep granite walls that surround the lake well into August. To camp, cross the lake's outlet and find a campsite away from the lake. From Gem Lakes you can explore the upper valley for an afternoon or even a few days, perhaps visiting the even more austere and beautiful alpine **Treasure Lakes** or remote **Dade Lake**, which is further south.

13 Return on the same route to the Little Lakes Valley Trailhead. If you feel like spending a night under the stars, without backpacking, consider one of the dozen **USFS campgrounds** (📞877-444-6777; www.recreation.gov; tent & RV sites from $22; ⏱late May-Sep; 🐾) nearby; most are along Rock Creek and a few are reservable.

Sierra Nevada

Geologists call the Sierra Nevada a tilted fault-block range – and it's a particularly impressive example at that, spreading 40 to 60 miles wide, with hundreds of peaks over 10,000ft. Picture a tilted fault block as an iceberg listing to one side while floating in the earth's crust. In the Sierra Nevada, that imaginary 'iceberg' is actually an immense body of granite known as a batholith that formed deep within the earth's crust, then 'floated' up and became exposed on the surface over millions of years. Today visitors can see the tip of this batholith, though it's obscured in places where older rocks (mostly metamorphic) still cling, like pieces of a torn cloak, or where newer rocks (mostly volcanic) have been added on top, like icing.

 TAKE A BREAK

Over a century old and still going strong, **Tom's Place Resort Cafe** (📞760-935-4239; www.tomsplace resort.com; 8180 Crowley Lake Dr; mains $10-19; ⏱8am-8pm daily mid-Apr–mid-Nov, 8am-8pm Thu-Sun mid-Nov–mid-Apr) off Rock Creek Rd is a classic. The decor is decidedly kitsch and brimming with Americana. Refuel in this friendly locals' joint with a stacked breakfast, or for dinner – country fried steak and burgers. A general store with food and other supplies is attached. Get three tacos for $8.25 on taco Thursdays in summer.

Also Try...

BRM/SHUTTERSTOCK ©

RAE LAKES LOOP

The best backpacking loop in Kings Canyon tours sun-blessed forests and meadows, crosses one mind-bending pass and skirts jewel-like lakes.

This multiday loop is deservedly popular. A clockwise circumambulation of a cluster of high peaks, the trail traverses the Rae Lakes (pictured above) – some of the most beautiful and picturesque lakes in the Sierra Nevada. They are named after Rachel 'Rae' Colby, wife of William E Colby, who joined the Sierra Club in 1889 and, as both its secretary and president, was instrumental in the founding of Kings Canyon National Park. The hiking season is from mid-June to September, although early in the season streams and rivers may be too high to cross. One of the bridges on this trail has washed out, making the loop impossible to complete unless you trek at the height of summer when the South Fork of the Kings River is at its lowest. Bridge construction was scheduled to start in 2021.

DURATION 5 days return
DIFFICULTY Hard
DISTANCE 41.4 miles

MT WHITNEY

This hugely popular trail rises more than 6000ft in 10.7 miles to the summit of Mt Whitney, the highest peak in the contiguous US.

The mystique of Mt Whitney (14,505ft) captures the imagination. It's a super-strenuous, really, really long walk that'll wear out even experienced mountaineers, but it doesn't require technical skills if attempted in summer or early fall. Earlier or later in the season, you'll likely need an ice axe and crampons, and to stay overnight. Many people in good physical condition make it to the top, although only superbly conditioned, previously acclimatized hikers should attempt this as a day hike. Breathing becomes difficult at these elevations, and altitude sickness is a common problem. Rangers recommend camping at the trailhead then at one of the two camps along the route. Get a permit at the Eastern Sierra Interagency Visitor Center in nearby Lone Pine, off US 395, and ask about weather and trail conditions.

DURATION 3 days return
DIFFICULTY Hard
DISTANCE 22 miles

BIG BALDY TRAIL

Rewarding climb to a granite dome with valley views and epic soaring vistas over Redwood Canyon, the Great Western Divide and Kings Canyon.

The trail begins in the forest and continues into the designated wilderness of Kings Canyon National Park. Views appear quickly on the trail, which climbs from 632ft to 8190ft via dirt paths, switchbacks, rocky ridges and granite surface. Take your time and be careful of your footing on the ridge sections, the drop is severe.

DURATION 2-3hr return
DIFFICULTY Moderate
DISTANCE 4.5 miles

CRESCENT MEADOW LOOP

A canopy of firs and sequoias (pictured above) rings this subalpine meadow in Sequoia National Park.

Downed logs make handy steps for peering over the high grass, but don't let your feet compact the fragile meadow itself. You may spy black bears ripping apart logs as they look for insects. Around the meadow's northeast corner, look up the hollow fire-scarred Chimney Tree. It's a 0.3-mile detour east toward Log Meadow to inspect Tharp's Log, a fallen giant sequoia that a 19th-century settler converted into a rustic cabin.

DURATION 1hr one way
DIFFICULTY Easy
DISTANCE 1.6 miles

MONARCH LAKES

This scenic – but steep! – out-and-back high-country route reaches two alpine lakes below jagged Sawtooth Peak.

A steep climb kicks off this higher altitude trek, which begins in Mineral King, a scenic subalpine valley. You'll pass a marmot-filled meadow and burbling creek then tackle a switchbacking ascent with views through red fir and pine forest before rounding a granite basin. Traverse a talus field and streams before reaching Lower Monarch Lake (10,400ft). The maintained trail stops here, but Upper Monarch Lake (10,640ft) can be reached by a steep trail up the hillside.

DURATION 4-6hr return
DIFFICULTY Hard
DISTANCE 8.4 miles

YOSEMITE NATIONAL PARK

Explore
YOSEMITE NATIONAL PARK

There's no better way – and often no other way – to see Yosemite than by hiking into it. Majestic domes. Plunging waterfalls. Soaring trees. It's nature on a grand and mesmerizing scale. And with more than 800 miles of trails, the park caters to hikers of all abilities. Yosemite Valley is accessible all year, while trailheads along Tioga Rd and Glacier Point Rd are open when roads are clear – usually late May through early November.

YOSEMITE VALLEY

The park's crown jewel, spectacular, meadow-carpeted Yosemite Valley stretches 7 miles long, bisected by the rippling Merced River and hemmed in by some of the most majestic chunks of granite anywhere on earth. Ribbons of water, including some of the highest waterfalls in the US, fall dramatically before crashing in thunderous displays. Some of the park's most recognizable natural features such as Half Dome, El Capitan and Yosemite Falls are here, as well as trailheads for popular hikes. Visitor activity for the park is concentrated here, especially in Yosemite Village, which has the main visitor center, a museum, eateries and other services. Curry Village is another hub.

Lodgings and campgrounds are scattered across the valley.

MARIPOSA

About halfway between Merced and Yosemite Valley, Mariposa (Spanish for 'butterfly') is the largest and most interesting town near Yosemite National Park. Established as a mining and railroad town during the gold rush, it has the oldest courthouse in continuous use (since 1854) west of the Mississippi, loads of Old West pioneer character and a couple of good museums dedicated to the area's heritage, plus annual festivals celebrating the history of the place. Sleeping options in town are primarily chains, with the exception of a creaky atmospheric historic hotel.

LEE VINING

Hwy 395 skirts the western bank of Mono Lake, rolling into the gateway town of Lee Vining, where you can eat, sleep, gas up (for a pretty penny) and catch Hwy 120 to Yosemite National Park when the road's open. A superb base for exploring Mono Lake, Lee Vining is only 12 miles (about a 30-minute drive) from Yosemite's Tioga Pass entrance. Most of the lodging options are fairly ordinary, but winter sports fans can find a few bargains in low season.

 ## WHEN TO GO

April, May and early June are great months to visit Yosemite Valley because the valley's

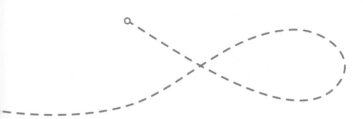

signature falls come fully alive from winter snowmelt. Crowds are brutal in the valley in July and August. Trailheads along Tioga Rd and Glacier Point Rd can be accessed when the roads are clear of snow, typically late May through early November. September and October are the best months to hit Tuolumne Meadows along Tioga Rd, when you'll enjoy fall foliage and pleasant temperatures.

 **WHERE TO STAY**

Camping, even if it's car camping in a campground near busy Yosemite Village, enhances the being-out-in-nature feeling. Backcountry wilderness camping is for the prepared and adventurous. All noncamping reservations within the park are handled by **Aramark/Yosemite Hospitality** (☏888-413-8869; www. travelyosemite.com) and can be made up to 366 days in advance; reservations are critical from May to early September. Rates – and demand – drop from October to April. Other park visitors overnight in nearby gateway towns like Fish Camp, Midpines, El Portal, Mariposa and Groveland; however, commute times into the park can be long.

 **WHAT'S ON**

Cascades These gush powerfully in May.

Tioga Rd Usually plowed and open by late May.

Tuolumne Meadows Poetry Festival (⊙Aug) Sit on the grass and listen to verse.

Bracebridge Dinner at the Ahwahnee (www.bracebridgedinners. com; ⊙Dec) Part feast and part Renaissance Fair.

 **TRANSPORT**

Yosemite is accessible year-round from the west (via Hwys 120 W and 140) and south (Hwy 41), and in summer also from the east (via Hwy 120 E). Roads are plowed in winter, but snow chains may be required at any time.

Yosemite is one of the few national parks that can easily be reached by public transportation. Greyhound buses and Amtrak trains serve Merced, west of the park, where they are met by buses operated by the Yosemite Area Regional Transportation System.

The free, air-conditioned Yosemite Valley Shuttle Bus is a comfortable and efficient way of traveling around the park. Cycling is an ideal way to explore Yosemite Valley. The entrance fee is $35 per vehicle.

45

MIRROR LAKE

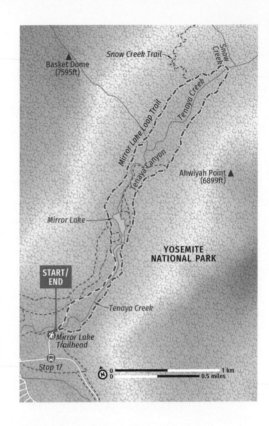

DURATION	DIFFICULTY	DISTANCE	START/END
1-2hr return	Easy	2-5 miles	Mirror Lake Trailhead

TERRAIN	Dirt lakeside path through the forest

Shallow Mirror Lake, reflecting Mt Watkins and Half Dome on its tranquil surface, is one of the Yosemite Valley's most photographed sights. Further northeast, Tenaya Canyon offers one of the quietest corners of the valley.

Formed when a rockfall dammed a section of Tenaya Creek, Mirror Lake has been slowly reverting to 'Mirror Meadow' ever since the park service stopped dredging it in 1971. Only folks who visit in spring and early summer see the splendid sight for which **Mirror Lake** is named. By midsummer it's just Tenaya Creek, and by fall the creek has sometimes dried up altogether. Spring is also marvelous because the dogwoods are in full bloom and Tenaya Creek becomes a lively torrent as you venture further up the canyon. The Ahwahneechee called Mirror Lake Ahwiyah, meaning 'quiet water.'

From the **Mirror Lake Trailhead**, near shuttle stop 17, follow the Mirror Lake road over Tenaya Creek. Take the old paved service road 1 mile to Mirror Lake (a parallel trail through the woods is also an option), where interpretive signs explain the area's natural history. From here you can return back to the shuttle stop, or journey up Tenaya Canyon for a little solitude.

The trail continues along Tenaya Creek into **Tenaya Canyon**, in 1 mile passing the Snow Creek Trail junction then crossing two footbridges. In 2009, a 115,000-ton rockfall cascaded almost 2000ft from Ahwiyah Point near Half Dome, burying a large section of the trail beyond here. A path now traverses the rockfall, and your heart may skip when you hear the pinging sound of loose rocks. From this opposite side of Tenaya Creek, the trail loops back through the canyon, passing Mirror Lake again. The trail can get buggy, so apply bug spray before starting.

46

LEMBERT DOME & DOG LAKE

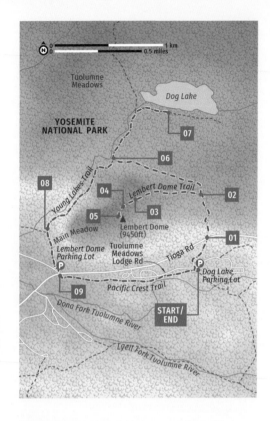

DURATION	DIFFICULTY	DISTANCE	START/END
2½-3hr return	Moderate	5 miles	Dog Lake parking lot

TERRAIN	Forest path & granite dome

Bang-for-your-buck is high on this moderate loop, which includes a thrilling scramble up a granite dome, lofty views of alpine meadows, and a tranquil pause by a scenic mountain lake. Wear your grippiest hiking shoes and bring your bathing suit.

GETTING HERE

Park in the Dog Lake parking lot, on the way to Tuolumne Meadows Lodge off Tioga Rd. The Tuolumne Meadows shuttle also stops here. The Dog Lake parking lot is a much better starting point for this loop than the Lembert Dome parking lot, where the trail is very steep and borderline unpleasant for an ascent.

STARTING POINT

The trailhead sits at the base of a wooded hill on the south side of Tioga Rd about 2 miles east of the Tuolumne Meadows Visitor Center.

01 This hike kicks off with a climb through lodgepole pines, crossing Tioga Rd, then switchbacking up a forested slope.

02 The trail levels off at 0.3 miles or so and continues through the pines. At a signed junction a half mile from the trailhead, turn left.

03 This easy westward path ends at the base of the granite **Lembert Dome** just under a mile from the trailhead. Hike west across the gently sloping granite until you see the small summit knob just ahead.

04 Those with a fear of heights can enjoy the **big views of the meadows** and surrounding mountain ranges at the top of a rise before the summit. Otherwise, onward. Note that tackling the summit dead-on from the top of the rise will require a skilled scramble beyond the abilities of most day

High Sierra Camps

The High Sierra camps are a more relaxing way to experience the backcountry, as you don't have to carry a tent or cooking gear – hearty meals and accommodations are provided.

There are five camps in the high country surrounding Tuolumne Meadows. Accommodations are canvas tent cabins. The seasons are short (roughly June through September) and the camps are very popular, so reservations are by lottery. For reservations visit www.travelyosemite.com/lodging/high-sierra-camps.

GUOQIANG XUE/SHUTTERSTOCK ©

hikers. Instead, walk southwest and approach the summit from the south, where the granite rises more gently.

05 The **360-degree views from the summit** (9450ft; pictured) are gobsmacking. The Sierra Crest stretches to the east. Look south to find the Cathedral Range. To the west lies the broad expanse of Tuolumne Meadows, the former homestead for the dome's namesake, 19th-century shepherd Jean-Baptiste Lembert.

06 Return to the trail junction and turn left. A half mile or so up the fairly flat trail is another junction. Turn

right toward **Dog Lake** (9170ft) and continue another half mile, following signage to the lake.

07 Be prepared to share this subalpine lake with fellow hikers, especially on weekends. A path meanders around the lake itself.

08 Return to the junction and head toward the Lembert Dome parking area. The trail is very steep and eroded, so watch your footing. A vast granite slab awaits at the bottom of the trail. Bear left across the slab to reach the parking lot.

09 From the parking lot, cross Tioga Rd at 4 miles and turn left to walk east on the **Pacific Cast Trail** to the **John Muir Trail** to complete the loop at about 5 miles. Do not walk east on Tioga Rd.

TAKE A BREAK

Refuel on juicy burgers, fries and thick shakes at **Mono Cone** (760-647-6606; 51508 Hwy 395; burgers $5-8; 11am-6pm mid-Apr–Oct;), a classic roadside joint in Lee Vining, about 20 miles east of Lembert Dome. Order at the window, wait to be called then chow down at a picnic table.

47

SENTINEL DOME & TAFT POINT

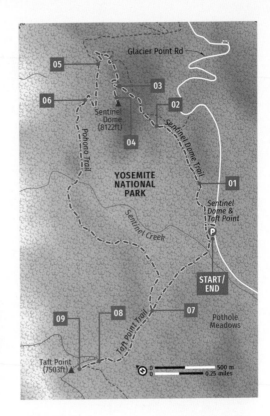

DURATION	DIFFICULTY	DISTANCE	START/END
3hr return	Moderate	5.1 miles	Glacier Point Rd

TERRAIN	Forest path & granite dome

For those who can't get to the top of Half Dome, Sentinel Dome offers an equally outstanding perspective on Yosemite's wonders, while Taft Point serves up a fantastic, hair-raising viewpoint at the edge of a sheer 4000ft vertical cliff.

GETTING HERE

From Hwy 41 (Wawona Rd), turn east onto Glacier Point Rd and drive 13 miles to the signed Sentinel Dome & Taft Point parking lot on the north (left) side of the road.

STARTING POINT

Just beyond the roadside parking lot, the trail divides. Take the right fork, heading north toward Sentinel Dome. The left fork leads to Taft Point. You'll be looping back here from Taft Point at the end of the hike.

01 The trail rises gently, contouring through an open area and then through a **mixed forest.**

02 Leave the forest for a short jaunt across **granite slabs** dotted with manzanita pines. Re-enter the forest, bending northwest before reaching the shoulder of **Sentinel Dome.**

03 Ascend the gentle granite slopes of the dome from the Glacier Point and Taft Point trail marker, reaching the top at 1.1 miles. The gnarled bleached bones of a Jeffrey pine crown the summit.

04 Soak up the **360-degree views**. To the west Cathedral Rock and El Capitan frame the Merced River and Yosemite Valley. Clouds Rest and Half Dome rise dramatically above Tenaya Canyon. Return to the trail sign for Glacier Point and Taft Point and bear left. Walk north, descending 300ft toward a small radio facility building.

 **Glacier Point**

Glacier Point is the final stop on the 16-mile Glacier Point Rd. From here the entire eastern Yosemite Valley spreads out before you, from Yosemite Falls to Half Dome, as well as the distant peaks that ring Tuolumne Meadows. From the railing, peer 3200ft straight down at Half Dome Village. Glacier Point has long been a popular destination. It used to be that getting up here was a major undertaking. That changed once the Four Mile Trail opened in 1872. A wagon road to the point was completed in 1882, and the current Glacier Point Rd was built in 1936. Another major reconstruction project is expected to begin in 2022. Glacier Point Rd is generally open from early May through mid-December.

Best for

BIG VIEWS

UNAI HUIZI PHOTOGRAPHY/SHUTTERSTOCK ©

05 At the trail junction at 1.8 miles, just beyond the radio facility, turn left onto the **Pohono Trail**. A right turn leads to Glacier Point. The near-level traverse ahead unfurls through a white-fir forest. Savor **breathtaking views** of the Merced River, lush meadows and **Yosemite Falls**.

06 Two switchbacks descend the soft, conifer-needle-covered trail. El Capitan and distant Mt Hoffmann are visible.

07 The trail climbs through a mixed forest dotted with boulders to a signed junction with the **Taft Point Trail** at about 3.7 miles.

08 Turn right and continue through the forest, eventually emerging to an open rocky slope. Descend and continue past the **fissures**. These narrow chimney-like slots drop hundreds of feet to Yosemite Valley.

09 Ahead, the sheer drop at **Taft Point** (7503ft) is guarded – in only one small area – by a dinky metal railing. Unless you have a profound fear of heights, approach and peer over the edge – the **sheer drop is mind-boggling**. Looking west through binoculars, you can spot climbers on El Capitan. Be careful near the open ledge. People have fallen to their

deaths. Return 1.1 miles on the forested Taft Point Trail to the parking lot.

 **TAKE A BREAK**

With a killer view of Yosemite Falls, the window tables at the casual yet elegantly contemporary **Mountain Room Restaurant** (☎209-372-1281; www.travelyosemite.com; Yosemite Valley Lodge, 9006 Yosemite Lodge Dr, Yosemite Valley; mains $22-50; ⏱5-9pm; 🖋 🚻) are a hot commodity. Plates of NY strip steak, roasted acorn squash and locally caught mountain trout woo diners, who are seated beside gallery-quality nature photographs.

48

CATHEDRAL LAKES

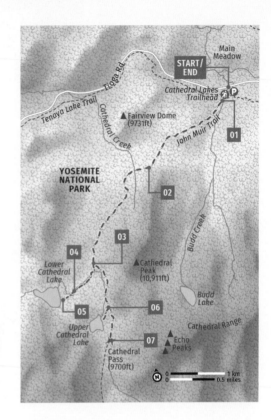

DURATION	DIFFICULTY	DISTANCE	START/END
4-6hr return	Moderate	7.6 miles	Tioga Rd

TERRAIN	Dirt path through forested slopes

Shimmering beneath the white granite flanks of the Cathedral Range, these sister pools are among the prettiest in the region. In addition to near-perfect scenery, the lakes promise fine – if chilly – swimming. There is some uphill climbing to get here, but views of the north mountains and double-pronged spire of Cathedral Peak should keep you going.

GETTING HERE

The hike starts from a parking area on the south side of Hwy 120 (Tioga Rd), 1.7 miles west of Tuolumne Meadows Visitor Center. Since this is a popular hike, and the parking lot and pullouts are often full, consider parking at the visitor center and taking the Tuolumne Meadows Shuttle Bus (7am to 7pm June to mid-September, $2 round trip), which stops at the trailhead.

STARTING POINT

From the Cathedral Lakes Trailhead on Tioga Rd, the hike heads southwest, mostly along John Muir Trail.

01 The trail joins the **John Muir Trail** and rises steadily through lodgepole pine, mountain hemlock and the occasional whitebark pine for the first half mile, then levels as a massive slab of granite – the northern flank of Cathedral Peak – slopes up from the left side of the trail. Soon you'll see **Fairview Dome** (9731ft) through the trees to your right.

02 Another ascent begins, with another long, steep and steady climb for nearly 600ft before leveling off and affording **outstanding views of Cathedral Peak** (pictured).

03 The trail flattens again, becoming a pleasant forest stroll as traffic noise disappears and quiet descends. Turn right at the trail junction at 2.8

Peaks & Domes

During the Tioga glacial period just 20,000 years ago, the massive Tuolumne Glacier, a 20,000ft-thick river of ice, coursed from the Sierra Crest through Tuolumne Meadows and completely filled Hetch Hetchy Valley. The contrasting shapes of peaks around Tuolumne are a record of this period – the smooth, domelike peaks were worn down beneath the glacier, while the sharp, jagged summits of the Cathedral Range and Sierra Crest remained above the ice that quarried their slopes.

AMY BALFOUR/LONELY PLANET ©

miles and walk for a half mile to Lower Cathedral Lake (9288ft), your best choice if you only have time for one lake.

04 After you leave the forest, follow the narrow trail as it bends right and cuts through a **stunning meadow**.

05 You'll emerge to a gorgeous granite bowl, or cirque, with the pointed spire of Cathedral Peak at your back and the **lake** spread out before you. Find a spot on the rocks and soak up this classic Sierra subalpine scene. Bring a jacket, too, as the winds keep temperatures a bit cool. Walk along the lake's edge

to get just the right shot of Cathedral Peak. Return to the junction and turn right to continue south on the John Muir Trail.

06 After about a half mile follow an unmarked side trail to your right to **Upper Cathedral Lake** (9585ft), the smaller of the two lakes. It's quieter here too. The view east toward craggy Echo Peaks is quite impressive.

07 Cap off the day by hiking another half mile on the John Muir Trail to **Cathedral Pass** (9700ft), which offers stunning views of the Cathedral Range. Retrace your steps to the trailhead. Note that mileage can

easily bump up a mile or two for this hike if you explore the shores of the lakes and include the hike to the pass.

TAKE A BREAK

A Mobil-gas-station restaurant off Hwy 120 in Lee Vining, the **Whoa Nellie Deli** (📞760-647-1088; www.whoanelliedeli.com; Tioga Gas Mart, 22 Vista Point Rd; mains $7.50-19; 🕐6:30am-9pm late Apr-Oct; 🍴) is a surprisingly darn good place to eat. Stop in for delicious burgers, fish tacos, wild-buffalo meatloaf and other tasty morsels, and Mono Lake views from outdoor picnic tables. The restaurant is 20 miles east of the Tuolumne Meadows Visitor Center.

49

VERNAL & NEVADA FALLS

DURATION	DIFFICULTY	DISTANCE	START/END
5-6hr return	Hard	6.7 miles	Happy Isles Trailhead

TERRAIN	Paved & dirt sections, steep steps

If you've only got time for one day hike in Yosemite Valley – and it's springtime – this splashy romp is the one. With challenges and rewards straight from an epic fantasy novel – a trailhead in Happy Isles, a sun-dappled footbridge, drenching mists, the Giant Staircase, the treacherous Emerald Pool and the majestic Liberty Cap dome – this thrilling loop will have you reminiscing for days. Or at least your calves will remember.

GETTING HERE

From Happy Isles (shuttle stop 16) in Yosemite Valley, cross the bridge over the Merced River and join the trail on the east side of the river.

STARTING POINT

At the start of the hike you will be on the Mist Trail, which overlaps with the John Muir Trail. Follow the riverbank upstream, passing the Happy Isles on your right.

01 Turn left at the informational bulletin board. The paved footpath ahead funnels hikers to several popular trails and various destinations, both inside and outside Yosemite Valley. Destinations include Vernal and Nevada Falls, Glacier Point, Half Dome and even Tuolumne Meadows, which borders Tioga Rd a mere 27.3 miles away.

02 A gentle-but-steep pathway ascends 400ft over 0.8-miles to the **Vernal Fall Bridge**. As the trail steepens, watch over your right shoulder for **Ililouette Fall** (often dry in summer), which peels over a 370ft cliff in the distance. From a lookout, you can gaze west and see Yosemite Falls. The trail is paved for about 1 mile and the stretch to the bridge is probably the most crowded part of this hugely popular trail.

03 Shortly beyond the Vernal Fall footbridge (just past the water fountain and restrooms), you'll reach the junction of the John Muir and Mist Trails. To do the trail clockwise, turn left and shortly begin the steep 0.3-mile ascent to the top of Vernal Fall by way of the **Mist Trail's granite steps**. You'll be looping back to this junction on the John Muir Trail later in the day.

04 In about 10 minutes Vernal Fall comes into view. But don't rest easy – you'll also be starting your climb up a very steep and narrow staircase of granite steps, the beginning of the **Giant Staircase**. Expect to get wet on the aptly named Mist Trail, as sheets of water from the falls spray your path. On sunny days the spray dances with rainbows. Vernal Fall, which the Miwok people called Pai-wai'-ak, tumbles 317ft over a vertical cliff.

05 A final short-but-steep rock staircase, protected by a railing, brings you to the **top of the falls**, where you can dry off and enjoy the views and a picnic. Pat yourself on the back – you climbed 1000ft. The top of the falls is about 1.3 miles from the trailhead.

06 Follow the river upstream, where the Merced whizzes down a long ramp of granite known as the **Silver Apron** and into the deceptively serene **Emerald Pool** before plunging over the cliff. No matter how fun the apron and pool look on a hot day, don't enter the water: underwater currents in Emerald Pool have whipped many swimmers over the falls.

⚠ Cliffs & Waterfalls

Smooth granite beside Yosemite's many rivers, streams and waterfalls is often slippery, even when dry. Tumbling over a fall is almost certain to be fatal. Despite warning signs in several languages and protective railings, people have died. Approach any waterfall with caution and, above all, don't get into the water. The current above Vernal Fall is stronger than it appears and hikers have been swept to their deaths over its precipice.

Use caution too when hiking to and around Glacier Point, Taft Point, and other precarious viewpoints. Some overlooks have railings but plenty of others don't. Also think carefully before taking an adventure selfie and assess the hazards.

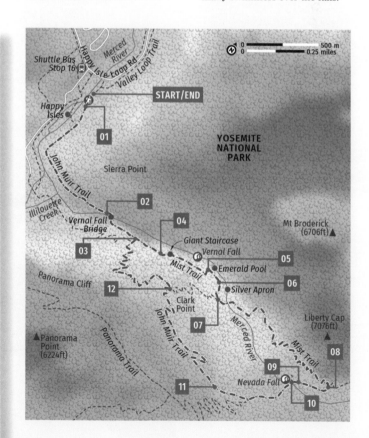

07 At the junction with the Clark Point cut-off, which connects with the John Muir Trail, continue straight. Nevada Fall tumbles into view just before another set of stone steps and their tight and twisting climb. You're going to have to muscle your way up this strenuous stretch, but the **plunging waterfall** is a breathtaking distraction as you climb.

08 The ascent ends at a signed junction with the John Muir Trail, about 0.2 miles northeast of the falls. A left turn on the famed path leads to Half Dome and Little Yosemite. Turn right to continue to the top of **Nevada Fall** (pictured), reaching it 2.7 miles from the trailhead.

09 Picnic or relax on a slab of granite bordering the river just ahead. Be prepared to fend off Steller's jays and squirrels that will have your jerky in their jaws in no time, should you let down your guard. An oft-overlooked **viewpoint** lies on a terrace that sits at the base of a short spur trail on the river's north side. Protected by an iron railing, it borders the very edge of the waterfall.

10 Follow the **footbridge** (elevation 5907ft) over the Merced River. Beneath it, the river whizzes through a chute before plunging 594ft over a polished cliff. Originally called Yo-wai'-yik by the Miwok people, Nevada Fall is the tallest fall on the Merced River.

John Muir Trail

The 211-mile John Muir Trail links Yosemite Valley and Mt Whitney, traveling through three national parks and two wilderness areas and offering what many consider to be the the very best mountain hiking in the US.

Uncrossed by any roads, the trail is a spectacular and pristine route through continental wilderness. It crosses 11 mountain passes, half of which are higher than 12,000ft and all but one of which are over 10,000ft. As it traverses the timberline country of the High Sierra, the trail passes thousands of lakes and numerous granite peaks between 13,000 and 14,000ft and takes in the Sierra's highest peak. The trail frequently descends from the Sierra Crest into forested areas of the western Sierra, with 5000ft deep canyons. Visit the Pacific Crest Trail Association website (www.pcta.org) for more information.

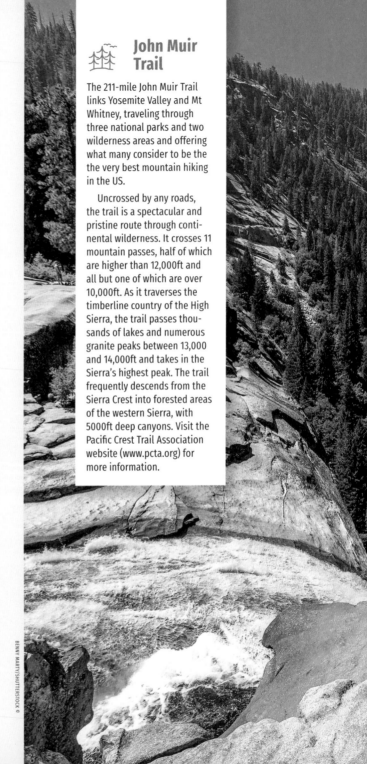

BENNY MARTY/SHUTTERSTOCK ©

11 Walk southwest on the **John Muir Trail**, passing the Panorama Trail junction. The trail then traverses a cliff with a stone wall. Stop here to look back at the **expansive view of Nevada Fall** and its neighbor, the **soaring Liberty Cap dome** (7076ft). Breathtaking.

12 From here, the trail switchbacks down the side of the gorge, passing Clark Point and the junction with the cut-off trail. Continue on the John Muir Trail to its junction with the Mist Trail. From the junction it's 1.1 miles down through Douglas firs and canyon live oaks to Yosemite Valley.

 **TAKE A BREAK**

Cap off your adventurous day with a celebratory dinner in the **Ahwahnee Dining Room** (📞209-372-1489; www.travelyosemite.com; Ahwahnee, 1 Ahwahnee Dr, Yosemite Valley; mains breakfast $14-18, lunch $16-19, dinner $31-49; ⏱7-10am, 11:30am-2pm & 5:30-8:30pm; 🍴). The formal ambience (mind your manners!) may not be for everybody, but few would not be awed by the sumptuous decor, soaring beamed ceiling and palatial chandeliers here. The menu is constantly in flux, but most dishes have perfect pitch and are beautifully presented.

Also Try...

OWEN REISER/SHUTTERSTOCK ©

HALF DOME

Rising 4800ft above the eastern end of Yosemite Valley is Half Dome, the most glorious granite dome on earth. The hike to its summit – with a 600ft climb up an exposed 45-degree rock face – is grueling, satisfying and potentially fatal.

The stand-alone summit of this glacier-carved chunk of granite offers awesome 360-degree views, and peering down its sheer 2000ft north face offers a once-in-a-lifetime thrill. But, unless you get a crack-of-dawn start, you'll have people aplenty to deal with. Most importantly, advance permits are required, making a Half Dome summit even harder to arrange. This rigorous hike is best done over two days but fit hikers can attempt it as a demanding 10- to 12-hour day hike. Hiking to the summit is only allowed when the protective cable route to the top has been installed on the rock face, typically between late May and mid-December. Begins near Happy Isles.

DURATION 10-12hr return
DIFFICULTY Hard
DISTANCE 14-16 miles

CLOUDS REST

Clouds Rest is Yosemite's largest expanse of granite and is arguably its finest panoramic viewpoint with breathtaking views of Half Dome and the valley.

Yosemite's largest granite peak, Clouds Rest (9926ft; pictured above), rises 4500ft above Tenaya Creek, with spectacular views from the summit and along the trail. The hike involves a strenuous ascent and equally significant descent (have a cold drink waiting for you!), but getting here is definitely worth the effort: more than 1000ft higher than nearby Half Dome, the Clouds Rest viewpoint is spectacular. The exposed summit path is a granite ridge which narrows thrillingly in one place. Never less than 5ft wide, the narrowest section may look intimidating but takes only five to 10 seconds to cross. Start from the Sunrise Lakes Trailhead at the western end of Tenaya Lake. Trailhead parking is limited, and the lot fills early.

DURATION 6-7hr return
DIFFICULTY Hard
DISTANCE 14.4 miles

CHRISTIAN_B/SHUTTERSTOCK ©

YOSEMITE FALLS

A classic hike to the top of Yosemite's most extraordinary waterfalls.

Yosemite Falls plunges 2425ft in three cascades, creating the world's fifth-highest free-leaping waterfall. An excellent trail climbs from the valley to the top of the falls along the valley's north rim. The stiff ascent of 2410ft and equivalent descent makes this a strenuous day hike. The side trip to spectacular Yosemite Point and its views of Half Dome, Clouds Rest and Glacier Point is an even stiffer 3000ft. The falls are often dry by midsummer, so May and June are the best times to visit.

DURATION 6-8hr return
DIFFICULTY Hard
DISTANCE 7.2 miles

PANORAMA TRAIL

This trail comprises several miles of Yosemite's most picture-perfect scenery, including eye-popping sightlines of Half Dome.

Panorama Trail (pictured above) connects Glacier Point and Nevada Fall. Hikers seeking a full loop from the valley must first tackle the steep 3200ft ascent on the Four Mile Trail. Those starting from Glacier Point and heading down to the valley must arrange a car shuttle or reserve a seat on the guided bus tour to Glacier Point. Or you can simply hike to Nevada Fall and return to Glacier Point the way you came.

DURATION 5hr one way
DIFFICULTY Moderate-hard
DISTANCE 8.5 miles

TUEEULALA & WAPAMA FALLS

This hike along the north shore of Hetch Hetchy Reservoir leads to the base of two neighboring falls.

Few trails in Yosemite bring you as close to the shower and roar of a giant waterfall as this one does to Wapama Falls. In springtime, after a good snowmelt, the enormous triple cascades can rage so mightily that the park has to close the trail as water rolls over the bridges. On your way, you'll pass wispy and free-leaping Tueeulala Falls (twee-la-la), which spring from more than 1000ft above the trail.

DURATION 2½-3hr return
DIFFICULTY Easy-moderate
DISTANCE 5.4 miles

LAKE TAHOE & GOLD COUNTRY

Explore
LAKE TAHOE
& GOLD COUNTRY

Soaring Sierra Nevada peaks flank the spectacular scenic drive that loops around clear-blue Lake Tahoe. Trails along the 72-mile loop hug the rugged coast, climb to rocky summits and impress with panoramic lake views. Gold once brought treasure hunters to the nearby foothills of the Gold Country. Today it's mighty sequoias.

TRUCKEE

Cradled by mountains and the Tahoe National Forest, Truckee is a thriving town steeped in Old West history. It was put on the map by the railroad, grew rich on logging and ice harvesting, and even had its brush with Hollywood during the 1924 filming of Charlie Chaplin's *The Gold Rush*. Today tourism fills much of the city's coffers, thanks to a well-preserved historical downtown and its proximity to Lake Tahoe and numerous ski and cross-country ski resorts.

SOUTH LAKE TAHOE

South Lake Tahoe is a chock-ablock commercial strip bordering the lake and framed by picture-perfect alpine mountains. It sits at the foot of the world-class **Heavenly** (☎775-586-7000; www.skiheavenly.com; 3860 Saddle Rd; adult/5-12yr/13-18yr $154/85/126; ☺9am-4pm Mon-Fri, 8:30am-4pm Sat, Sun & holidays; ♿) mountain resort, and buzzes from the gambling tables in the casinos just across the border in Stateline, NV. Lake Tahoe's south shore draws visitors with a cornucopia of activities, lodging and restaurant options, especially for summer beach access and tons of powdery winter snow.

MURPHYS

With its white picket fences, historic downtown and old-world charm, Murphys is one of the more scenic communities along the southern stretch of Gold Country, befitting its nickname as 'Queen of the Sierra.' It lies 8 miles east of Hwy 49 on Murphys Grade Rd, and is named for Daniel and John Murphy, who founded a trading post and mining operation on Murphy Creek in 1848. The town's refined Main St is lined with wine-tasting rooms, boutiques, galleries. There's lots of good strolling. For information and a town overview, look to www.visitmurphys.com.

☀ WHEN TO GO

Hiking trails fully open in July and August and you'll likely see wildflowers blooming. Since this is the summer holiday season and kids are out of school, expect crowded parking lots and trails. Hotels and campgrounds will also be busy and lodging prices at a premium. September and October are a great time to hike, with cooler temperatures and colorful foliage and fewer tourists after Labor Day.

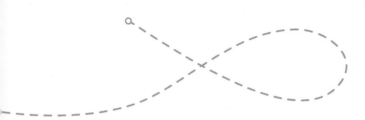

Resources

Explore Tahoe (www.cityofslt.us) Interpretive exhibits and recreational and transportation information at a multipurpose 'urban trailhead' in South Lake Tahoe.

Lake Tahoe Visitors Authority (www.tahoesouth.com) Tourist information, maps, brochures and money-saving coupons in South Lake Tahoe, with a second center in Stateline.

USDA Lake Tahoe Basin Management Unit (www.fs.usda.gov/ltbmu) Wilderness permits and camping and outdoor recreation information.

USFS Truckee District Ranger Station (www.fs.usda.gov/tahoe) Tahoe National Forest information.

Calaveras Big Trees State Park Visitor Center www.bigtrees.org) As well as information on the trees, staff at the visitor center will tell you about the Native American Miwoks, mountain lions and how to cope with bear encounters.

WHERE TO STAY

South Lake Tahoe has lots of choices. Lodging options line Lake Tahoe Blvd (Hwy 50) between Stateline and Ski Run Blvd. Further west, closer to the intersection of Hwys 50 and 89, a string of budget motels ranges from adequate to inexcusable. Inns and cabins border the highway around the lake, and you'll find casino-hotels in Stateline, NV, beside South Lake Tahoe. A few dependable midrange chain motels and hotels are found off I-80 exits near Truckee. There's also a hostel behind the train station and a historic hotel downtown. The Gold Country is loaded with boutique inns and gold-rush-era hotels.

WHAT'S ON

First Fridays Truckee (◷5-8pm 1st Fri monthly) Stroll downtown for complimentary art, food and drinks.

Wildflower season (◷Apr-Aug) Peaks in spring at lower elevations and in late summer in the High Sierra.

Donner Party Hike (www.donnerpartyhike.com; ◷Sep) Retrace the steps of the ill-fated Donner Party on a historian-led hike.

TRANSPORT

From Reno-Tahoe International Airport, South Tahoe Airporter (www.southtahoeairporter.com) operates several daily shuttle buses to Stateline casinos. Amtrak www.amtrak.com) has a daily Thruway bus service between Sacramento and South Lake Tahoe ($34, 2½ hours), stopping at the South Y Transit Center. Tahoe Transportation District (www.tahoetransportation.org/transit) local buses operate year-round. The Route 50/South Shore Daily runs from around 6am to 8pm daily, stopping all along Hwy 50 in South Lake Tahoe between the South Y Transit Center and the Stateline Transit Center.

Truckee straddles I-80 and is connected to the lakeshore via Hwy 89 to Tahoe City or Hwy 267 to Kings Beach. The main drag through downtown Truckee is Donner Pass Rd, where you'll find the Amtrak depot.

For a helpful overview of all transit options year-round around the lake, visit www.linkingtahoe.com.

50

SOUTH GROVE TRAIL

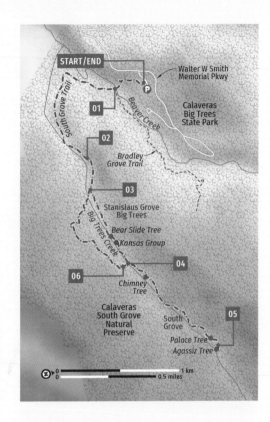

DURATION	DIFFICULTY	DISTANCE	START/END
3hr return	Easy	5.5 miles	South Grove parking lot

TERRAIN	Dirt forest path, can be dusty

The ancient sequoias in Calaveras Big Trees State Park are too big around for tree huggers to do their thing. But go ahead, put your hand against a chunk of cinnamon-brown bark. Leave it there a second. Is it us, or does it feel like that tree is breathing? Getting up close with the big trees in a tranquil setting is a highlight of a hike in the South Grove.

GETTING HERE

From the city of Angels Camp, which straddles Hwy 49, follow Hwy 4 east 22 miles to the state park. Once inside the park, it's 8.5 miles to the South Grove parking lot.

STARTING POINT

Calaveras Big Trees State Park is home to two groves of sequoias, the bustling North Grove and the quiet South Grove. The North Grove borders the entrance station while the latter sits in the southern reaches of the park.

01 The South Grive Trail twists into the trees, soon crossing a bridge over **Beaver Creek**. Just ahead, look for the start of the **Bradley Grove Trail** on your left. The young sequoias on this 2.5-mile loop were planted in the 1950s. The trail climbs for a mile or so through a mixed conifer forest.

02 The trail crosses an old logging road at 1.2 miles, where a sign marks the entrance to the **Calaveras South Grove Natural Preserve**. The grove was owned by a logging company in the early 1900s, and plans were once afoot to log the sugar pines here. Environmentalists saved the day.

03 Enter the preserve and follow the trail, which tracks **Big Trees Creek**. At your first

Spotlight on Sequoias

Sequoias in the South Grove are tucked among other soaring trees in a mixed conifer forest, and it's a bit of a scavenger hunt to pick them out. First check out the bark, which is cinnamon brown or red, and sometimes violet. The bark is also soft to the touch. Older sequoias have rounded tops, large branches and many are charred from past fires. Some reach 300ft. Younger sequoias are v-shaped, like Christmas trees. Sequoia cones are about the same size and shape as chicken eggs. A type of redwood, giant sequoias are also among the world's oldest trees, and can live more than 3000 years. Some in the South Grove may have reached the ripe old age of 2000.

Best for

ESCAPING THE CROWDS

AMY BALFOUR/LONELY PLANET ©

trail junction, stay left. Sequoias appear here and there as you walk. Kids will get a kick out of the **Bear Slide Tree** (pictured). This enormous fallen sequoia is hollow, and its interior 'tunnel' is fun to explore. Ahead on the right is a cluster of giant sequoias known as the **Kansas Group**.

04 Walk straight at the junction. Step inside the **Chimney Tree** and look up. Fire ripped out its core and top, but the tree remains alive because its sapwood still delivers life-preserving nutrients and water. Next up is the **Palace Tree**, named by visitors in the 1870s because the large opening at

its base reminded them of the courtyard carriage entrance at the Palace Hotel in San Francisco.

05 The South Grove's star attraction awaits at the end of the trail: the **Agassiz Tree** (aģ-uh-see), the largest tree in the park. Its estimated dimensions are a diameter of 25ft across at 6ft up, and a height of 250ft. The tree is named for Louis Agassiz, a well-known 18th-century naturalist.

06 Retrace your steps then turn left at the first trail junction, to add a short loop to your return. Just ahead is an

enormous **fallen sequoia**, slowly decaying but providing sunlight and shelter for sequoia seeds. Continue along the loop to the next trail junction. Turn left and return to the parking lot.

 TAKE A BREAK

Stop by a wine-tasting room or two then wander to **Murphys Historic Hotel** (☎ 209-728-3444; www. murphyshotel.com; 457 Main St; historic rooms $139-215, annex rooms $149-255; P) for conviviality in the saloon and fried chicken in the dining room.

51

EAGLE FALLS & EAGLE LAKE

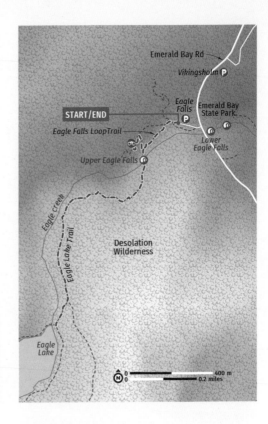

DURATION	DIFFICULTY	DISTANCE	START/END
2hr return	Easy	2 miles	Eagle Falls parking lot

TERRAIN	Dirt with stair sections

Families and photographers, this short-but-sweet Tahoe hike is for you. You'll climb stone steps to big views of Emerald Bay then cross a rocky waterfall. A final huff-and-puff through the evergreens in the Desolation Wilderness drops you beside a secluded alpine lake.

The most challenging part of this day hike is finding a parking spot in the Eagle Falls Trailhead lot ($5 per day) or the nearby Vikingsholm lot ($5 to $10 per day). On the western shore of Lake Tahoe beside Hwy 89, these two lots are popular jumping-off points for hikes in the Desolation Wilderness and Emerald Bay State Park. The wilderness area requires a free day-use permit, available at the wilderness information signboard.

Just beyond the signboard, you'll kick off the Eagle Falls Loop Trail at a set of **rough granite steps**.

Though steep, they do set the stage for adventure, and sheer curiosity should have you up them in no time. At the top, a short spur trail climbs to a **scenic vista** with **fine views of Emerald Bay** and tiny Fannette Island. Return to the base of the spur trail and turn right. You'll be leaving the loop trail (which returns to the parking lot). The bridge just ahead crosses **Upper Eagle Falls**, which tumbles down a rocky gorge through the pine trees.

Another stone staircase awaits just beyond the falls, tunneling into the evergreens and the **Desolation Wilderness**. Listen for the sounds of Eagle Creek as you climb. Cross a flattened boulder patch, where you'll have more **fine views of Lake Tahoe**. To continue on the trail, follow the left side of the boulder patch. At about 1 mile look for a post. Turn right here and walk the final steps to **Eagle Lake**, a serene spot surrounded by granite peaks – reflected in the lake – and whisper-thin beaches.

52

PACIFIC COAST TRAIL & MT JUDAH LOOP

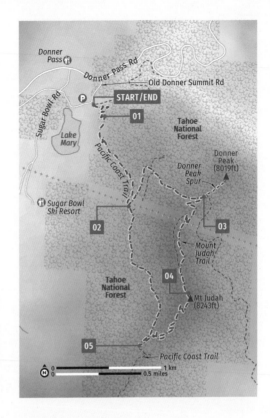

DURATION	DIFFICULTY	DISTANCE	START/END
1½hr return	Moderate	5.5 miles	Off Old Donner Summit Rd

TERRAIN	Rocky switchbacks & dirt path

This lasso loop wins Best in Show for its visual diversity and winning personality – its lake-and-mountain views are nothing short of charming. A rocky climb up the Pacific Coast Trail (PCT) leads to the upper slopes of Sugar Bowl Ski Resort, where a loop trail shoots through a forest, opens up to ridgeline views of Donner Lake then climbs to the windy summit of Mt Judah.

GETTING HERE

From Truckee, follow I-80 west to exit 184 to Donner Pass Rd. Turn left and drive up Donner Pass Rd to Summit Haus – about 6.7 miles – then turn left onto Old Donner Summit Rd. Follow the road as it bends right and look for the parking area, also on your right. To reach the trailhead, walk back toward the bend in the road and turn right on the Pacific Coast Trail.

STARTING POINT

This hike starts beside an information board beside the Pacific Coast Trail (PCT), which crosses Donner Pass on its epic north–south journey across California. A weathered map shows the basic routes of the many trails surrounding the pass. From here you'll follow the PCT south.

01 There's no goofing around at the start of this hike, which starts a switchbacking heavy-breathing ascent just beyond the trailhead. Watch your footing while powering up this section of the trail – it's hard to keep your eyes on the rock-strewn path as **views of Donner Pass and Sugar Bowl Ski Resort** open up below you.

The Doomed Donner Party

At the eastern end of Donner Lake, **Donner Memorial State Park** (📞530-582-7892; www.parks.ca.gov; Donner Pass Rd; per car May-Sep $10, Oct-Apr $5; 🕐visitor center 10am-5pm, day use 7am-8pm; P⚡) occupies one of the sites where the doomed Donner Party got trapped while migrating west during the fateful winter of 1846. The ill-fated pioneers attempted a shortcut over the roadless pass here after hearing it would save them 200 miles. An exceptionally fierce winter came early, stranding the group in late fall. When rescuers arrived in March, evidence of cannibalism was everywhere. In the end, only 47 of the 89 members of the Donner Party survived.

Best for

BIG VIEWS

02 Follow the ridgeline, where you'll have a **bird's-eye view of Lake Mary** just west. Mossy pines and empty chairlifts – hanging above the ski runs – are your next distraction, and at 1 mile you'll reach the **Mt Judah Trail** on your left, marked by a small sign.

03 Ascend gently through the forest on the Mt Judah Trail along a forested path, which will bring you to a saddle between Donner Peak (8019ft) and Mt Judah (8243ft). If you have time for a detour, the **rocky summit of Donner Peak** to the north offers excellent views of Lake Donner below.

04 The trail turns south and climbs gently along a ridge to the broad **summit of Mt Judah**, which is 2.7 miles from the trailhead. It's a nice spot for a picnic and photographs, and the **mountain-and-lake views** (pictured) are some of the most expansive anywhere in the northern Sierra. In July, numerous varieties of pink and purple penstemons and bright red-purple rock fringe flowers dot Mt Judah's eastern slopes.

05 Descend south through **hemlock forest** to rejoin the PCT and return to the parking area.

TAKE A BREAK

A festive mix of locals and tourists drop in nightly at the bar at **Pianeta** (📞530-587-4694; www.pianeta restauranttahoe.com; 10096 Donner Pass Rd; mains $22-49; 🕐5-9pm) in Truckee for happy-hour cocktails ($7), good conversation and top-notch service. Thick stone walls, intimate booths and mountain-cool decor provide an inviting backdrop. The northern Italian dishes shine, and appreciative diners dig into pastas, steaks and seafood with gusto. Reservations recommended or try to snag a seat early at the bar.

53

RUBICON TRAIL

DURATION	DIFFICULTY	DISTANCE	START/END
4½hr return	Moderate	10 miles	Calawee Cove parking lot

TERRAIN	Dirt path through forest

This exhilarating hike swerves through the trees like a kiddie-coaster, swooping up and down coastal bluffs as it passes secluded coves, historic buildings and family-friendly campsites, with Lake Tahoe a near-constant companion.

GETTING HERE

The Rubicon Trail links DL Bliss State Park and Emerald Bay State Park. Both parks border the western shores of Lake Tahoe. The best way to reach the trailhead is by car via Hwy 89. Begin at DL Bliss State Park to avoid a long and steep hike between the lofty Vikingsholm parking lot for Emerald Bay State Park and the trailhead down by the lake (2 miles round trip).

STARTING POINT

Follow the main park road through DL Bliss State Park all the way to the very last parking lot, which overlooks Lake Tahoe and popular Calawee Cove. The trailhead is at the southern end of the lot. Arrive before 9am for parking near the trailhead. You'll find restrooms here and a separate path down to the cove. The Lighthouse Trail also ends here.

01 The trail stays high above **Calawee Cove** as you walk east from the trailhead, and you'll be passing pine trees and boulders as you begin to ascend. You'll soon swing south above **Rubicon Point**. The Rubicon Trail has 1000ft of elevation change, and most of it is experienced on short uphill and downhill sections just south of the point.

02 The trail stays from 200ft to 300ft above the rugged shoreline for the next 30 minutes. In places where it skirts the rocky bluffs above the deep blue lake, a chain railing protects you from the edge. The **views across Lake Tahoe are stunning** but most impressive is the visibility – up to 70% in a recent test – into Tahoe's depths. Visibility has been reduced about 30% by algae growth. Along the trail grow pinemat manzanitas, alpine prickly currants and tobacco brushes and in wetter areas look for stands of aspen, mountain alder and creek dogwood. Osprey may nest in the tops of trees.

03 The **Lighthouse Trail** links with the Rubicon Trail at two junctions as you walk south. The lighthouse (pictured), which unfortunately looks like a wooden outhouse, was in use only for a year or two starting in 1919. Its light was visible for 7 miles. The lighthouse predates the park, which was established when Duane Leroy Bliss and his wife Elizabeth Tobey Bliss donated more than 700 acres to the state in 1929. Consider stopping by for a look on your return. The Lighthouse Trail adds a nice short loop at the end of the hike. It runs parallel to the

Rubicon Trail and links back to the Calawee Cove parking lot.

04 You'll come to a clearing and trail junction about 1 mile from the trailhead. A short spur trail leads to another parking area and the Lower Pine Campground. This parking area is a good back-up if the lots along the lake are full, but you will want to make time on your return for the bluff-top views along the first mile of trail.

05 Continuing south on the Rubicon Trail, the path cuts inland for a pleasant **forest ramble** through cedars, pine

Emerald Bay Maritime Heritage Trail

Established in 2018, this unusual path (www.parks.ca.gov) takes divers to sunken barges and recreational boats, complete with underwater interpretive markers. Elsewhere in the bay divers can find a submerged rockslide and a historic dumping ground, all part of the unique Underwater State Parks of Emerald Bay and DL Bliss State Park. Divers should be prepared for a chilly high-altitude plunge. Reno-based Sierra Diving Center (www.sierradive.com) and Adventure Scuba Center (www.renoscuba.com) offer classes and trips.

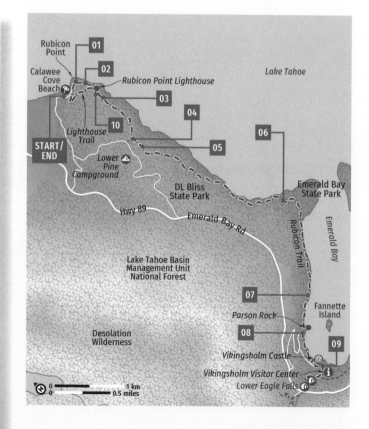

trees and firs. From here the trail is broader, less rocky and basically level, until you begin switchbacking down to the lake at 2 miles. You'll soon pass a **bluff-top overlook** – a nice spot for a snack – and a quiet sandy cove.

06 After entering **Emerald Bay State Park**, the trail curves southwest, bypassing Emerald Point as it enters the teardrop bay. The quiet of the forest disappears as you approach the bustling boat campground, used by boaters and hikers at 3.6 miles.

07 Look south for **Fannette Island** (pictured) as you walk along the shoreline. This uninhabited granite speck in Emerald Bay State Park is Lake Tahoe's only island. It holds the vandalized remains of a tiny 1920s teahouse belonging to heir Lora Knight, who would occasionally motorboat guests to the island from Vikingsholm Castle, her Scandinavian-style mansion on the bay.

08 Just after passing **Parson Rock** on your left, you'll reach the **Vikingsholm area**. A separate trail heads off to the right and eventually leads to the parking area for the state park after a nearly mile-long climb.

09 Continue straight ahead past the dock along the swimming beach to the striking **mansion**, a replica of a 9th-century Norse fortress. The mansion is 4.5 miles from the DL Bliss State Park trailhead.

AMY BALFOUR/LONELY PLANET ©

Here you'll also find picnic tables, restrooms and lots of coastal activity. The visitor center has exhibits about local characters and the castle. A trail behind the visitor center leads to Lower Eagle Falls. From the falls it's 1.6 miles to Eagle Point Campground.

10 Return the way you came, detouring onto the **Lighthouse Loop** for a change of scenery. If you started in the early morning and it's a nice day, the convivial beach scene will be a jarring change from the morning's quiet – but it also looks rather fun.

 TAKE A BREAK

For a post-hike brew, travel 12 miles south to the beer garden at **South Lake Brewing Co** (☎530-578-0087; www.southlakebeer.com; 1920 Lake Tahoe Blvd; ⏱noon-8pm Mon-Thu, 11am-8pm Fri-Sun), where flights of craft beer are served on old snow skis. Up to 16 beers are on tap, and there's a food truck Thursday through Monday in warmer months.

54

MT ROSE

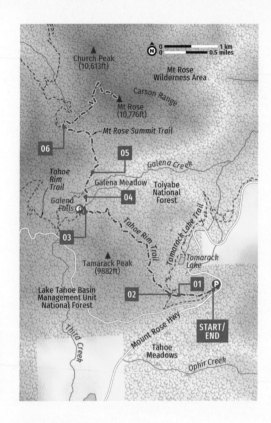

DURATION	DIFFICULTY	DISTANCE	START/END
6-8hr return	Hard	11 miles	Mt Rose Summit Parking Area

TERRAIN	Dirt path & a rocky climb

This popular day hike climbs 1930ft on its journey to the summit of Mt Rose (10,776ft), the highest peak in the Carson Range. Expect some huffing and puffing, but the trip is a visual feast, with abundant wildflowers, evergreen forests, a sassy little waterfall and sweeping bird's-eye views of Tahoe Meadows, Lake Tahoe and the Carson Range.

GETTING HERE

The parking area at the Mt Rose Summit Welcome Plaza is 8 miles northeast of Incline Village, NV, via Hwy 431, which is also known as the Mt Rose Scenic Byway. From Truckee, which is 25 miles west of the welcome plaza, follow Hwy 267 southeast to Incline Village then hop onto the scenic byway.

STARTING POINT

The trail begins at the western end of the parking area. Look for a dirt path a few steps beyond the restrooms. Follow it a short distance to an information board for the Tahoe Rim Trail (www.tahoerim trail.org). The rim trail is a 165-mile loop around the lake, and it overlaps the Mt Rose Summit Trail from here to Galena Falls at 2.5 miles.

01 The trail slowly bends north, offering **splendid views of Tahoe Meadows and Lake Tahoe** to the west. Far below, an interpretive trail and three loop trails meander through the alpine wonders of Tahoe Meadows, a family-friendly spot where you'll pass boulders, pine trees and firs. It's also a fun place for sledding in winter.

02 After a half-mile or so the trail starts an easy ramble through the forest. A spur trail on your right leads to Tamarack Lake, but you'll contin-

Alpine Wildflowers

Blue and white lupines, bright yellow mountain mule ears and purple pentsemons are common. Close to the dry ground look for the broad, coconut-scented yellow flowers of the unusual woody-fruited evening primrose, and on sunny midsummer days inhale the minty fragrances of sagebrush and mountain pennyroyal.

AMY BALFOUR/LONELY PLANET ©

ue straight through the woods. Views of peaks and cliffs in the **Mt Rose Wilderness** play peekaboo through the evergreens as you walk.

03 You'll hear the sound of rushing water before you reach **Galena Falls** (pictured) and Galena Creek at about 2.5 miles. The falls – found just a few steps beyond the trail junction signs – splash down a rocky cliff face that's dotted with greenery. This is a pleasant spot for a picnic, with some shade. The falls are also a good place to turn around if you're just looking for an easy day hike.

04 At the trail junction, follow the path heading north to Mt Rose. The summit is about 3 miles away, and the trail begins to rise from here. There will be several creek crossings as you pass **Galena Meadow** on your right. Keep watch for wildflowers.

05 The trail begins climbing steadily, with steep sections. You'll enter the 30,000-acre **Mt Rose Wilderness**.

06 Next up is a saddle and trail junction. Turn right at the junction and follow switchbacks up the slope, ascending above the tree line

to the summit ridge. The trail follows the ridge to the **summit**, with **views of Lake Tahoe, Truckee Meadows and Reno**. Retrace your steps to the parking lot.

 **TAKE A BREAK**

A kitschy log cabin is home to **Soule Domain** (☎530-546-7529; www. souledomain.com; 9983 Cove St; mains $25-41; ⏱5-8pm), the most elegant restaurant on Tahoe's north shore. Chef Charlie Soule puts a delicious, light-handed global spin on an appealing array of seafood and meat dishes, from sea scallops poached in champagne to curried almond chicken sautéed with snow peas and shiitake mushrooms.

Also Try...

MT TALLAC

Climb to the summit of a rocky peak on Tahoe's southwestern lakeshore, with stunning vistas of Fallen Leaf Lake, the Desolation Wilderness and Lake Tahoe.

The rocky summit of Mt Tallac (9735ft) is a popular destination for serious day hikers. No other high peak is so close to Lake Tahoe and therefore so easily accessible, with its incomparable views (pictured above) of the vast lake and adjacent granite landscape of the Desolation Wilderness. Tallac, the only peak around Tahoe with a Washoe name, means 'great mountain.' Its greatness is evident once you're at the commanding summit. The trail is steep in places, gaining 3255ft over 4.5 miles, with an equally knee-pounding descent to the trailhead. Bring a jacket, even on warm days, and watch for afternoon thunderstorms. A free day-use permit is required – get one by simply registering at the trailhead.

DURATION 7-9hr return
DIFFICULTY Hard
DISTANCE 9.6 miles

SIERRA BUTTES FIRE LOOKOUT

This 5-miler joins the Pacific Coast Trail (PCT) before a 1500ft elevation gain to epic views from a lookout tower.

See those jagged rock formations as you approach Sierra City on Hwy 49 west? That striking spot is where you're headed. And luckily for hikers, the steep path is short and not overly strenuous. Look for wildflowers like mule's ear and paintbrush as you climb. The terrain along the way is mixed: exposed rock and boulders, and pine forest. The hike ends with a dramatic 150ft climb up a metal stairway to a locked fire tower at 8587ft.. From the grated catwalk on top, savor sweeping views of alpine lakes and, on a clear day, Lassen Peak.

DURATION 4hr return
DIFFICULTY Moderate
DISTANCE 5 miles

ANNE08/SHUTTERSTOCK ©

ELLIS PEAK

Hike along a panoramic ridge, ascending 1390ft to a scenic peak above Lake Tahoe's west shore with 360-degree views.

Ellis Peak (8740ft; pictured above) offers remarkable views of the Desolation Wilderness, Granite Chief Wilderness and Lake Tahoe from high above its west shore. Views are surpassed only by those attained on the much more strenuous Mt Tallac, making this hike a nice alternative for vast bird's-eye views if you only have a half day. Look for a veritable garden of wildflowers on the sandy slopes of the ridge, which is reached via a nearly 500ft climb.

DURATION 3-3½hr return
DIFFICULTY Moderate
DISTANCE 6 miles

NOBLE LAKE

Wildflowers line the forested upper slopes of Noble Canyon under dramatic Highland Peak.

Noble Canyon in Carson-Iceberg Wilderness is wilder and more rugged than Mokelumne Wilderness and the Lake Tahoe area, offering more solitude and more open, broader vistas for those who make the drive up Hwy 4. The fairly gentle trail contours south above the deep and forested Noble Canyon between Ebbetts Pass and scenic Noble Lake. Striking volcanic peaks, pleasant flower-lined trails and cascading streams should delight most hikers.

DURATION 3½-4½hr return
DIFFICULTY Moderate
DISTANCE 7.6 miles

ST MARY'S PASS

Fabulous viewpoint above Sonora Pass on the Sierra Crest, with a side trip up Sonora Peak.

With views not only of the wilderness to the north, but of nearby Levitt Peak and the more distant Yosemite High Country to the south, the pass is one of the Sierra Nevada's most scenic. Wildflowers add to the enjoyment. From the pass you can hike to the top of nearby Sonora Peak (11,459ft) for even more views. You can also drop down into the beautiful Clark Fork Meadow just north to spend the night in a granite-encircled campsite. The pass is 1.3 miles north of Hwy 108.

DURATION 1-1½hr return
DIFFICULTY Easy
DISTANCE 2.6 miles

NORTHERN MOUNTAINS

Explore
NORTHERN MOUNTAINS ←- - - -

From the dramatic crags and volcanic formations of Lassen Volcanic National Park to the high desert plateaus and the ancient granite spires of the northern Sierra, these mountains don't look the way people envision California. The topography resembles the older mountains of the Rockies more than the relatively young granite of Yosemite, with raging rivers, cobalt alpine lakes and conifer forests thrown in for good measure. The towns are tiny but friendly, with few comforts; come to get lost in vast remoteness.

REDDING

A tourist destination it is not, though it is the major gateway city to the northeast corner of the state and a useful spot for restocking before long jaunts into the wilderness. Redding's many motels and hotels (most large chains are represented and have swimming pools) huddle around noisy thoroughfares and some downtown options have photogenic, retro neon signs. Aim for the ones on less busy N Market St.

MT LASSEN REGION

From the north on Hwy 89, you won't see many gas/food/lodgings signs after Mt Shasta City. Aside from the eight developed campgrounds in the park, there are many more in the surrounding Lassen National Forest. The nearest hotels and motels are in Chester, which accesses the south entrance of the park. There are also some motels and basic services near the split of Hwy 89 and Hwy 44, in the north. You'll find a few modest places to eat in the small towns surrounding the park but you'll want to pack provisions.

MT SHASTA CITY

Comfortable and practical Mt Shasta City glows in the shadow of the white pyramid of Mt Shasta. The downtown is enchanting; you can spend hours poking around crystal shops and galleries. There are tons of places to stay, from rustic campgrounds to plush boutique B&Bs (reserve ahead), along with trendy restaurants and cafes that come and go with the snowmelt.

DUNSMUIR

This town is home to a spirited set of artists, naturalists, urban refugees and native Dunsmuirians, who are rightly proud of the fish-stocked rivers around their little community. Its downtown streets – once a bawdy gold-rush district – hold clean and friendly motels, cafes and galleries.

MCCLOUD

This tiny, historic mill town sits at the foot of the south slope of Mt Shasta, and is an alternative to staying in Mt Shasta City. Quiet streets retain an easygoing charm, and lodgings in McCloud

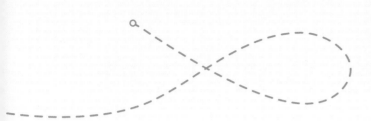

Resources

Lassen Volcanic National Park
(📞 530-595-4480; www.nps.
gov/lavo; 7-day entry per car
mid-Apr–Nov $30, Dec–mid-
Apr $10)

Visit Redding (www.visit
redding.com) Redding's tourism
bureau.

Visit Mt Shasta (www.visit
mtshasta.com) Mt Shasta's
tourism bureau.

Hike Mt Shasta (www.hike
mtshasta.com) Excellent online
hiking resource for the Mt
Shasta area.

Mt Shasta Trail Association
(www.mountshastatrail
association.org) Nonprofit that
builds trails, advocates for
access and conservation, and
publishes information about
area hiking.

Outdoor Project (www.
outdoorproject.com) Nonprofit
promoting outdoor recreation.

are desirable (reserve ahead).
For camping, the McCloud Ranger District Office has information on the half-dozen campgrounds nearby, and Fowlers
Camp is the most popular. The
town's eating options are pricey
and few.

WHEN TO GO

Warm weather and snow-free
passes are ideal for summer day
hikes, while scattered showers and snow descend on the
higher elevations in the shoulder
months (October, November,
April and May). Lassen Volcanic
National Park has a short season
from around the beginning of
June to the beginning of September. Lower elevations open up
earlier but you can expect many
services to be shut between
October and May. That said, the
winter is an incredibly peaceful
time to snowshoe as long as the
roads are open.

WHERE TO STAY

Rest your head on a feather
pillow in a B&B or snuggle up in
a sleeping bag under the stars
deep in the forest. If you're visiting Lassen, think woodsy lodges,
RV parks and camping, oftentimes next to beautiful alpine
lakes. In and around Mt Shasta
you'll find everything from backcountry camping to lovely B&Bs,
although the cheapest option for
a bed is often a roadside motel.

WHAT'S ON

Ski Season (www.skipark.com;
🕙late fall to early summer) Fly
down the slopes of Mt Shasta.

Mushroom Festival (🕙May) Mc-
Cloud hosts its annual mushroom foraging event.

Montague Balloon Fair (www.face
book.com/montagueballoonfair;
🕙late Sep) In Mt Shasta City,
hot-air balloons take to the skies.

TRANSPORT

There are a few bus services
and Amtrak runs through Redding and the Mt Shasta region,
but for the most part you'll
need your own wheels to really
explore this region (especially
for Lassen Volcanic National
Park).

55

BUMPASS HELL TRAIL

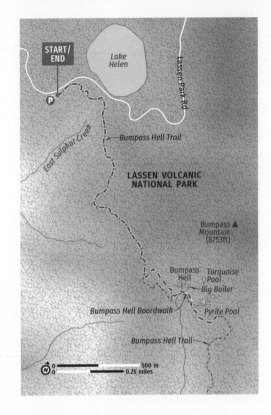

DURATION	DIFFICULTY	DISTANCE	START/END
2hr return	Easy	3 miles	Bumpass Hell parking area

TERRAIN	Rock & boardwalk

An active hydrothermal basin with pale blue pools and billowing clouds of steam, Bumpass Hell is the crown jewel of Lassen Volcanic National Park. And it's got the crowds to prove it. Try to arrive early in the morning to easily secure a parking spot and have the raised boardwalk and its boiling mud pots, fizzy fumaroles and sulfuric gasses all to yourself. Extending this hike to Cold Boiling and Crumbaugh Lakes and ending at the Kohm Yah-mah-nee Visitor Center is also highly recommended, but you'll need a plan for returning to your car.

From the Bumpass Hell parking area (which is about 6 miles north of the park's southwest entrance), the trail gradually climbs the rocky rim of a large valley offering **views of crystal clear Lake Helen**

and Lassen Peak soaring above it. After about a mile, the trail dips 250ft into an entirely new landscape buzzing with hydrothermal activity.

A wide, even **boardwalk** allows hikers to explore the **volatile, mineral-rich pools** and **effervescent mud pots**, admiring the unusual landscape with its muted colors and strange, sulfuric aroma. It's all a very visceral reminder that the nearby volcanos are not dormant, but simply resting.

It's worth noting that the hissing basin was first discovered in 1864 by mountaineer Kendall Vanhook Bumpass. He claimed the springs and intended to mine the minerals and develop the area into a tourist site. Unfortunately, while guiding some visitors, Bumpass stepped through the crust and sunk into the boiling mud, resulting in the loss of his leg.

Stay on the boardwalk, folks.

56

MCCLOUD RIVER TRAIL

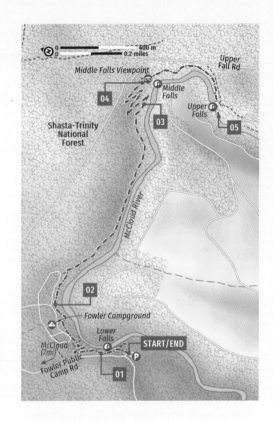

DURATION	DIFFICULTY	DISTANCE	START/END
2-3hr return	Easy	3.5 miles	Lower Falls parking lot

TERRAIN	Pavement, packed dirt, some stairs

An accessible and easy jaunt along the spellbinding McCloud River brings visitors to three jaw-dropping waterfalls. Yes, the crowds tend to gather for summer swims and cliff jumps. But things quiet considerably when the forest foliage goes technicolor in fall, and even more so after snow blankets the dreamy winter landscape.

GETTING HERE

You'll need a car to reach this hike. From McCloud, drive 5 miles southeast on Hwy 89. When you reach the sign for Fowlers and Lower Falls, turn right onto Fowler Public Camp Rd. Continue through an intersection and stay right at the fork and soon you will arrive at the Lower Falls parking area.

STARTING POINT

The out-and-back trail begins at the staircase next to the Lower Falls overlook, and there's also a ramp for visitors with mobility issues. Frequently packed with visitors, this day-use area features restrooms, picnic tables and BBQ grills.

01 The paved path runs parallel to the **river**, with views of the 15ft Lower Falls and an option for a cool dip. Originally, this area was the home of the Wintu tribe, and they referred to the falls as 'Nurum-wit-ti-dekki' (falls where the salmon turn back). Folks may be trout fishing here, and although this was once a popular spot for diving from rocks, submerged boulders have made it dangerous.

02 The path climbs gently and veers away from the river, then back toward it. Heavily trafficked Fowler Campground will soon appear on the left and a railing comes up on the right, tracing the

rim of a canyon. Thereafter the path turns to dirt but remains wide and even, with the scenic river again visible on the right.

03 Large boulders and old-growth trees flank the path as it meanders by a fern-shrouded river toward thundering **Middle Falls** (pictured). At 50ft high and 100ft across, this is the hike's most awe-inspiring attraction, and a few brave souls may be scaling the rocks beside it to hurl themselves from an adjacent ledge into an incredibly cold (but highly refreshing!) pool.

04 The trail switches back, climbing out of the canyon. It's a short climb, and the only uphill section of the trail. A wooden staircase takes hikers the rest of the way to the rim and its **stunning views over Middle Falls**. A paved trail here connects to a parking lot and some restrooms, but also continues east towards Upper Falls.

05 The trail follows the rim of the canyon high above the river, eventually approaching the **Upper Falls**. This dazzling 25-footer flows through a rocky channel carved out of a basalt wall. There's an unofficial path that leads to the base, but it's very steep (and therefore not recommended). Continuing upstream, white water plunges over rocks and through small pools within the canyon. Most hikers turn back here, but some continue to **Bigelow Meadow** to look for migratory birds.

TAKE A BREAK

Cruise over to **Axe & Rose Public House** (☏530-859-8500; www. mccloudhotel.com; 424 Main St; ⏰4-8pm Wed-Sun; 📶) in McCloud to sample a local beer, cider or fancy cocktail. The cozy, modern pub also offers a good menu of soups, salads, sandwiches and fancier main dishes like glazed salmon or rib-eye steaks. There's a great outdoor patio for when the weather is warm.

57

CINDER CONE TRAIL

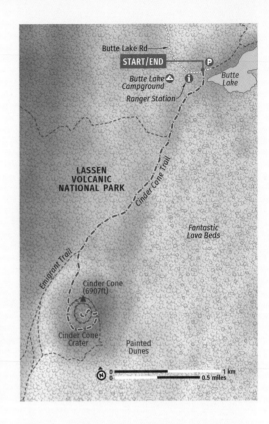

DURATION	DIFFICULTY	DISTANCE	START/END
2hr return	Moderate	3 miles	Butte Lake parking lot

TERRAIN	Sand, cinders & volcanic rock

Have you ever felt like scaling the ashy flank of a perfectly formed, 750ft cinder cone volcano then descending into its terrifying crater? This trail does that, with scenery that calls to mind Mordor's Mt Doom in *The Lord of the Rings*. As the path climbs up the volcano, it offers views of a unique and awe-inspiring landscape of multicolored dunes, expanses of hardened lava, vast pine forests and cool mountain lakes.

Drive along Hwy 44 to the northeast area of **Lassen Volcanic National Park** and turn right onto Butte Lake Rd, which ends at the Butte Lake parking area. The trail begins at the southwest side of the lot and quickly arrives at a **woodland area** traversed in the 1850s by wagons full of California emigrants (hence the former name, Nobels' Emigrant Trail).

The trail inclines gently past solidified lava flows known as the **Fantastic Lava Beds**, which you'll want to stop and gawk at. The magma that created these jagged volcanic rocks broke through the base of the volcano sometime around 1650 and flowed outward, then hardened.

After about a mile, you'll reach the base of the decided symmetrical volcano along with the **Painted Dunes**, rolling pumice fields with vivid red and orange coloration created by oxidized volcanic ash. From there, you'll make the sweaty ascent up the **cone** (pictured), with **stunning views** in all directions. At the top, you can trace the rim and look out over the lava flows, the dunes, Lassen Peak and Snag Lake. Then you can spiral into the crater.

There's another way down the volcano on the southeastern flank, and the trail then loops around to send you back.

58

LASSEN PEAK

DURATION	DIFFICULTY	DISTANCE	START/END
4-5hr return	Moderate-hard	5 miles	Lassen Peak parking area

TERRAIN	Dirt, rubble & rock (can be very steep)

The world's largest plug dome volcano last blew its top less than 100 years ago, but today fit and fearless hikers can scale its flanks and stand triumphant at the top of still-active Lassen Peak. Highlights of the hike include rare alpine plants, occasional snow patches and evidence of glacial episodes, and as you climb, the stunning views of volcanically active surrounds and distant lakes become increasingly epic. After all, at 10,457ft, Lassen Peak is the highest point in the park.

GETTING HERE

You'll need to enter Lassen Volcanic National Park (p201) with a car (and plenty of gas in the tank) from either the northwest or the southwest entrance, which are connected by a 30-mile section of SR-89. The Lassen Peak Trailhead is a winding, 15-minute drive from the southwest entrance, and an equally winding 35-minute drive from the northwest entrance. Although both entrances are open year-round, SR-89 closes to through traffic during the winter due to snow, from approximately November to May.

STARTING POINT

Originating in the parking lot, where you'll also find the area's only restrooms, the trail inclines steeply from 8500ft and is composed mainly of loose rock. You'll notice an even steeper looking path to your left, but don't wander over – that's actually a scar created by careless hikers, and it's illegal to leave the trail. Be sure to set out with plenty of water.

01 The lower stretch of the trail offers some sparse tree cover, along with opportunities to rest in the shade and gaze out at nearby pinnacles and peaks. Keep your eyes peeled for the **American pika**, a high-elevation mammal related to rabbits but more closely resembling a mouse. Park biologists monitor pika populations because they're worried that as climate change warms their habitat, the creatures may have nowhere else to go. In this area you might also notice some sloping blankets of rock known as talus, which were once lava that emerged through the volcano's surface.

02 Continuing along several lengthy and steeply inclining switchbacks, the sapphire-colored **Lake Helen** (pictured) will come into view to the south, and the hardy purple lupine flowers will dangle prettily from rock crevices. To the northeast, a glacier-carved depression within the rock contains the only permanent snowfield on Lassen Peak. From here on up, there's only limited shade available. Be sure you've got plenty of water and adequate sun protection, including a hat, sunglasses and sunscreen. As the air gets thinner, you may want to consider taking frequent rests. And while the climb isn't exactly easy, hikers of all levels of athlet-icism (including children) tend to do just fine.

03 As you continue your ascent, patches of snow and ice may remain alongside the trail, and particularly steep or slick areas feature helpful stairs. Be sure to look down at what's beneath your feet – the dark rocks are actually the youngest rocks in California. Known as black dacite, they were formed when lava shot violently out of the crater in 1915, setting off an avalanche and a mudflow that took down forests, pastures and even six homes in the valley beneath the

Lassen Peak in Winter

Lassen Volcanic National Park becomes a winter wonderland starting in October, and the snow often doesn't recede until July. During these months, experienced hikers tackle the challenging but magical ascent up Lassen Peak, and snow-shoers and cross-county skiers circle Manzanita Lake for views of snow-blanketed volcanoes. The trails near the northwest park entrance are classified as beginner and intermediate, while those near the southwest entrance are intermediate to advanced. Call the **Kohm Yah-mah-nee Visitor Center** (☏530-595-4480; www.nps.gov/lavo; 21820 Lassen National Park Hwy, Mineral; ⏱9am-5pm, closed Mon & Tue Nov-Apr; ♿) to check on conditions.

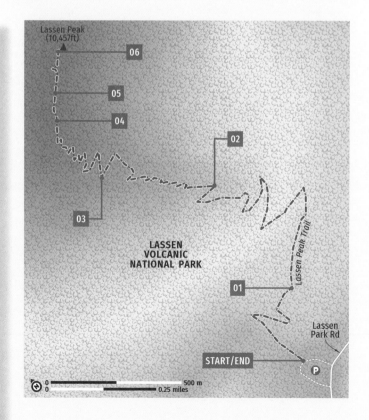

volcano's northeastern slope. Three days later, lava again filled the crater and the volcano exploded a second avalanche of hot ash, rock fragments and gasses down the mountain (which set off another highly destructive mudflow). Those two blows solidified the volcano's notoriety and led to its establishment as a national park by Congress on August 9, 1916.

04 Less-agile hikers will likely complete their journey here, at a **prime lookout point** with a panoramic view of Brokeoff Mountain, Manzanita Lake and Mt Shasta in one direction, and the Cinder Cone, Juniper Lake and Mt Harkness in another. Signage identifies and explains all, including the roped-off rare plant habitat, which is home to golden draba as well as a species of smelowskia found only here and on the saddle between Lassen Peak and Chaos Crags. In earlier times, the whole region was a summer encampment and meeting point for the Atsugewi, Yana, Yahi and Maidu Native American tribes. They hunted deer and gathered plants for basketmaking. Some indigenous people still live nearby and work closely with the park to help educate visitors on their ancient history and contemporary culture.

05 Depending on the conditions and time of year you visit, this next leg of the trail may take you through a short but slippery patch of ice and snow. Hiking poles are helpful in navigating this, and hikers with devious companions may find themselves involved in snowball fights. Early in the season you'll need snow and ice-climbing equipment to reach the summit.

06 A rock scamper to the jagged **summit** rewards with sweeping views of all the land. The terrain is steep and exposed, the air is thin and the feeling upon arrival at the top of this active volcano is nothing short of sublime. This is also the best spot to view the hilariously named **Devastated Area** to the northeast of the peak. Although the 1915 blast did a number on it, the area has recovered well and doesn't exactly appear 'devastated' anymore. If you're planning to make it all the way to the top, note that the temperature drops and strong winds are a possibility. Consider carrying a windbreaker with you.

☕ TAKE A BREAK

The cafe at the Kohm Yah-mah-nee Visitor Center (p209) sells espresso, snacks, sandwiches and other healthy bites. It's open daily from 9am to 5pm in summer and fall, and has limited offerings in winter and spring, when it's open only Saturdays and Sundays from 11am to 2pm.

A snack bar at the Manzanita Lake Camper Store offers sandwiches, hot dogs, and other meals at the park's north entrance. It's open June to early October, daily from 8am to 8pm.

Eruptions of Lassen Peak

Lassen Peak hadn't made a peep for something like 27,000 years. But on May 30, 1914, it awoke from the long slumber and expelled steam out of newly formed vent at its summit. A year later, 180 more violent upheavals of steam and rock had formed a wide crater and captured the country's collective imagination: at the time, Lassen Peak was the only erupting volcano in the United States.

The eruptions spawned the development of the first US Geological Survey (USGS) volcano observatory. Today, USGS scientists monitor several locations throughout the park with seismometers, hoping to predict hazardous conditions. Lassen Peak remains active, and scientists say it will one day erupt again.

59

CASTLE CRAGS TRAIL

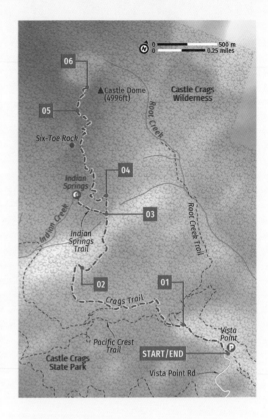

DURATION	DIFFICULTY	DISTANCE	START/END
4-5hr return	Moderate-hard	5.5 miles	Vista Point

TERRAIN	Woodland & rocks, sometimes steep

Soaring granite spires and unsurpassed views of Mt Shasta and Gray Rocks shouldn't be this easy to come by. But right off I-5, this steep forest climb and rock scramble traverses the region's most majestic pinnacles and culminates at the base of an awe-inspiring pluton, Castle Dome (4996ft). Thirsty? A short spur trail leads to the verdant and potable Indian Springs.

GETTING HERE

You'll need your own wheels. Castle Crags State Park is located right off the I-5 at the Castella exit (725), from which you'll head west on Castle Creek Rd before turning right into the park. At the guard station, a ranger will collect an $8 entrance fee and offer maps covering the park's 28 miles of hiking trails. You'll turn right and drive about a mile up a winding, one-lane road to the Vista Point parking lot, where only about 20 cars fit (arrive early on weekends).

STARTING POINT

The out-and-back trail begins at the southern end of Vista Point's parking lot. Before setting out on the main trail, consider taking the short, accessible path from the parking lot's north end, which leads to a lookout point. Although this adds half a mile (total) to your hike, it offers a stunning view of Gray Rocks, Mt Shasta and the Castle Crags, which you're about to scale.

01 Things start out easy, with a wide path through unremarkable woodlands at only a slight incline. After 0.3 miles, the trail splits (stay to the left) and steepens significantly, with switchbacks aiding in the elevation gain. The soft forest floor is easy on the feet and the thick canopy keeps things cool.

ASHLEY HARRELL/LONELY PLANET ©

02 The steep climb continues northward until the path switches back to the east, and just after the bend a small clearing offers an initial opportunity to behold the **dramatic spires of Castle Crags**. Some hikers use this area as a campsite.

03 After still more climbing, the trail emerges from the forest and flattens out, offering lovely **views of Gray Rocks** and some of the Castle Crags. **Six-Toe Rock**, the most popular crag for rock climbing, comes into view, and the spur trail to Indian Springs appears on the left. Just 0.2 miles off the main trail, the **bubbling, fern-shrouded spring** contains drinkable water.

04 Continuing north from the junction, you'll approach a sign signaling your exit from the state park and entrance into **Castle Crags Wilderness** (part of Shasta-Trinity National Forest). The views here are astounding, with the iconic **Castle Dome** (pictured) looming over snowcapped **Mt Shasta**.

05 The trail gets rockier, more exposed, and increasingly epic as you make the ascent, weaving through towering granite spires. Be careful scampering over rocks as you continue skyward toward Castle Dome.

06 Approaching a dusty saddle at the base of the dome, the vegetation gets brushy and manzanitas are ubiquitous. The maintained trail ends here, but adventurous hikers often explore adjacent rock formations. From here, retrace your steps back to the parking lot.

TAKE A BREAK

Fuel up on baked wings, bratwurst or a veggie nut burger at **Dunsmuir Brewery Works** (☏530-235-1900; www.dunsmuirbreweryworks.com; 5701 Dunsmuir Ave; mains $13-15; ⊙noon-6pm Wed & Thu, to 7pm Fri-Sun, extended hours Apr-Sep; 🖥) before an afternoon climb. Or toast your return from Castle Crags with a crisp ale or perfectly balanced IPA. The buzzing patio and aw-shucks staff round out the experience.

60

CANYON CREEK TRAIL

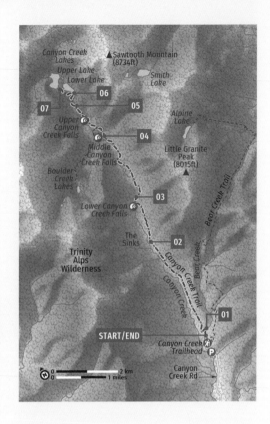

DURATION	DIFFICULTY	DISTANCE	START/END
1-2 days return	Moderate-hard	16 miles	Canyon Creek Trailhead

TERRAIN	Woodland, rocks; some creek crossings

With a granite canyon carved by glaciers, gushing waterfalls, serene forests and two subalpine lakes, this Trinity Alps trek is the stuff of legends. Hikers will need considerable stamina to complete this out-and-back trail in a day, but the views of pine-dotted mountains towering over shimmering blue-green lakes make it more than worthwhile. Shorter hikes to the waterfalls are also recommended.

GETTING HERE

A car is required. Coming from the Weaverville Ranger Station (where you must pick up a wilderness permit from the self-serve kiosk if you are camping), it's just 8 miles west to the town of Junction City. When you reach the General Store, take a right to head north on scenic Canyon Creek Rd. Continue for 13.5 miles until you reach the parking lot and trailhead.

STARTING POINT

From the parking lot you'll head northwest, passing a turnoff for Bear Creek Trail and signage for Boulder Lakes, yet another destination. There's plenty of wilderness to explore in the Trinity Alps, but the Canyon Creek Lakes are the prettiest (and the most sought-after). Onward!

01 Initially, you'll trudge through a quiet forest, crossing **Bear Creek** and continuing north with Canyon Creek to the west. The trail is even and a thick canopy provides plenty of shade, but there's little to see.

02 A spur trail to the west leads to the creek and over a log bridge to a **small island**, which offers decent camping. Upstream you'll notice a rockslide over the creek that's referred to as the **Sinks** (rocks disappear when the water rises).

03 The trail becomes more exposed and steepens, switching back as it climbs. Large granite boulders flank the trail and after a creek crossing an unmaintained path doglegs to the southwest, finishing at the base of the spectacular **Lower Canyon Creek Falls**.

04 Continue north to a series of clearings and meadows. You'll then reach two more **majestic waterfalls**, along with massive granite slabs and conifers. In summer the **wildflowers** pop and the creek offers swimming holes.

05 Continue through the forestlands along the creek, being sure to follow any signs or cairns. Eventually you'll need to hopscotch the creek over logs and large stones, after which the boulder scramble begins, with high exposure and Sierra Nevada–like surrounds.

06 Approaching **Lower Lake** (pictured), the sun glitters off its tranquil waters, and pine-covered **Sawtooth Mountain** soars at 8400ft above. Take a dip in the clear, icy lake, then stretch out over a toasty granite slab beneath the afternoon sun.

07 Hike along the western side of Lower Lake before breaking off to the northwest to rock scamper to **Upper Lake**. There's no specific path, so use your best judgment. Upper Lake is the larger and brighter blue lake.

 **TAKE A BREAK**

Fuel up on espresso and a tasty breakfast from **Mamma Llama** (www.mammallama.com; 490 Main St, Weaverville; breakfasts & sandwiches $5-9; ⏰7:30am-4pm Mon-Fri, 10am-3pm Sat; 🛜), a local institution that also does wraps, sandwiches and microbrew beer available by the bottle, along with green smoothies and plenty of vegetarian options.

Also Try...

GRIZZLY CREEK TRAIL

Advanced hikers willing to take on this remote and challenging trail in the Trinity Alps will be rewarded with a stunning arrangement of granite cliffs, a unique glacier, an expansive alpine lake and the highest waterfall in Northern California.

The Grizzly Creek Trail is the only route that reaches the magnificent Grizzly Lake (and its falls), but it cannot be accessed by car. A hiker must approach the trail via either the North Fork Trinity River Trail (a 15-mile journey) or the China Spring Trail, a brutal 2 miles of steep climbs and steeper descents. The Grizzly Creek Trail itself is only slightly less demanding, with a final rock scramble that's notoriously dicey. After a jaunt through forestland and meadow, over sedimentary rock and past innumerable cataracts, this grueling trail delivers its trekkers to one of the most awe-inspiring natural places in all the American West.

DURATION 1-2 days return
DIFFICULTY Hard
DISTANCE 14 miles

MANZANITA LAKE TRAIL

This easy, family-friendly loop within Lassen Volcanic National Park begins (and ends) near the park's northwestern entrance, and meanders through forestland around a picturesque lake (pictured above) with a classic view of Lassen Peak.

Beginning from the Manzanita Lake Picnic Area, this mostly flat trail follows the lake's shoreline and offers superior views of Lassen Peak and Chaos Crags over the gloriously reflective lake, particularly in the morning. Some stretches of the trail are flanked by Jeffrey pines, and in the quieter areas away from crowds it may be possible to view ducks, woodpeckers and sometimes deer. Rowboating is common and although swimming is normally permitted, during research the activity had been banned due to an otter attack. Yes, you read that right. Apparently the swimmer got between the mother otter and her pups.

DURATION 1-2hr return
DIFFICULTY Easy
DISTANCE 1.5 miles

MEF13/GETTY IMAGES ©

DEADFALL LAKES & MT EDDY TRAIL

A wildflower meadow and some mountain lakes are only the beginning on this out-of-the-way trek culminating atop Mt Eddy, the highest point in the Klamath Mountains, with views for days.

Park at the Deadfall Meadows Trailhead. The first mile or so may be a bit slick and muddy, but a gradual ascent brings you to the dryer ground of the Deadfall Basin, which was carved out by glaciers. The two lakes are excellent stops to snack before ascending 9025ft Mt Eddy. Views stretch from Lassen Peak all the way to Oregon.

DURATION 7-8hr return
DIFFICULTY Moderate-hard
DISTANCE 10 miles

JAMES K CARR TRAIL

The most sought-after waterfall in Whiskeytown Recreation Area is the 220ft Whiskeytown Falls (pictured above), and reaching it requires only a short uphill hike through an old-growth forest.

From the visitor center, drive 9 miles west on Hwy 299 to Crystal Creek Rd. Turn left and drive 3.5 miles to the parking lot. Mill Creek Trail leads downhill and over a footbridge crossing Crystal Creek, after which you'll ascend through a forested ravine alongside thundering cascades, arriving at the base of three-tiered, 220ft falls. Stone stairs lead up the cliff.

DURATION 2-3hr return
DIFFICULTY Moderate
DISTANCE 3.4 miles

WHITNEY BUTTE TRAIL

For a different hiking experience of NorCal, consider the high desert of Lava Beds National Monument and its famous lava tubes, yawning caves and tribal rock art.

We like the Whitney Butte Trail for the mix of environments: the trail begins in an ice cave before meandering over a collapsed lava tube system and through meadows of wildflowers, sage and juniper. Eventually snow-capped Mt Shasta comes into view, and you'll traverse the flanks of Whitney Butte before finishing up at an expansive lava flow.

DURATION 3-4hr return
DIFFICULTY Moderate
DISTANCE 6.6 miles

Behind the Scenes

Send us your feedback

We love to hear from travelers – your comments help make our books better. We read every word, and we guarantee that your feedback goes straight to the authors. Visit **lonelyplanet.com/ contact** to submit your updates and suggestions. We may edit, reproduce and incorporate your comments in Lonely Planet products such as guidebooks, websites and digital products, so let us know if you don't want your comments reproduced or your name acknowledged. For a copy of our privacy policy visit lonelyplanet.com/privacy.

ACKNOWLEDGEMENTS

Cover photograph Sequoia State Park, Ingus Kruklitis/ Shutterstock ©

Digital Model Elevation Data U.S. Geological Survey Department of the Interior/USGS U.S. Geological Survey

Photographs pp6–11
Jimmy W, Alizada Studios, Cassiohabib, canadastock, salilbhatt, AJ9, Underswestern-sky, Joanne T/Shutterstock ©; scott sady/tahoelight.com, Ed Callaert/Alamy Stock Photo ©

WRITER THANKS

AMY BALFOUR

A big thank you to the friends who shared their favorite hikes and insider tips: Chris & Amy Rose, Lynn Neumann, Randy Propster, Tom Pettus, and Trudie Grattan. Special thanks to my trackers, who made sure Waldo returned from her daily adventures: John Crumpler, Lori Jarvis, Kathleen Graves, Katherine Londos, Sara Winn and the DSF Girls. Thank you Michael and Melissa Peeler for your always fun hospitality.

RAY BARTLETT

Huge thanks to my family and wonderful friends for making this such an epic journey, as well as to Lonely Planet editors and staff, and the various fun, quirky, fascinating people I met along the way. May the road always rise to meet you all.

GREGOR CLARK

Thanks to Caitlin Swalec, Keasley Jones, Patrick Goodrich, Anita Liboff, Jim Sternberg and all the other Californians who offered their sage advice and helped me discover new trails to complement all my old favorites. Special thanks to all the many old friends and relatives who opened their homes and actually came out walking with me, even in the middle of a pandemic: Carl, April, Jim, Nicia, Ted, Jennifer, Martha, Kelly and Pam – you totally made my trip, and it wouldn't have been the same without you!

ASHLEY HARRELL

Thanks to my coauthors and editors for all their support, and to Justin Legge, Carolyn Belak, Dave Feral, Rowdy Kelley, Kevin Fredrickson, Matt LaFever, Britt Corkey, Joseph Tyler and the nice people over at Cave Springs resort for sharing their knowledge. Thanks also to those who accompanied me on the trails: Richard and Joey Stenger, Blu Graham, Amy Benziger, Matt Penfold, Paul Olejarczuk, Lois Beckett, Terrell Liedstrand, Osa Peligrosa and Steven Sparapani, the best boy scout I've ever known.

THIS BOOK

This Lonely Planet guidebook was researched and written by Amy Balfour, Ray Bartlett, Gregor Clark and Ashley Harrell.

This guidebook was produced by:

Senior Product Editors Daniel Bolger, Martine Power

Coordinating Editor Andrea Dobbin

Product Editor Kate James

Book Designer Virginia Moreno

Assisting Editors Kate Kiely, Gabbi Stefanos

Cartographer Alison Lyall

Cover Researcher & Design Ania Bartoszek

Product Development Imogen Bannister, Liz Heynes, Anne Mason, Dianne Schallmeiner, John Taufa, Juan Winata

Design Development Virginia Moreno

Cartographic Series Designer Wayne Murphy

Thanks to Angela Tinson, Karen Henderson, Anne Mason, Genna Patterson

By Difficulty

Index

RAY BARTLETT

Ray Bartlett (@kaisoradotcom on Instagram) has been travel writing for nearly two decades, bringing Japan, Korea, Mexico, Tanzania, Guatemala, Indonesia, and many parts of the United States to life in rich detail for Lonely Planet and other publishers, newspapers, and magazines. His second novel, *Celadon,* is set in southern Japan, and his debut novel, *Sunsets of Tulum,* set in Yucatán, was a Midwest Book Review 2016 Fiction pick. Among other pursuits, he surfs regularly and is an accomplished Argentine tango dancer. Ray currently divides his time between homes in the USA, Japan, and Mexico.

My favorite walk is Wildrose Peak, since it was such a beautiful view from the top and not as hot as some, with a wonderful variety of landscapes and terrains. There's the chance to see mountain lions (I didn't, sigh) and vultures and hawks soar above. I had the mountain to myself, too.

GREGOR CLARK

Gregor Clark is a US-based writer whose love of foreign languages and curiosity about what's around the next bend have taken him to dozens of countries on five continents. Chronic wanderlust has also led him to visit all 50 states and most Canadian provinces on countless road trips through his native North America. Since 2000, Gregor has regularly contributed to Lonely Planet guides, with a focus on Europe and the Americas. A polyglot since early childhood, Gregor earned his degree in Romance Languages at Stanford University and has remained an avid linguist throughout careers in international publishing, teaching, translation and tour leadership. He lived in California, France, Spain and Italy prior to settling with his wife and two daughters in his current home state of Vermont.

My favorite walk is Big Sur Bluffs & Beaches. Big Sur is my spiritual homeland, and Andrew Molera State Park's trails offer rapturous immersion in its coastal bluffs, hidden beaches, remnants of redwood forest, and panoramic views stretching from the Santa Lucia Mountains to the Pacific.

ASHLEY HARRELL

After a brief stint selling day spa coupons door-to-door in South Florida, Ashley decided she'd rather be a writer. She went to journalism grad school, convinced a newspaper to hire her, and starting covering wildlife, crime and tourism, sometimes all in the same story. Fueling her zest for storytelling and the unknown, she traveled widely and moved often, from a tiny NYC apartment to a vast California ranch to a jungle cabin in Costa Rica, where she started writing for Lonely Planet. From there her travels became more exotic and farther flung, and she still laughs when paychecks arrive.

My favorite walk is the Cinder Cone Trail. Hiking up and into an ash-covered volcano, I was mesmerized by the views of alpine lakes, pine forests and multi-colored dunes.

Our Story

A beat-up old car, a few dollars in the pocket and a sense of adventure. In 1972 that's all Tony and Maureen Wheeler needed for the trip of a lifetime – across Europe and Asia overland to Australia. It took several months, and at the end – broke but inspired – they sat at their kitchen table writing and stapling together their first travel guide, *Across Asia on the Cheap*. Within a week they'd sold 1500 copies. Lonely Planet was born.

Today, Lonely Planet has offices in the US, Ireland and China with a network of over 2000 contributors in every corner of the globe. We share Tony's belief that 'a great guidebook should do three things: inform, educate and amuse'.

Our Writers

AMY BALFOUR

Amy has hiked, biked and paddled across the United States. Her top picks for US adventure include the cables of Half Dome, the South Kaibab Trail to Phantom Ranch, the road to the Racetrack Playa in Death Valley, the Gauley River during dam release, and the doorbell at the Museum of Jurassic Technology. Books authored or co-authored include *USA, Western USA, Southwest USA, Hawaii* and *California*. Her stories have appeared in *Backpacker, Sierra, Southern Living* and *Women's Health*.

My favorite walk is Vernal & Nevada Fall because it's jam-packed with big views, lurking dangers and invigorating challenges – I'm looking at you Giant Staircase!

← MORE WRITERS ─ ─ ─ ─ ─ ─ ─ ─ ─ ─ ─ ─ ─ ─ ─ ○

STAY IN TOUCH LONELYPLANET.COM/CONTACT

IRELAND Digital Depot, Roe Lane (off Thomas St), Digital Hub, Dublin 8, D08 TCV4, Ireland

 twitter.com/ lonelyplanet

 facebook.com/ lonelyplanet

 instagram.com/ lonelyplanet

 youtube.com/ lonelyplanet

 lonelyplanet.com/ newsletter